The Busy Coder's Guide to Android Development

by Mark L. Murphy

CommonsWare

The Busy Coder's Guide to Android Development
by Mark L. Murphy

CommonsWare books may be purchased in printed (bulk) or digital form for educational or business use. For more information, contact *direct@commonsware.com*.

Printing History:
   Jul 2008:   Version 1.0   ISBN: 978-0-9816780-0-9

Table of Contents

Preface

Welcome to the Book!

Thanks!

Thanks for your interest in developing applications for Android! Increasingly, people will access Internet-based services using so-called "non-traditional" means, such as mobile devices. The more we do in that space now, the more that people will help invest in that space to make it easier to build more powerful mobile applications in the future. Android is new – at the time of this writing, there are no shipping Android-powered devices – but it likely will rapidly grow in importance due to the size and scope of the Open Handset Alliance.

And, most of all, thanks for your interest in this book! I sincerely hope you find it useful and at least occasionally entertaining.

Prerequisites

If you are interested in programming for Android, you will need at least basic understanding of how to program in Java. Android programming is done using Java syntax, plus a class library that resembles a subset of the Java SE library (plus Android-specific extensions). If you have not programmed in Java before, you probably should quick learn how that works before attempting to dive into programming for Android.

The book does not cover in any detail how to download or install the Android development tools, either the Eclipse IDE flavor or the standalone flavor. The Android Web site[1] covers this quite nicely. The material in the book should be relevant whether you use the IDE or not. You should download, install, and test out the Android development tools from the Android Web site before trying any of the examples listed in this book.

Some chapters may reference material in previous chapters, though usually with a link back to the preceding section of relevance.

Warescription

This book will be published both in print and in digital (ebook) form. The ebook versions of all CommonsWare titles are available via an annual subscription – the Warescription.

The Warescription entitles you, for the duration of your subscription, to ebook forms of *all* CommonsWare titles, not just the one you are reading. Presently, CommonsWare offers PDF and Kindle; other ebook formats will be added based on interest and the openness of the format.

Each subscriber gets personalized editions of all editions of each title: both those mirroring printed editions and in-between updates that are only available in ebook form. That way, your ebooks are never out of date for long, and you can take advantage of new material as it is made available instead of having to wait for a whole new print edition. For example, when new releases of the Android SDK are made available, this book will be quickly updated to be accurate with changes in the APIs.

From time to time, subscribers will also receive access to subscriber-only online material, both short articles and not-yet-published new titles.

Also, if you own a print copy of a CommonsWare book, and it is in good clean condition with no marks or stickers, you can exchange that copy for a discount off the Warescription price.

---

1   http://code.google.com/android/index.html

If you are interested in a Warescription, visit the Warescription section of the CommonsWare Web site[2].

Book Bug Bounty

Find a problem in one of our books? Let us know!

Be the first to report a unique concrete problem, and we'll give you a coupon for a six-month Warescription as a bounty for helping us deliver a better product. You can use that coupon to get a new Warescription, renew an existing Warescription, or give the coupon to a friend, colleague, or some random person you meet on the subway.

By "concrete" problem, we mean things like:

- Typographical errors
- Sample applications that do not work as advertised, in the environment described in the book
- Factual errors that cannot be open to interpretation

By "unique", we mean ones not yet reported. Each book has an errata page on the CommonsWare Web site; most known problems will be listed there.

We appreciate hearing about "softer" issues as well, such as:

- Places where you think we are in error, but where we feel our interpretation is reasonable
- Places where you think we could add sample applications, or expand upon the existing material
- Samples that do not work due to "shifting sands" of the underlying environment (e.g., changed APIs with new releases of an SDK)

However, those "softer" issues do not qualify for the formal bounty program.

---

2   http://commonsware.com/warescription.html

Questions about the bug bounty, or problems you wish to report for bounty consideration, should be sent to bounty@commonsware.com[3].

Source Code License

The source code samples shown in this book are available for download from the CommonsWare Web site. All of the Android projects are licensed under the Apache 2.0 License[4], in case you have the desire to reuse any of it.

Creative Commons and the Four-to-Free (42F) Guarantee

Each CommonsWare book edition will be available for use under the Creative Commons Attribution-Noncommercial-Share Alike 3.0[5] license as of the fourth anniversary of its publication date, or when 4,000 copies of the edition have been sold, whichever comes first. That means that, once four years have elapsed (perhaps sooner!), you can use this prose for non-commercial purposes. That is our Four-to-Free Guarantee to our readers and the broader community. For the purposes of this guarantee, new Warescriptions and renewals will be counted as sales of this edition, starting from the time the edition is published.

This edition of this book will be available under the aforementioned Creative Commons license on **July 1, 2012**. Of course, watch the CommonsWare Web site, as this edition might be relicensed sooner based on sales.

For more details on the Creative Commons Attribution-Noncommercial-Share Alike 3.0 license, visit the Creative Commons Web site.

Note that future editions of this book will become free on later dates, each four years from the publication of that edition or based on sales of that specific edition. Releasing one edition under the Creative Commons license does not automatically release *all* editions under that license.

---

3   mailto:bounty@commonsware.com
4   http://www.apache.org/licenses/LICENSE-2.0.html
5   http://creativecommons.org/licenses/by-nc-sa/3.0/

PART I – Core Concepts

CHAPTER 1

The Big Picture

Android devices, by and large, will be mobile phones. While the Android technology is being discussed for use in other areas (e.g., car dashboard "PCs"), for the most part, you can think of Android as being used on phones.

For developers, this has benefits and drawbacks.

On the plus side, circa 2008, Android-style smartphones are sexy. Offering Internet services over mobile devices dates back to the mid-1990's and the Handheld Device Markup Language (HDML). However, only in recent years have phones capable of Internet access taken off. Now, thanks to trends like text messaging and to products like Apple's iPhone, phones that can serve as Internet access devices are rapidly gaining popularity. So, working on Android applications gives you experience with an interesting technology (Android) in a fast-moving market segment (Internet-enabled phones), which is always a good thing.

The problem comes when you actually have to program the darn things.

Anyone with experience in programming for PDAs or phones has felt the pain of phones simply being *small* in all sorts of dimensions:

- Screens are small (you won't get comments like, "is that a 24-inch LCD in your pocket, or...?")
- Keyboards, if they exist, are small

- Pointing devices, if they exist, are annoying (as anyone who has lost their stylus will tell you) or inexact (large fingers and "multi-touch" LCDs are not a good mix)

- CPU speed and memory are tight compared to desktops and servers you may be used to

- You can have any programming language and development framework you want, so long as it was what the device manufacturer chose and burned into the phone's silicon

- And so on

Moreover, applications running on a phone have to deal with the fact that they're *on a phone*.

People with mobile phones tend to get very irritated when those phones don't work, which is why the "can you hear me now?" ad campaign from Verizon Wireless has been popular for the past few years. Similarly, those same people will get irritated at you if your program "breaks" their phone:

- ...by tying up the CPU such that calls can't be received

- ...by not working properly with the rest of the phone's OS, such that your application doesn't quietly fade to the background when a call comes in or needs to be placed

- ...by crashing the phone's operating system, such as by leaking memory like a sieve

Hence, developing programs for a phone is a different experience than developing desktop applications, Web sites, or back-end server processes. You wind up with different-looking tools, different-behaving frameworks, and "different than you're used to" limitations on what you can do with your program.

What Android tries to do is meet you halfway:

- You get a commonly-used programming language (Java) with some commonly used libraries (e.g., some Apache Commons APIs), with support for tools you may be used to (Eclipse)

- You get a fairly rigid and uncommon framework in which your programs need to run so they can be "good citizens" on the phone and not interfere with other programs or the operation of the phone itself

As you might expect, much of this book deals with that framework and how you write programs that work within its confines and take advantage of its capabilities.

What Androids Are Made Of

When you write a desktop application, you are "master of your own domain". You launch your main window and any child windows – like dialog boxes – that are needed. From your standpoint, you are your own world, leveraging features supported by the operating system, but largely ignorant of any other program that may be running on the computer at the same time. If you do interact with other programs, it is typically through an API, such as using JDBC (or frameworks atop it) to communicate with MySQL or another database.

Android has similar concepts, but packaged differently, and structured to make phones more crash-resistant.

Activities

The building block of the user interface is the **activity**. You can think of an activity as being the Android analogue for the window or dialog in a desktop application.

While it is possible for activities to not have a user interface, most likely your "headless" code will be packaged in the form of content providers or services, described below.

Content Providers

Content providers provide a level of abstraction for any data stored on the device that is accessible by multiple applications. The Android development model encourages you to make your own data available to other applications, as well as your own – building a content provider lets you do that, while maintaining complete control over how your data gets accessed.

Intents

Intents are system messages, running around the inside of the device, notifying applications of various events, from hardware state changes (e.g., an SD card was inserted), to incoming data (e.g., an SMS message arrived), to application events (e.g., your activity was launched from the device's main menu). Not only can you respond to intents, but you can create your own, to launch other activities, or to let you know when specific situations arise (e.g., raise such-and-so intent when the user gets within 100 meters of this-and-such location).

Services

Activities, content providers, and intent receivers are all short-lived and can be shut down at any time. Services, on the other hand, are designed to keep running, if needed, independent of any activity. You might use a service for checking for updates to an RSS feed, or to play back music even if the controlling activity is no longer operating.

Stuff At Your Disposal

Storage

You can package data files with your application, for things that do not change, such as icons or help files. You also can carve out a small bit of space on the device itself, for databases or files containing user-entered or retrieved data needed by your application. And, if the user supplies bulk storage, like an SD card, you can read and write files on there as needed.

Network

Android devices will generally be Internet-ready, through one communications medium or another. You can take advantage of the Internet access at any level you wish, from raw Java sockets all the way up to a built-in WebKit-based Web browser widget you can embed in your application.

Multimedia

Android devices have the ability to play back and record audio and video. While the specifics may vary from device to device, you can query the device to learn its capabilities and then take advantage of the multimedia capabilities as you see fit, whether that is to play back music, take pictures with the camera, or use the microphone for audio note-taking.

GPS

Android devices will frequently have access to location providers, such as GPS, that can tell your applications where the device is on the face of the Earth. In turn, you can display maps or otherwise take advantage of the location data, such as tracking a device's movements if the device has been stolen.

Phone Services

And, of course, Android devices are typically phones, allowing your software to initiate calls, send and receive SMS messages, and everything else you expect from a modern bit of telephony technology.

CHAPTER 2

Project Structure

The Android build system is organized around a specific directory tree structure for your Android project, much like any other Java project. The specifics, though, are fairly unique to Android and what it all does to prepare the actual application that will run on the device or emulator. Here's a quick primer on the project structure, to help you make sense of it all, particularly for the sample code referenced in this book.

Root Contents

When you create a new Android project (e.g., via `activityCreator.py`), you get five key items in the project's root directory:

- `AndroidManifest.xml`, which is an XML file describing the application being built and what components – activities, services, etc. – are being supplied by that application

- `build.xml`, which is an Ant[6] script for compiling the application and installing it on the device

- `bin/`, which holds the application once it is compiled

- `src/`, which holds the Java source code for the application

- `res/`, which holds "resources", such as icons, GUI layouts, and the like, that get packaged with the compiled Java in the application

---

6 http://ant.apache.org/

- assets/, which hold other static files you wish packaged with the application for deployment onto the device

The Sweat Off Your Brow

When you created the project (e.g., via activityCreator.py), you supplied the fully-qualified class name of the "main" activity for the application (e.g., com.commonsware.android.SomeDemo). You will then find that your project's src/ tree already has the namespace directory tree in place, plus a stub Activity subclass representing your main activity (e.g., src/com/commonsware/android/SomeDemo.java). You are welcome to modify this file and add others to the src/ tree as needed to implement your application.

The first time you compile the project (e.g., via ant), out in the "main" activity's namespace directory, the Android build chain will create R.java. This contains a number of constants tied to the various resources you placed out in the res/ directory tree. You should not modify R.java yourself, letting the Android tools handle it for you. You will see throughout many of the samples where we reference things in R.java (e.g., referring to a layout's identifier via R.layout.main).

And Now, The Rest of the Story

You will also find that your project has a res/ directory tree. This holds "resources" – static files that are packaged along with your application, either in their original form or, occasionally, in a preprocessed form. Some of the subdirectories you will find or create under res/ include:

- res/drawable/ for images (PNG, JPEG, etc.)

- res/layout/ for XML-based UI layout specifications

- res/raw/ for general-purpose files (e.g,. a CSV file of account information)

- res/values/ for strings, dimensions, and the like

- res/xml/ for other general-purpose XML files you wish to ship

We will cover all of these, and more, in later chapters of this book.

What You Get Out Of It

When you compile your project (via ant or the IDE), the results go into the bin/ directory under your project root. Specifically:

- bin/classes/ holds the compiled Java classes
- bin/classes.dex holds the executable created from those compiled Java classes
- bin/yourapp.apk is the actual Android application (where yourapp is the name of your application)

The .apk file is a ZIP archive containing the .dex file, the compiled edition of your resources (resources.arsc), any un-compiled resources (such as what you put in res/raw/) and the AndroidManifest.xml file.

CHAPTER 3

Inside the Manifest

The foundation for any Android application is the manifest file: AndroidManifest.xml in the root of your project. Here is where you declare what all is inside your application – the activities, the services, and so on. You also indicate how these pieces attach themselves to the overall Android system; for example, you indicate which activity (or activities) should appear on the device's main menu (a.k.a., launcher).

When you create your application, you will get a starter manifest generated for you. For a simple application, offering a single activity and nothing else, the auto-generated manifest will probably work out fine, or perhaps require a few minor modifications. On the other end of the spectrum, the manifest file for the Android API demo suite is over 1,000 lines long. Your production Android applications will probably fall somewhere in the middle.

Most of the interesting bits of the manifest will be described in greater detail in the chapters on their associated Android features. For example, the service element will be described in greater detail in the chapter on creating services. For now, we just need to understand what the role of the manifest is and its general overall construction.

In The Beginning, There Was the Root, And It Was Good

The root of all manifest files is, not surprisingly, a manifest element:

```
<manifest xmlns:android="http://schemas.android.com/apk/res/android"
  package="com.commonsware.android.search">
...
</manifest>
```

Note the namespace declaration. Curiously, the generated manifests only apply it on the attributes, not the elements (e.g., it's manifest, not android:manifest). However, that pattern works, so unless Android changes, stick with their pattern.

The biggest piece of information you need to supply on the manifest element is the package attribute (also curiously not-namespaced). Here, you can provide the name of the Java package that will be considered the "base" of your application. Then, everywhere else in the manifest file that needs a class name, you can just substitute a leading dot as shorthand for the package. For example, if you needed to refer to com.commonsware.android.Snicklefritz in this manifest shown above, you could just use .Snicklefritz, since com.commonsware.android is defined as the application's package.

Permissions, Instrumentations, and Applications (Oh, My!)

Underneath the manifest element, you will find:

- uses-permission elements, to indicate what permissions your application will need in order to function properly – see the chapter on permissions for more details

- permission elements, to declare permissions that activities or services might require other applications hold in order to use your application's data or logic – again, more details are forthcoming in the chapter on permissions

- instrumentation elements, to indicate code that should be invoked on key system events, such as starting up activities, for the purposes of logging or monitoring

- an application element, defining the guts of the application that the manifest describes

```
<manifest xmlns:android="http://schemas.android.com/apk/res/android"
  package="com.commonsware.android">
  <uses-permission
    android:name="android.permission.ACCESS_LOCATION" />
  <uses-permission
    android:name="android.permission.ACCESS_GPS" />
  <uses-permission
    android:name="android.permission.ACCESS_ASSISTED_GPS" />
  <uses-permission
    android:name="android.permission.ACCESS_CELL_ID" />
  <application>
...
  </application>
</manifest>
```

In the preceding example, the manifest has uses-permission elements to indicate some device capabilities the application will need – in this case, permissions to allow the application to determine its current location. And, there is the application element, whose contents will describe the activities, services, and whatnot that make up the bulk of the application itself.

Your Application Does Something, Right?

The real meat of the manifest file are the children of the application element.

By default, when you create a new Android project, you get a single activity element:

```
<manifest xmlns:android="http://schemas.android.com/apk/res/android"
    package="com.commonsware.android.skeleton">
    <application>
        <activity android:name=".Now" android:label="Now">
            <intent-filter>
                <action android:name="android.intent.action.MAIN" />
                <category android:name="android.intent.category.LAUNCHER" />
            </intent-filter>
        </activity>
    </application>
</manifest>
```

This element supplies android:name for the class implementing the activity, android:label for the display name of the activity, and (frequently) an intent-filter child element describing under what conditions this activity will be displayed. The stock `activity` element sets up your activity to appear in the launcher, so users can choose to run it. As we'll see later in this book, you can have several activities in one project, if you so choose.

You may also have one or more `receiver` elements, indicating non-activities that should be triggered under certain conditions, such as when an SMS message comes in. These are called intent receivers and are described midway through the book.

You may have one or more `provider` elements, indicating content providers – components that supply data to your activities and, with your permission, other activities in other applications on the device. These wrap up databases or other data stores into a single API that any application can use. Later, we'll see how to create content providers and how to use content providers that you or others create.

Finally, you may have one or more `service` elements, describing services – long-running pieces of code that can operate independent of any activity. The quintessential example is the MP3 player, where you want the music to keep playing even if the user pops open other activities and the MP3 player's user interface is "misplaced". Two chapters late in the book cover how to create and use services.

PART II – Activities

CHAPTER 4

Creating a Skeleton Application

Every programming language or environment book starts off with the ever-popular "Hello, World!" demonstration: just enough of a program to prove you can build things, not so much that you cannot understand what is going on. However, the typical "Hello, World!" program has no interactivity (e.g., just dumps the words to a console), and so is really boring.

This chapter demonstrates a simple project, but one using Advanced Push-Button Technology™ and the current time, to show you how a simple Android activity works.

Begin at the Beginning

To work with anything in Android, you need a project. With ordinary Java, if you wanted, you could just write a program as a single file, compile it with `javac`, and run it with `java`, without any other support structures. Android is more complex, but to help keep it manageable, Google has supplied tools to help create the project. If you are using an Android-enabled IDE, such as Eclipse with the Android plugin, you can create a project inside of the IDE (e.g., select **File > New > Project**, then choose **Android > Android Project**).

If you are using tools that are not Android-enabled, you can use the `activityCreator.py` script, found in the `tools/` directory in your SDK installation. Just pass `activityCreator.py` the package name of the activity you want to create and a --out switch indicating where the project files should be generated. For example:

```
./activityCreator.py --out /path/to/my/project/dir \
com.commonsware.android.Now
```

You will wind up with a handful of pre-generated files, as described in a previous chapter.

For the purposes of the samples shown in this book, you can download their project directories in a ZIP file on the CommonsWare Web site. These projects are ready for use; you do not need to run activityCreator.py on those unpacked samples.

The Activity

Your project's src/ directory contains the standard Java-style tree of directories based upon the Java package you chose when you created the project (e.g., com.commonsware.android results in src/com/commonsware/android/). Inside the innermost directory you should find a pre-generated source file named Now.java, which where your first activity will go.

Open Now.java in your editor and paste in the following code:

```java
package com.commonsware.android.skeleton;

import android.app.Activity;
import android.os.Bundle;
import android.view.View;
import android.widget.Button;
import java.util.Date;

public class Now extends Activity implements View.OnClickListener {
  Button btn;

  @Override
  public void onCreate(Bundle icicle) {
    super.onCreate(icicle);

    btn = new Button(this);
    btn.setOnClickListener(this);
```

```
      updateTime();
      setContentView(btn);
    }

    public void onClick(View view) {
      updateTime();
    }

    private void updateTime() {
      btn.setText(new Date().toString());
    }
}
```

Or, if you download the source files off the Web site, you can just use the Now project directly.

Dissecting the Activity

Let's examine this piece by piece:

```
package com.commonsware.android.skeleton;

import android.app.Activity;
import android.os.Bundle;
import android.view.View;
import android.widget.Button;
import java.util.Date;
```

The package declaration needs to be the same as the one you used when creating the project. And, like any other Java project, you need to import any classes you reference. Most of the Android-specific classes are in the android package.

Remember that not every Java SE class is available to Android programs! Visit the Android class reference[7] to see what is and is not available.

```
public class Now extends Activity implements View.OnClickListener {
  Button btn;
```

Activities are public classes, inheriting from the android.Activity base class. In this case, the activity holds a button (btn). Since, for simplicity, we want

---

7   http://code.google.com/android/reference/packages.html

to trap all button clicks just within the activity itself, we also have the activity class implement OnClickListener.

```
@Override
public void onCreate(Bundle icicle) {
  super.onCreate(icicle);

  btn = new Button(this);
  btn.setOnClickListener(this);
  updateTime();
  setContentView(btn);
}
```

The onCreate() method is invoked when the activity is started. The first thing you should do is chain upward to the superclass, so the stock Android activity initialization can be done.

In our implementation, we then create the button instance (new Button(this)), tell it to send all button clicks to the activity instance itself (via setOnClickListener()), call a private updateTime() method (see below), and then set the activity's content view to be the button itself (via setContentView()).

We will discuss that magical Bundle icicle in a later chapter. For the moment, consider it an opaque handle that all activities receive upon creation.

```
public void onClick(View view) {
  updateTime();
}
```

In Swing, a JButton click raises an ActionEvent, which is passed to the ActionListener configured for the button. In Android, a button click causes onClick() to be invoked in the OnClickListener instance configured for the button. The listener is provided the view that triggered the click (in this case, the button). All we do here is call that private updateTime() method:

```
private void updateTime() {
  btn.setText(new Date().toString());
}
```

When we open the activity (onCreate()) or when the button is clicked (onClick()), we update the button's label to be the current time via setText(), which functions much the same as the JButton equivalent.

Building and Running the Activity

To build the activity, either use your IDE's built-in Android packaging tool, or run ant in the base directory of your project. Then, to run the activity:

- Launch the emulator (e.g., run tools/emulator from your Android SDK installation)

- Install the package (e.g., run tools/adb install /path/to/this/example/bin/Now.apk from your Android SDK installation)

- View the list of installed applications in the emulator and find the "Now" application

Figure 1. The Android application "launcher"

- Open that application

You should see an activity screen akin to:

Figure 2. The Now demonstration activity

Clicking the button – in other words, pretty much anywhere on the phone's screen – will update the time shown in the button's label.

Note that the label is centered horizontally and vertically, as those are the default styles applied to button captions. We can control that formatting, which will be covered in a later chapter.

After you are done gazing at the awesomeness of Advanced Push-Button Technology™, you can click the back button on the emulator to return to the launcher.

CHAPTER 5

Using XML-Based Layouts

While it is technically possible to create and attach widgets to our activity purely through Java code, the way we did in the preceding chapter, the more common approach is to use an XML-based layout file. Dynamic instantiation of widgets is reserved for more complicated scenarios, where the widgets are not known at compile-time (e.g., populating a column of radio buttons based on data retrieved off the Internet).

With that in mind, it's time to break out the XML and learn out to lay out Android activity views that way.

What Is an XML-Based Layout?

As the name suggests, an XML-based layout is a specification of widgets' relationships to each other – and to containers – encoded in XML format. Specifically, Android considers XML-based layouts to be resources, and as such layout files are stored in the res/layout directory inside your Android project.

Each XML file contains a tree of elements specifying a layout of widgets and containers that make up one View. The attributes of the XML elements are properties, describing how a widget should look or how a container should behave. For example, if a Button element has an attribute value of android:textStyle = "bold", that means that the text appearing on the face of the button should be rendered in a boldface font style.

Android's SDK ships with a tool (aapt) which uses the layouts. This tool should be automatically invoked by your Android tool chain (e.g., Eclipse, Ant's build.xml). Of particular importance to you as a developer is that aapt generates the R.java source file within your project, allowing you to access layouts and widgets within those layouts directly from your Java code, as will be demonstrated .

Why Use XML-Based Layouts?

Most everything you do using XML layout files can be achieved through Java code. For example, you could use setTypeface() to have a button render its text in bold, instead of using a property in an XML layout. Since XML layouts are yet another file for you to keep track of, we need good reasons for using such files.

Perhaps the biggest reason is to assist in the creation of tools for view definition, such as a GUI builder in an IDE like Eclipse or a dedicated Android GUI designer like DroidDraw[8]. Such GUI builders could, in principle, generate Java code instead of XML. The challenge is re-reading the definition in to support edits – that is far simpler if the data is in a structured format like XML than in a programming language. Moreover, keeping the generated bits separated out from hand-written code makes it less likely that somebody's custom-crafted source will get clobbered by accident when the generated bits get re-generated. XML forms a nice middle ground between something that is easy for tool-writers to use and easy for programmers to work with by hand as needed.

Also, XML as a GUI definition format is becoming more commonplace. Microsoft's XAML[9], Adobe's Flex[10], and Mozilla's XUL[11] all take a similar approach to that of Android: put layout details in an XML file and put programming smarts in source files (e.g., Javascript for XUL). Many less-well-known GUI frameworks, such as ZK[12], also use XML for view definition. While "following the herd" is not necessarily the best policy, it does have the

8   http://droiddraw.org/
9   http://windowssdk.msdn.microsoft.com/en-us/library/ms752059.aspx
10   http://www.adobe.com/products/flex/
11   http://www.mozilla.org/projects/xul/
12   http://www.zkoss.org/

advantage of helping to ease the transition into Android from any other XML-centered view description language.

OK, So What Does It Look Like?

Here is the Button from the previous chapter's sample application, converted into an XML layout file:

```
<?xml version="1.0" encoding="utf-8"?>
<Button xmlns:android="http://schemas.android.com/apk/res/android"
    android:id="@+id/button"
    android:text=""
    android:layout_width="fill_parent"
    android:layout_height="fill_parent"/>
```

The class name of the widget – Button – forms the name of the XML element. Since Button is an Android-supplied widget, we can just use the bare class name. If you create your own widgets as subclasses of android.view.View, you would need to provide a full package declaration as well (e.g., com.commonsware.android.MyWidget).

The root element needs to declare the Android XML namespace:

```
xmlns:android="http://schemas.android.com/apk/res/android"
```

All other elements will be children of the root and will inherit that namespace declaration.

Because we want to reference this button from our Java code, we need to give it an identifier via the android:id attribute. We will cover this concept in greater detail .

The remaining attributes are properties of this Button instance:

- android:text indicates the initial text to be displayed on the button face (in this case, an empty string)

- android:layout_width and android:layout_height tell Android to have the button's width and height fill the "parent", in this case the entire screen – these attributes will be covered in greater detail in a later chapter

Since this single widget is the only content in our activity's view, we only need this single element. Complex views will require a whole tree of elements, representing the widgets and containers that control their positioning. All the remaining chapters of this book will use the XML layout form whenever practical, so there are dozens of other examples of more complex layouts for you to peruse.

What's With the @ Signs?

Many widgets and containers only need to appear in the XML layout file and do not need to be referenced in your Java code. For example, a static label (TextView) frequently only needs to be in the layout file to indicate where it should appear. These sorts of elements in the XML file do not need to have the android:id attribute to give them a name.

Anything you *do* want to use in your Java source, though, needs an android:id.

The convention is to use @+id/... as the id value, where the ... represents your locally-unique name for the widget in question. In the XML layout example in the preceding section, @+id/button is the identifier for the Button widget.

Android provides a few special android:id values, of the form @android:id/... – we will see some of these in various chapters of this book.

And We Attach These to the Java...How?

Given that you have painstakingly set up the widgets and containers for your view in an XML layout file named snicklefritz.xml stored in res/layout, all you need is one statement in your activity's onCreate() callback to use that layout:

This is the same `setLayoutView()` we used earlier, passing it an instance of a `View` subclass (in that case, a `Button`). The Android-built `View`, constructed from our layout, is accessed from that code-generated `R` class. All of the layouts are accessible under `R.layout`, keyed by the base name of the layout file – `snicklefritz.xml` results in `R.layout.snicklefritz`.

To access our identified widgets, use `findViewById()`, passing it the numeric identifier of the widget in question. That numeric identifier was generated by Android in the `R` class as `R.id.something` (where `something` is the specific widget you are seeking). Those widgets are simply subclasses of `View`, just like the `Button` instance we created in the previous chapter.

The Rest of the Story

In the original `Now` demo, the button's face would show the current time, which would reflect when the button was last pushed (or when the activity was first shown, if the button had not yet been pushed).

Most of that logic still works, even in this revised demo (`NowRedux`). However, rather than instantiating the `Button` in our activity's `onCreate()` callback, we can reference the one from the XML layout:

```
package com.commonsware.android.layouts;

import android.app.Activity;
import android.os.Bundle;
import android.view.View;
import android.widget.Button;
import java.util.Date;

public class NowRedux extends Activity
  implements View.OnClickListener {
  Button btn;

  @Override
  public void onCreate(Bundle icicle) {
    super.onCreate(icicle);

    setContentView(R.layout.main);

    btn=(Button)findViewById(R.id.button);
    btn.setOnClickListener(this);
    updateTime();
```

```
    }

    public void onClick(View view) {
        updateTime();
    }

    private void updateTime() {
        btn.setText(new Date().toString());
    }
}
```

The first difference is that rather than setting the content view to be a view we created in Java code, we set it to reference the XML layout (setContentView(R.layout.main)). The R.java source file will be updated when we rebuild this project to include a reference to our layout file (stored as main.xml in our project's res/layout directory).

The other difference is that we need to get our hands on our Button instance, for which we use the findViewById() call. Since we identified our button as @+id/button, we can reference the button's identifier as R.id.button. Now, with the Button instance in hand, we can set the callback and set the label as needed.

The results look the same as with the original Now demo:

Figure 3. The NowRedux sample activity

CHAPTER 6

Employing Basic Widgets

Every GUI toolkit has some basic widgets: fields, labels, buttons, etc. Android's toolkit is no different in scope, and the basic widgets will provide a good introduction as to how widgets work in Android activities.

Assigning Labels

The simplest widget is the label, referred to in Android as a TextView. Like in most GUI toolkits, labels are bits of text not editable directly by users. Typically, they are used to identify adjacent widgets (e.g., a "Name:" label before a field where one fills in a name).

In Java, you can create a label by creating a TextView instance. More commonly, though, you will create labels in XML layout files by adding a TextView element to the layout, with an android:text property to set the value of the label itself. If you need to swap labels based on certain criteria, such as internationalization, you may wish to use a resource reference in the XML instead, as will be described later in this book.

TextView has numerous other properties of relevance for labels, such as:

- android:typeface to set the typeface to use for the label (e.g., monospace)

- android:textStyle to indicate that the typeface should be made bold (bold), italic (italic), or bold and italic (bold_italic)

- android:textColor to set the color of the label's text, in RGB hex format (e.g., #FF0000 for red)

For example, in the Label project, you will find the following layout file:

```
<?xml version="1.0" encoding="utf-8"?>
<TextView xmlns:android="http://schemas.android.com/apk/res/android"
  android:layout_width="fill_parent"
  android:layout_height="wrap_content"
  android:text="You were expecting something profound?"
  />
```

Just that layout alone, with the stub Java source provided by Android's project builder (e.g., activityCreator), gives you:

Figure 4. The LabelDemo sample application

Button, Button, Who's Got the Button?

We've already seen the use of the Button widget in the previous two chapters. As it turns out, Button is a subclass of TextView, so everything discussed in the preceding section in terms of formatting the face of the button still holds.

Fleeting Images

Android has two widgets to help you embed images in your activities: ImageView and ImageButton. As the names suggest, they are image-based analogues to TextView and Button, respectively.

Each widget takes an android:src attribute (in an XML layout) to specify what picture to use. These usually reference a drawable resource, described in greater detail in the chapter on resources. You can also set the image content based on a Uri from a content provider via setImageURI().

ImageButton, a subclass of ImageView, mixes in the standard Button behaviors, for responding to clicks and whatnot.

Fields of Green. Or Other Colors.

Along with buttons and labels, fields are the third "anchor" of most GUI toolkits. In Android, they are implemented via the EditView widget, which is a subclass of the TextView used for labels.

Along with the standard TextView properties (e.g., android:textStyle), EditView has many others that will be useful for you in constructing fields, including:

- android:autoText, to control if the field should provide automatic spelling assistance
- android:capitalize, to control if the field should automatically capitalize the first letter of entered text (e.g., first name, city)
- android:digits, to configure the field to accept only certain digits
- android:singleLine, to control if the field is for single-line input or multiple-line input (e.g., does <Enter> move you to the next widget or add a newline?)

Beyond those, you can configure fields to use specialized input methods, such as android:numeric for numeric-only input, android:password for shrouded password input, and `android:phoneNumber` for entering in phone numbers. If you want to create your own input method scheme (e.g., postal codes, Social Security numbers), you need to create your own implementation of the `InputMethod` interface, then configure the field to use it via `android:inputMethod`. You can see an example of this in the appendix discussing the TourIt sample application.

For example, from the `Field` project, here is an XML layout file showing an `EditView`:

```
<?xml version="1.0" encoding="utf-8"?>
<EditText xmlns:android="http://schemas.android.com/apk/res/android"
  android:id="@+id/field"
  android:layout_width="fill_parent"
  android:layout_height="fill_parent"
  android:singleLine="false"
  />
```

Note that `android:singleLine` is false, so users will be able to enter in several lines of text.

For this project, the `FieldDemo.java` file populates the input field with some prose:

```
package com.commonsware.android.basic;

import android.app.Activity;
import android.os.Bundle;
import android.widget.EditText;

public class FieldDemo extends Activity {
  @Override
  public void onCreate(Bundle icicle) {
    super.onCreate(icicle);
    setContentView(R.layout.main);

    EditText fld=(EditText)findViewById(R.id.field);
    fld.setText("Licensed under the Apache License, Version 2.0 " +
            "(the \"License\"); you may not use this file " +
            "except in compliance with the License. You may " +
            "obtain a copy of the License at " +
            "http://www.apache.org/licenses/LICENSE-2.0");
  }
}
```

The result, once built and installed into the emulator, is:

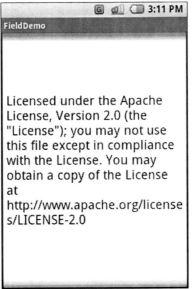

Figure 5. The FieldDemo sample application

NOTE: Android's emulator only allows one application in the launcher per unique Java package. Since all the demos in this chapter share the com.commonsware.android.basic package, if you have the LabelDemo application installed, you will not see the FieldDemo application in the launcher. To remove the LabelDemo application – or any application – use adb shell "rm /data/app/...", where ... is the name of the application's APK file (e.g., LabelDemo.apk). Then, reinstall the formerly-hidden application, and it will show up in the launcher.

Another flavor of field is one that offers auto-completion, to help users supply a value without typing in the whole text. That is provided in Android as the AutoCompleteTextView widget, discussed in greater detail later in this book.

Just Another Box to Check

The classic checkbox has two states: checked and unchecked. Clicking the checkbox toggles between those states to indicate a choice (e.g., "Add rush delivery to my order").

In Android, there is a CheckBox widget to meet this need. It has TextView as an ancestor, so you can use TextView properties like android:textColor to format the widget.

Within Java, you can invoke:

- isChecked() to determine if the checkbox has been checked

- setChecked() to force the checkbox into a checked or unchecked state

- toggle() to toggle the checkbox as if the user checked it

Also, you can register a listener object (in this case, an instance of OnCheckedChangeListener) to be notified when the state of the checkbox changes.

For example, from the CheckBox project, here is a simple checkbox layout:

```xml
<?xml version="1.0" encoding="utf-8"?>
<CheckBox xmlns:android="http://schemas.android.com/apk/res/android"
    android:id="@+id/check"
    android:layout_width="wrap_content"
    android:layout_height="wrap_content"
    android:text="This checkbox is: unchecked" />
```

The corresponding CheckBoxDemo.java retrieves and configures the behavior of the checkbox:

```java
package com.commonsware.android.basic;

import android.app.Activity;
import android.os.Bundle;
import android.widget.CheckBox;
import android.widget.CompoundButton;
```

```
public class CheckBoxDemo extends Activity
  implements CompoundButton.OnCheckedChangeListener {
  CheckBox cb;

  @Override
  public void onCreate(Bundle icicle) {
    super.onCreate(icicle);
    setContentView(R.layout.main);

    cb=(CheckBox)findViewById(R.id.check);
    cb.setOnCheckedChangeListener(this);
  }

  public void onCheckedChanged(CompoundButton buttonView,
                                boolean isChecked) {
    if (isChecked) {
      cb.setText("This checkbox is: checked");
    }
    else {
      cb.setText("This checkbox is: unchecked");
    }
```

Note that the activity serves as its own listener for checkbox state changes since it implements the OnCheckedChangeListener interface (via cb.setOnCheckedChangeListener(this)). The callback for the listener is onCheckedChanged(), which receives the checkbox whose state has changed and what the new state is. In this case, we update the text of the checkbox to reflect what the actual box contains.

The result? Clicking the checkbox immediately updates its text, as shown below:

Figure 6. The CheckBoxDemo sample application, with the checkbox unchecked

Figure 7. The same application, now with the checkbox checked

Turn the Radio Up

As with other implementations of radio buttons in other toolkits, Android's radio buttons are two-state, like checkboxes, but can be grouped such that only one radio button in the group can be checked at any time.

Like CheckBox, RadioButton inherits from CompoundButton, which in turn inherits from TextView. Hence, all the standard TextView properties for font face, style, color, etc. are available for controlling the look of radio buttons. Similarly, you can call isChecked() on a RadioButton to see if it is selected, toggle() to select it, and so on, like you can with a CheckBox.

Most times, you will want to put your RadioButton widgets inside of a RadioGroup. The RadioGroup indicates a set of radio buttons whose state is tied, meaning only one button out of the group can be selected at any time. If you assign an android:id to your RadioGroup in your XML layout, you can access the group from your Java code and invoke:

- check() to check a specific radio button via its ID (e.g., group.check(R.id.rb1))

- clearCheck() to clear all radio buttons, so none in the group are checked

- getCheckedRadioButtonId() to get the ID of the currently-checked radio button (or -1 if none are checked)

For example, from the RadioButton sample application, here is an XML layout showing a RadioGroup wrapping a set of RadioButton widgets:

```xml
<?xml version="1.0" encoding="utf-8"?>
<RadioGroup
  xmlns:android="http://schemas.android.com/apk/res/android"
  android:orientation="vertical"
  android:layout_width="fill_parent"
  android:layout_height="fill_parent"
  >
    <RadioButton android:id="@+id/radio1"
      android:layout_width="wrap_content"
      android:layout_height="wrap_content"
      android:text="Rock" />
```

```
    <RadioButton android:id="@+id/radio2"
      android:layout_width="wrap_content"
      android:layout_height="wrap_content"
      android:text="Scissors" />

    <RadioButton android:id="@+id/radio3"
      android:layout_width="wrap_content"
      android:layout_height="wrap_content"
      android:text="Paper" />
</RadioGroup>
```

Using the stock Android-generated Java for the project and this layout, you get:

Figure 8. The RadioButtonDemo sample application

Note that the radio button group is initially set to be completely unchecked at the outset. To pre-set one of the radio buttons to be checked, use either setChecked() on the RadioButton or check() on the RadioGroup from within your onCreate() callback in your activity.

It's Quite a View

All widgets, including the ones shown above, extend View, and as such give all widgets an array of useful properties and methods beyond those already described.

Useful Properties

Some of the properties on View most likely to be used include:

- Controls the focus sequence:
  - android:nextFocusDown
  - android:nextFocusLeft
  - android:nextFocusRight
  - android:nextFocusUp
- android:visibility, which controls whether the widget is initially visible
- android:background, which typically provides an RGB color value (e.g., #00FF00 for green) to serve as the background for the widget

Useful Methods

You can toggle whether or not a widget is enabled via setEnabled() and see if it is enabled via isEnabled(). One common use pattern for this is to disable some widgets based on a CheckBox or RadioButton selection.

You can give a widget focus via requestFocus() and see if it is focused via isFocused(). You might use this in concert with disabling widgets as mentioned above, to ensure the proper widget has the focus once your disabling operation is complete.

To help navigate the tree of widgets and containers that make up an activity's overall view, you can use:

- `getParent()` to find the parent widget or container

- `getParentOfType()` to search upwards in the tree to find a container of a certain class (e.g., find the `RadioGroup` for a `RadioButton`)

- `findViewById()` to find a child widget with a certain ID

- `getRootView()` to get the root of the tree (e.g., what you provided to the activity via `setContentView()`)

CHAPTER 7

Working with Containers

Containers pour a collection of widgets (and possibly child containers) into specific layouts you like. If you want a form with labels on the left and fields on the right, you will need a container. If you want OK and Cancel buttons to be beneath the rest of the form, next to one another, and flush to right side of the screen, you will need a container. Just from a pure XML perspective, if you have multiple widgets (beyond RadioButton widgets in a RadioGroup), you will need a container just to have a root element to place the widgets inside.

Most GUI toolkits have some notion of layout management, frequently organized into containers. In Java/Swing, for example, you have layout managers like BoxLayout and containers that use them (e.g., Box). Some toolkits stick strictly to the box model, such as XUL and Flex, figuring that any desired layout can be achieved through the right combination of nested boxes.

Android, through LinearLayout, also offers a "box" model, but in addition supports a range of containers providing different layout rules. In this chapter, we will look at three commonly-used containers: LinearLayout (the box model), RelativeLayout (a rule-based model), and TableLayout (the grid model), along with ScrollView, a container designed to assist with implementing scrolling containers. In the next chapter, we will examine some more esoteric containers.

Thinking Linearly

As noted above, LinearLayout is a box model – widgets or child containers are lined up in a column or row, one after the next. This works similar to FlowLayout in Java/Swing, vbox and hbox in Flex and XUL, etc.

Flex and XUL use the box as their primary unit of layout. If you want, you can use LinearLayout in much the same way, eschewing some of the other containers. Getting the visual representation you want is mostly a matter of identifying where boxes should nest and what properties those boxes should have, such as alignment vis a vis other boxes.

Concepts and Properties

To configure a LinearLayout, you have five main areas of control besides the container's contents: the orientation, the fill model, the weight, the gravity, and the padding.

Orientation

Orientation indicates whether the LinearLayout represents a row or a column. Just add the android:orientation property to your LinearLayout element in your XML layout, setting the value to be horizontal for a row or vertical for a column.

The orientation can be modified at runtime by invoking setOrientation() on the LinearLayout, supplying it either HORIZONTAL or VERTICAL.

Fill Model

Let's imagine a row of widgets, such as a pair of radio buttons. These widgets have a "natural" size based on their text. Their combined sizes probably do not exactly match the width of the Android device's screen – particularly since screens come in various sizes. We then have the issue of what to do with the remaining space.

All widgets inside a LinearLayout must supply android:layout_width and android:layout_height properties to help address this issue. These properties' values have three flavors:

- You can provide a specific dimension, such as 125px to indicate the widget should take up exactly 125 pixels

- You can provide wrap_content, which means the widget should fill up its natural space, unless that is too big, in which case Android can use word-wrap as needed to make it fit

- You can provide fill_parent, which means the widget should fill up all available space in its enclosing container, after all other widgets are taken care of

The latter two flavors are the most common, as they are independent of screen size, allowing Android to adjust your view to fit the available space.

Weight

But, what happens if we have two widgets that should split the available free space? For example, suppose we have two multi-line fields in a column, and we want them to take up the remaining space in the column after all other widgets have been allocated their space.

To make this work, in addition to setting android:layout_width (for rows) or android:layout_height (for columns) to fill_parent, you must also set android:layout_weight. This property indicates what proportion of the free space should go to that widget. If you set android:layout_weight to be the same value for a pair of widgets (e.g., 1), the free space will be split evenly between them. If you set it to be 1 for one widget and 2 for another widget, the second widget will use up twice the free space that the first widget does. And so on.

Gravity

By default, everything is left- and top-aligned. So, if you create a row of widgets via a horizontal LinearLayout, the row will start flush on the left side of the screen.

If that is not what you want, you need to specify a gravity. Using android:layout_gravity on a widget (or calling setGravity() at runtime on the widget's Java object), you can tell the widget and its container how to align it vis a vis the screen.

For a column of widgets, common gravity values are left, center_horizontal, and right for left-aligned, centered, and right-aligned widgets respectively.

For a row of widgets, the default is for them to be aligned so their texts are aligned on the baseline (the invisible line that letters seem to "sit on"), though you may wish to specify a gravity of center_vertical to center the widgets along the row's vertical midpoint.

Padding

By default, widgets are tightly packed next to each other. If you want to increase the whitespace between widgets, you will want to use the android:padding property (or by calling setPadding() at runtime on the widget's Java object).

The padding specifies how much space there is between the boundaries of the widget's "cell" and the actual widget contents. Padding is analogous to the margins on a word processing document – the page size might be 8.5"x11", but 1" margins would leave the actual text to reside within a 6.5"x9" area.

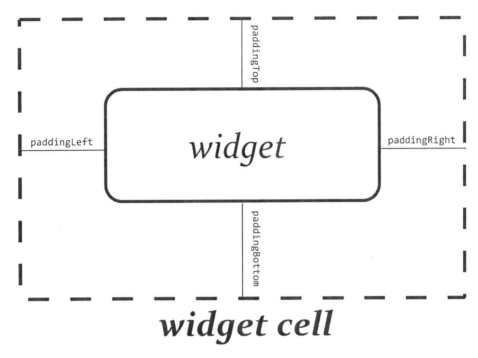

Figure 9. The relationship between a widget, its cell, and the padding values

The android:padding property allows you to set the same padding on all four sides of the widget, with the widget's contents itself centered within that padded-out area. If you want the padding to differ on different sides, use android:paddingLeft, android:paddingRight, android:paddingTop, and android:paddingBottom.

The value of the padding is a dimension, such as 5px for 5 pixels' worth of padding.

Example

Let's look at an example (Linear) that shows LinearLayout properties set both in the XML layout file and at runtime.

Here is the layout:

```
<?xml version="1.0" encoding="utf-8"?>
<LinearLayout
  xmlns:android="http://schemas.android.com/apk/res/android"
  android:orientation="vertical"
  android:layout_width="fill_parent"
  android:layout_height="fill_parent"
  >
  <RadioGroup android:id="@+id/orientation"
    android:orientation="horizontal"
    android:layout_width="wrap_content"
    android:layout_height="wrap_content"
    android:padding="5px">
    <RadioButton
      android:id="@+id/horizontal"
      android:text="horizontal" />
    <RadioButton
      android:id="@+id/vertical"
      android:text="vertical" />
  </RadioGroup>
  <RadioGroup android:id="@+id/gravity"
    android:orientation="vertical"
    android:layout_width="fill_parent"
    android:layout_height="wrap_content"
    android:padding="5px">
    <RadioButton
      android:id="@+id/left"
      android:text="left" />
    <RadioButton
      android:id="@+id/center"
      android:text="center" />
    <RadioButton
      android:id="@+id/right"
      android:text="right" />
  </RadioGroup>
</LinearLayout>
```

Note that we have a LinearLayout wrapping two RadioGroup sets. RadioGroup is a subclass of LinearLayout, so our example demonstrates nested boxes as if they were all LinearLayout containers.

The top RadioGroup sets up a row (android:orientation = "horizontal") of RadioButton widgets. The RadioGroup has 5px of padding on all sides, separating it from the other RadioGroup. The width and height are both set to wrap_content, so the radio buttons will only take up the space that they need.

The bottom RadioGroup is a column (android:orientation = "vertical") of three RadioButton widgets. Again, we have 5px of padding on all sides and a "natural" height (android:layout_height = "wrap_content"). However, we have set `android:layout_width` to be `fill_parent`, meaning the column of radio buttons "claims" the entire width of the screen.

To adjust these settings at runtime based on user input, we need some Java code:

```
package com.commonsware.android.containers;

import android.app.Activity;
import android.os.Bundle;
import android.text.TextWatcher;
import android.widget.LinearLayout;
import android.widget.RadioGroup;
import android.widget.EditText;

public class LinearLayoutDemo extends Activity
  implements RadioGroup.OnCheckedChangeListener {
  RadioGroup orientation;
  RadioGroup gravity;

  @Override
  public void onCreate(Bundle icicle) {
    super.onCreate(icicle);
    setContentView(R.layout.main);

    orientation=(RadioGroup)findViewById(R.id.orientation);
    orientation.setOnCheckedChangeListener(this);
    gravity=(RadioGroup)findViewById(R.id.gravity);
    gravity.setOnCheckedChangeListener(this);
  }

  public void onCheckedChanged(RadioGroup group, int checkedId) {
    if (group==orientation) {
      if (checkedId==R.id.horizontal) {
        orientation.setOrientation(LinearLayout.HORIZONTAL);
      }
      else {
        orientation.setOrientation(LinearLayout.VERTICAL);
      }
    }
    else if (group==gravity) {
      if (checkedId==R.id.left) {
        gravity.setGravity(0x03);    // left
      }
      else if (checkedId==R.id.center) {
        gravity.setGravity(0x01);    // center_horizontal
      }
      else if (checkedId==R.id.right) {
        gravity.setGravity(0x05);    // right
      }
    }
```

```
    }
}
```

In onCreate(), we look up our two RadioGroup containers and register a listener on each, so we are notified when the radio buttons change state (setOnCheckedChangeListener(this)). Since the activity implements OnCheckedChangeListener, the activity itself is the listener.

In onCheckedChanged() (the callback for the listener), we see which RadioGroup had a state change. If it was the orientation group, we adjust the orientation based on the user's selection. If it was the gravity group, we adjust the gravity based on the user's selection.

Here is the result when it is first launched inside the emulator:

Figure 10. The LinearLayoutDemo sample application, as initially launched

If we toggle on the "vertical" radio button, the top RadioGroup adjusts to match:

Figure 11. The same application, with the vertical radio button selected

If we toggle the "center" or "right" radio buttons, the bottom RadioGroup adjusts to match:

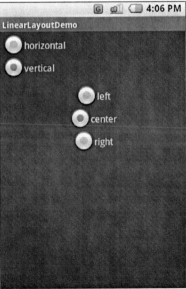

Figure 12. The same application, with the vertical and center radio buttons selected

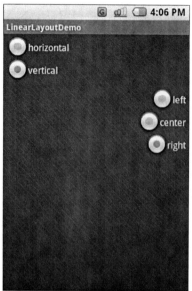

Figure 13. The same application, with the vertical and right radio buttons selected

All Things Are Relative

RelativeLayout, as the name suggests, lays out widgets based upon their relationship to other widgets in the container and the parent container. You can place Widget X below and to the left of Widget Y, or have Widget Z's bottom edge align with the bottom of the container, and so on.

This is reminiscent of James Elliot's RelativeLayout[13] for use with Java/Swing.

Concepts and Properties

To make all this work, we need ways to reference other widgets within an XML layout file, plus ways to indicate the relative positions of those widgets.

---

13 http://www.onjava.com/pub/a/onjava/2002/09/18/relativelayout.html

Positions Relative to Container

The easiest relations to set up are tying a widget's position to that of its container:

- `android:layout_alignParentTop` says the widget's top should align with the top of the container

- `android:layout_alignParentBottom` says the widget's bottom should align with the bottom of the container

- `android:layout_alignParentLeft` says the widget's left side should align with the left side of the container

- `android:layout_alignParentRight` says the widget's right side should align with the right side of the container

- `android:layout_centerHorizontal` says the widget should be positioned horizontally at the center of the container

- `android:layout_centerVertical` says the widget should be positioned vertically at the center of the container

- `android:layout_centerInParent` says the widget should be positioned both horizontally and vertically at the center of the container

All of these properties take a simple boolean value (`true` or `false`).

Note that the padding of the widget is taken into account when performing these various alignments. The alignments are based on the widget's overall cell (combination of its natural space plus the padding).

Relative Notation in Properties

The remaining properties of relevance to `RelativeLayout` take as a value the identity of a widget in the container. To do this:

1. Put identifiers (`android:id` attributes) on all elements that you will need to address, of the form `@+id/...`

2. Reference other widgets using the same identifier value without the plus sign (@id/...)

For example, if Widget A is identified as @+id/widget_a, Widget B can refer to Widget A in one of its own properties via the identifier @id/widget_a.

Positions Relative to Other Widgets

There are four properties that control position of a widget vis a vis other widgets:

- android:layout_above indicates that the widget should be placed above the widget referenced in the property

- android:layout_below indicates that the widget should be placed below the widget referenced in the property

- android:layout_toLeft indicates that the widget should be placed to the left of the widget referenced in the property

- android:layout_toRight indicates that the widget should be placed to the right of the widget referenced in the property

Beyond those four, there are five additional properties that can control one widget's alignment relative to another:

- android:layout_alignTop indicates that the widget's top should be aligned with the top of the widget referenced in the property

- android:layout_alignBottom indicates that the widget's bottom should be aligned with the bottom of the widget referenced in the property

- android:layout_alignLeft indicates that the widget's left should be aligned with the left of the widget referenced in the property

- android:layout_alignRight indicates that the widget's right should be aligned with the right of the widget referenced in the property

- android:layout_alignBaseline indicates that the baselines of the two widgets should be aligned

The last one is useful for aligning labels and fields so that the text appears "natural". Since fields have a box around them and labels do not, android:layout_alignTop would align the top of the field's box with the top of the label, which will cause the text of the label to be higher on-screen than the text entered into the field.

So, if we want Widget B to be positioned to the right of Widget A, in the XML element for Widget B, we need to include android:layout_toRight = "@id/widget_a" (assuming @id/widget_a is the identity of Widget A).

Order of Evaluation

What makes this even more complicated is the order of evaluation. Android makes a single pass through your XML layout and computes the size and position of each widget in sequence. This has a few ramifications:

- You cannot reference a widget that has not been defined in the file yet
- You must be careful that any uses of fill_parent in android:layout_width or android:layout_height do not "eat up" all the space before subsequent widgets have been defined

Example

With all that in mind, let's examine a typical "form" with a field, a label, plus a pair of buttons labeled "OK" and "Cancel".

Here is the XML layout, pulled from the Relative sample project:

```
<?xml version="1.0" encoding="utf-8"?>
<RelativeLayout
  xmlns:android="http://schemas.android.com/apk/res/android"
  android:layout_width="fill_parent"
  android:layout_height="wrap_content"
  android:padding="5px">
  <TextView android:id="@+id/label"
    android:layout_width="wrap_content"
    android:layout_height="wrap_content"
    android:text="URL:"
```

```
          android:paddingTop="5px"/>
  <EditText
      android:id="@+id/entry"
      android:layout_width="fill_parent"
      android:layout_height="wrap_content"
      android:layout_toRight="@id/label"
      android:layout_alignBaseline="@id/label"/>
  <Button
      android:id="@+id/ok"
      android:layout_width="wrap_content"
      android:layout_height="wrap_content"
      android:layout_below="@id/entry"
      android:layout_alignRight="@id/entry"
      android:text="OK" />
  <Button
      android:layout_width="wrap_content"
      android:layout_height="wrap_content"
      android:layout_toLeft="@id/ok"
      android:layout_alignTop="@id/ok"
      android:text="Cancel" />
</RelativeLayout>
```

First, we open up the RelativeLayout. In this case, we want to use the full width of the screen (android:layout_width = "fill_parent"), only as much height as we need (android:layout_height = "wrap_content"), and have a 5-pixel pad between the boundaries of the container and its contents (android:padding = "5px").

Next, we define the label, which is fairly basic, except for its own 5-pixel padding (android:padding = "5px"). More on that in a moment.

After that, we add in the field. We want the field to be to the right of the label, have their texts aligned along the baseline, and for the field to take up the rest of this "row" in the layout. Those are handled by three properties:

- android:layout_toRight = "@id/label"
- android:layout_alignBaseline = "@id/label"
- android:layout_alignBaseline = "@id/label"

If we were to skip the 5-pixel padding on the label, we would find that the top of the field is clipped off. That's because of the 5-pixel padding on the container itself. The android:layout_alignBaseline = "@id/label" simply aligns the baselines of the label and field. The label, by default, has its top aligned with the top of the parent. But the label is shorter than the field because of the field's box. Since the field is dependent on the label's position, and the label's position is already defined (because it appeared first in the XML), the field winds up being too high and has the top of its box clipped off by the container's padding.

You may find yourself running into these sorts of problems as you try to get your RelativeLayout to behave the way you want it to.

The solution to this conundrum, used in the XML layout shown above, is to give the label 5 pixels' of padding on the top. This pushes the label down far enough that the field will not get clipped.

Here are some "solutions" that do not work:

- You cannot use android:layout_alignParentTop on the field, because you cannot have two properties that both attempt to set the vertical position of the field. In this case, android:layout_alignParentTop conflicts with the later android:layout_alignBaseline = "@id/label" property, and the last one in wins. So, you either have the top aligned properly or the baselines aligned properly, but not both.

- You cannot define the field first, then put the label to the left of the field, as the android:layout_width = "fill_parent" "eats up" the width of the "row", leaving no room for the label, so the label does not appear

Going back to the example, the OK button is set to be below the field (android:layout_below = "@id/entry") and have its right side align with the right side of the field (android:layout_alignRight = "@id/entry"). The Cancel button is set to be to the left of the OK button (android:layout_toLeft = "@id/ok") and have its top aligned with the OK button (android:layout_alignTop = "@id/ok").

With no changes to the auto-generated Java code, the emulator gives us:

Figure 14. The RelativeLayoutDemo sample application

Tabula Rasa

If you like HTML tables, spreadsheet grids, and the like, you will like Android's TableLayout – it allows you to position your widgets in a grid to your specifications. You control the number of rows and columns, which columns might shrink or stretch to accommodate their contents, and so on.

TableLayout works in conjunction with TableRow. TableLayout controls the overall behavior of the container, with the widgets themselves poured into one or more TableRow containers, one per row in the grid.

Concepts and Properties

For all this to work, we need to figure out how widgets work with rows and columns, plus how to handle widgets that live outside of rows.

Putting Cells in Rows

Rows are declared by you, the developer, by putting widgets as children of a TableRow inside the overall TableLayout. You, therefore, control directly how many rows appear in the table.

The number of columns are determined by Android; you control the number of columns in an indirect fashion.

First, there will be at least one column per widget in your longest row. So if you have three rows, one with two widgets, one with three widgets, and one with four widgets, there will be at least four columns.

However, a widget can take up more than one column by including the android:layout_span property, indicating the number of columns the widget spans. This is akin to the colspan attribute one finds in table cells in HTML:

```
<TableRow>
  <TextView android:text="URL:" />
  <EditText
    android:id="@+id/entry"
    android:layout_span="3"/>
</TableRow>
```

In the above XML layout fragment, the field spans three columns.

Ordinarily, widgets are put into the first available column. In the above fragment, the label would go in the first column (column 0, as columns are counted starting from 0), and the field would go into a spanned set of three columns (columns 1 through 3). However, you can put a widget into a different column via the android:layout_column property, specifying the 0-based column the widget belongs to:

```
<TableRow>
  <Button
    android:id="@+id/cancel"
    android:layout_column="2"
    android:text="Cancel" />
  <Button android:id="@+id/ok" android:text="OK" />
</TableRow>
```

In the preceding XML layout fragment, the Cancel button goes in the third column (column 2). The OK button then goes into the next available column, which is the fourth column.

Non-Row Children of TableLayout

Normally, TableLayout contains only TableRow elements as immediate children. However, it is possible to put other widgets in between rows. For those widgets, TableLayout behaves a bit like LinearLayout with vertical orientation. The widgets automatically have their width set to fill_parent, so they will fill the same space that the longest row does.

One pattern for this is to use a plain View as a divider (e.g., <View android:layout_height = "2px" android:background = "#0000FF" /> as a two-pixel-high blue bar across the width of the table).

Stretch, Shrink, and Collapse

By default, each column will be sized according to the "natural" size of the widest widget in that column (taking spanned columns into account). Sometimes, though, that does not work out very well, and you need more control over column behavior.

You can place an android:stretchColumns property on the TableLayout. The value should be a single column number (again, 0-based) or a comma-delimited list of column numbers. Those columns will be stretched to take up any available space yet on the row. This helps if your content is narrower than the available space.

Conversely, you can place a android:shrinkColumns property on the TableLayout. Again, this should be a single column number or a comma-delimited list of column numbers. The columns listed in this property will try to word-wrap their contents to reduce the effective width of the column – by default, widgets are not word-wrapped. This helps if you have columns with potentially wordy content that might cause some columns to be pushed off the right side of the screen.

You can also leverage an `android:collapseColumns` property on the `TableLayout`, again with a column number or comma-delimited list of column numbers. These columns will start out "collapsed", meaning they will be part of the table information but will be invisible. Programmatically, you can collapse and un-collapse columns by calling `setColumnCollapsed()` on the `TableLayout`. You might use this to allow users to control which columns are of importance to them and should be shown versus which ones are less important and can be hidden.

You can also control stretching and shrinking at runtime via `setColumnStretchable()` and `setColumnShrinkable()`.

Example

The XML layout fragments shown above, when combined, give us a `TableLayout` rendition of the "form" we created for `RelativeLayout`, with the addition of a divider line between the label/field and the two buttons (found in the `Table` demo):

```
<?xml version="1.0" encoding="utf-8"?>
<TableLayout
  xmlns:android="http://schemas.android.com/apk/res/android"
  android:layout_width="fill_parent"
  android:layout_height="fill_parent"
  android:stretchColumns="1">
  <TableRow>
    <TextView
        android:text="URL:" />
    <EditText android:id="@+id/entry"
      android:layout_span="3"/>
  </TableRow>
  <View
    android:layout_height="2px"
    android:background="#0000FF" />
  <TableRow>
    <Button android:id="@+id/cancel"
      android:layout_column="2"
      android:text="Cancel" />
    <Button android:id="@+id/ok"
      android:text="OK" />
  </TableRow>
</TableLayout>
```

When compiled against the generated Java code and run on the emulator, we get:

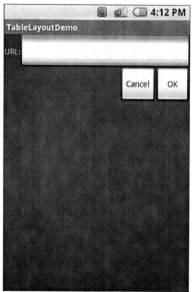

Figure 15. The TableLayoutDemo sample application

Scrollwork

Phone screens tend to be small, which requires developers to use some tricks to present a lot of information in the limited available space. One trick for doing this is to use scrolling, so only part of the information is visible at one time, the rest available via scrolling up or down.

ScrollView is a container that provides scrolling for its contents. You can take a layout that might be too big for some screens, wrap it in a ScrollView, and still use your existing layout logic. It just so happens that the user can only see part of your layout at one time, the rest available via scrolling.

For example, here is a ScrollView used in an XML layout file (from the Scroll demo):

```xml
<?xml version="1.0" encoding="utf-8"?>
<ScrollView
  xmlns:android="http://schemas.android.com/apk/res/android"
  android:layout_width="fill_parent"
  android:layout_height="wrap_content">
  <TableLayout
    android:layout_width="fill_parent"
    android:layout_height="fill_parent"
    android:stretchColumns="0">
    <TableRow>
      <View
        android:layout_height="80px"
        android:background="#000000"/>
      <TextView android:text="#000000"
        android:paddingLeft="4px"
        android:layout_gravity="center_vertical" />
    </TableRow>
    <TableRow>
      <View
        android:layout_height="80px"
        android:background="#440000" />
      <TextView android:text="#440000"
        android:paddingLeft="4px"
        android:layout_gravity="center_vertical" />
    </TableRow>
    <TableRow>
      <View
        android:layout_height="80px"
        android:background="#884400" />
      <TextView android:text="#884400"
        android:paddingLeft="4px"
        android:layout_gravity="center_vertical" />
    </TableRow>
    <TableRow>
      <View
        android:layout_height="80px"
        android:background="#aa8844" />
      <TextView android:text="#aa8844"
        android:paddingLeft="4px"
        android:layout_gravity="center_vertical" />
    </TableRow>
    <TableRow>
      <View
        android:layout_height="80px"
        android:background="#ffaa88" />
      <TextView android:text="#ffaa88"
        android:paddingLeft="4px"
        android:layout_gravity="center_vertical" />
    </TableRow>
    <TableRow>
      <View
        android:layout_height="80px"
        android:background="#ffffaa" />
      <TextView android:text="#ffffaa"
```

```
        android:paddingLeft="4px"
        android:layout_gravity="center_vertical" />
    </TableRow>
    <TableRow>
      <View
        android:layout_height="80px"
        android:background="#ffffff" />
      <TextView android:text="#ffffff"
        android:paddingLeft="4px"
        android:layout_gravity="center_vertical" />
    </TableRow>
  </TableLayout>
</ScrollView>
```

Without the `ScrollView`, the table would take up at least 560 pixels (7 rows at 80 pixels each, based on the `View` declarations). There may be some devices with screens capable of showing that much information, but many will be smaller. The `ScrollView` lets us keep the table as-is, but only present part of it at a time.

On the stock Android emulator, when the activity is first viewed, you see:

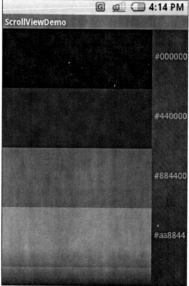

Figure 16. The ScrollViewDemo sample application

Notice how only four rows and part of the fifth are visible. By pressing the up/down buttons on the directional pad, you can scroll up and down to see the remaining rows.

CHAPTER 8

Using Selection Widgets

Back in the chapter on basic widgets, you saw how fields could have constraints placed upon them to limit possible input, such as numeric-only or phone-number-only. These sorts of constraints help users "get it right" when entering information, particularly on a mobile device with cramped keyboards.

Of course, the ultimate in constrained input is to select a choice from a set of items, such as the radio buttons seen earlier. Classic UI toolkits have listboxes, comboboxes, drop-down lists, and the like for that very purpose. Android has many of the same sorts of widgets, plus others of particular interest for mobile devices (e.g., the Gallery for examining saved photos).

Moreover, Android offers a flexible framework for determining what choices are available in these widgets. Specifically, Android offers a framework of data adapters that provide a common interface to selection lists ranging from static arrays to database contents. Selection views – widgets for presenting lists of choices – are handed an adapter to supply the actual choices.

Adapting to the Circumstances

In the abstract, adapters provide a common interface to multiple disparate APIs. More specifically, in Android's case, adapters provide a common interface to the data model behind a selection-style widget, such as a listbox.

This use of Java interfaces is fairly common (e.g., Java/Swing's model adapters for JTable), and Java is far from the only environment offering this sort of abstraction (e.g., Flex's XML data-binding framework accepts XML inlined as static data or retrieved from the Internet).

Android's adapters are responsible for providing the roster of data for a selection widget plus converting individual elements of data into specific views to be displayed inside the selection widget. The latter facet of the adapter system may sound a little odd, but in reality it is not that different from other GUI toolkits' ways of overriding default display behavior. For example, in Java/Swing, if you want a JList-backed listbox to actually be a checklist (where individual rows are a checkbox plus label, and clicks adjust the state of the checkbox), you inevitably wind up calling setCellRenderer() to supply your own ListCellRenderer, which in turn converts strings for the list into JCheckBox-plus-JLabel composite widgets.

Using ArrayAdapter

The easiest adapter to use is ArrayAdapter – all you need to do is wrap one of these around a Java array or java.util.List instance, and you have a fully-functioning adapter:

```
String[] items={"this", "is", "a",
                "really", "silly", "list"};
new ArrayAdapter<String>(this,
  android.R.layout.simple_list_item_1, items);
```

The ArrayAdapter constructor takes three parameters:

- The Context to use (typically this will be your activity instance)
- The resource ID of a view to use (such as a built-in system resource ID, as shown above)
- The actual array or list of items to show

By default, the ArrayAdapter will invoke toString() on the objects in the list and wrap each of those strings in the view designated by the supplied resource. android.R.layout.simple_list_item_1 simply turns those strings into TextView objects. Those TextView widgets, in turn, will be shown the list or spinner or whatever widget uses this ArrayAdapter.

You can subclass ArrayAdapter and override getView() to "roll your own" views:

```
public View getView(int position, View convertView,
                     ViewGroup parent) {
  if (convertView==null) {
    convertView=new TextView(this);
  }

  convertView.setText(buildStringFor(position));

  return(convertView);
}
```

Here, getView() receives three parameters:

- The index of the item in the array to show in the view
- An existing view to update with the data for this position (if one already existed, such as from scrolling – if null, you need to instantiate your own)
- The widget that will contain this view, if needed for instantiating the view

In the example shown above, the adapter still returns a TextView, but uses a different behavior for determining the string that goes in the view. The TourIt sample application demonstrates using a more complicated custom view for a list adapter.

Other Key Adapters

Here are some other adapters in Android that you will likely use, each of which will be covered in greater detail later in this book:

- CursorAdapter converts a Cursor, typically from a content provider, into something that can be displayed in a selection view
- SimpleAdapter converts data found in XML resources

- `ActivityAdapter` and `ActivityIconAdapter` provide you with the names or icons of activities that can be invoked upon a particular intent

Lists of Naughty and Nice

The classic listbox widget in Android is known as `ListView`. Include one of these in your layout, invoke `setAdapter()` to supply your data and child views, and attach a listener via `setOnItemSelectedListener()` to find out when the selection has changed. With that, you have a fully-functioning listbox.

However, if your activity is dominated by a single list, you might well consider creating your activity as a subclass of `ListActivity`, rather than the regular `Activity` base class. If your main view is just the list, you do not even need to supply a layout – `ListActivity` will construct a full-screen list for you. If you do want to customize the layout, you can, so long as you identify your `ListView` as `@android:id/list`, so `ListActivity` knows which widget is the main list for the activity.

For example, here is a layout pulled from the `List` sample project:

```
<?xml version="1.0" encoding="utf-8"?>
<LinearLayout
  xmlns:android="http://schemas.android.com/apk/res/android"
  android:orientation="vertical"
  android:layout_width="fill_parent"
  android:layout_height="fill_parent" >
  <TextView
    android:id="@+id/selection"
    android:layout_width="fill_parent"
    android:layout_height="wrap_content"/>
  <ListView
    android:id="@android:id/list"
    android:layout_width="fill_parent"
    android:layout_height="fill_parent"
    android:drawSelectorOnTop="false"
    />
</LinearLayout>
```

It is just a list with a label on top to show the current selection.

The Java code to configure the list and connect the list with the label is:

```
public class ListViewDemo extends ListActivity {
  TextView selection;
  String[] items={"lorem", "ipsum", "dolor", "sit", "amet",
          "consectetuer", "adipiscing", "elit", "morbi", "vel",
          "ligula", "vitae", "arcu", "aliquet", "mollis",
          "etiam", "vel", "erat", "placerat", "ante",
          "porttitor", "sodales", "pellentesque", "augue", "purus"};

  /** Called with the activity is first created. */
  @Override
  public void onCreate(Bundle icicle) {
    super.onCreate(icicle);
    setContentView(R.layout.main);
    setListAdapter(new ArrayAdapter<String>(this,
                      android.R.layout.simple_list_item_1,
                      items));
    selection=(TextView)findViewById(R.id.selection);
  }

  public void onListItemClick(ListView parent, View v, int position,
                      long id) {
    selection.setText(items[position]);
  }
}
```

With `ListActivity`, you can set the list adapter via `setListAdapter()` – in this case, providing an `ArrayAdapter` wrapping an array of nonsense strings. To find out when the list selection changes, override `onListItemClick()` and take appropriate steps based on the supplied child view and position (in this case, updating the label with the text for that position).

The results?

Figure 17. The ListViewDemo sample application

Spin Control

In Android, the Spinner is the equivalent of the drop-down selector you might find in other toolkits (e.g., JComboBox in Java/Swing). Pressing the left and right buttons on the D-pad iterates over children. Pressing the center button on the D-pad displays, by default, a small list (akin to a ListView) appears to show a few items at a time, instead of the one-item-at-a-time perspective the unexpanded Spinner itself provides.

As with ListView, you provide the adapter for data and child views via setAdapter() and hook in a listener object for selections via setOnItemSelectedListener().

If you want to tailor the view used when displaying the drop-down perspective, you need to configure the adapter, not the Spinner widget. Use the setDropDownViewResource() method to supply the resource ID of the view to use.

For example, culled from the Spinner sample project, here is an XML layout for a simple view with a Spinner:

```
<?xml version="1.0" encoding="utf-8"?>
<LinearLayout
  xmlns:android="http://schemas.android.com/apk/res/android"
  android:orientation="vertical"
  android:layout_width="fill_parent"
  android:layout_height="fill_parent"
  >
  <TextView
    android:id="@+id/selection"
    android:layout_width="fill_parent"
    android:layout_height="wrap_content"
    />
  <Spinner android:id="@+id/spinner"
    android:layout_width="fill_parent"
    android:layout_height="wrap_content"
    android:drawSelectorOnTop="true"
    />
</LinearLayout>
```

This is the same view as shown in the previous section, just with a Spinner instead of a ListView. The Spinner property android:drawSelectorOnTop controls whether the arrows are drawn on the selector button on the right side of the Spinner UI.

To populate and use the Spinner, we need some Java code:

```
public class SpinnerDemo extends Activity
  implements AdapterView.OnItemSelectedListener {
  TextView selection;
  String[] items={"lorem", "ipsum", "dolor", "sit", "amet",
          "consectetuer", "adipiscing", "elit", "morbi", "vel",
          "ligula", "vitae", "arcu", "aliquet", "mollis",
          "etiam", "vel", "erat", "placerat", "ante",
          "porttitor", "sodales", "pellentesque", "augue", "purus"};

  @Override
  public void onCreate(Bundle icicle) {
    super.onCreate(icicle);
    setContentView(R.layout.main);
    selection=(TextView)findViewById(R.id.selection);

    Spinner spin=(Spinner)findViewById(R.id.spinner);
    spin.setOnItemSelectedListener(this);

    ArrayAdapter<String> aa=new ArrayAdapter<String>(this,
                    android.R.layout.simple_list_item_1,
```

```
                            items);

  aa.setDropDownViewResource(
    android.R.layout.simple_spinner_dropdown_item);
  spin.setAdapter(aa);
}

public void onItemSelected(AdapterView parent, View v,
                           int position, long id) {
  selection.setText(items[position]);
}

public void onNothingSelected(AdapterView parent) {
  selection.setText("");
}
}
```

Here, we attach the activity itself as the selection listener
(spin.setOnItemSelectedListener(this)). This works because the activity
implements the OnItemSelectedListener interface. We configure the adapter
not only with the list of fake words, but also with a specific resource to use
for the drop-down view (via aa.setDropDownViewResource()). Finally, we
implement the callbacks required by OnItemSelectedListener to adjust the
selection label based on user input.

What we get is:

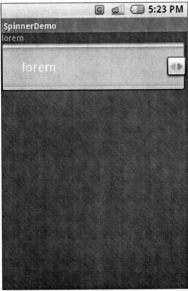

Figure 18. The SpinnerDemo sample application, as initially launched

Figure 19. The same application, with the spinner drop-down list displayed

Grid Your Lions (Or Something Like That...)

As the name suggests, GridView gives you a two-dimensional grid of items to choose from. You have moderate control over the number and size of the columns; the number of rows is dynamically determined based on the number of items the supplied adapter says are available for viewing.

There are a few properties which, when combined, determine the number of columns and their sizes:

- android:numColumns spells out how many columns there are, or, if you supply a value of auto_fit, Android will compute the number of columns based on available space and the properties listed below.

- android:verticalSpacing and its counterpart android:horizontalSpacing indicate how many pixels of whitespace there should be between items in the grid.

- android:columnWidth indicates how many pixels wide each column should be.

- android:stretchMode indicates, for grids with auto_fit for android:numColumns, what should happen for any available space not taken up by columns or spacing – this should be columnWidth to have the columns take up available space or spacingWidth to have the whitespace between columns absorb extra space. For example, suppose the screen is 320 pixels wide, and we have android:columnWidth set to 100 and android:horizontalSpacing set to 5. Three columns would use 310 pixels (three columns of 100 pixels and two whitespaces of 5 pixels). With android:stretchMode set to columnWidth, the three columns will each expand by 3-4 pixels to use up the remaining 10 pixels. With android:stretchMode set to spacingWidth, the two whitespaces will each grow by 5 pixels to consume the remaining 10 pixels.

Note that the properties android:verticalSpacing, android:horizontalSpacing, and android:columnWidth all take a simple number pixels, not a dimension, at the time of this writing.

Otherwise, the GridView works much like any other selection widget – use setAdapter() to provide the data and child views, invoke setOnItemSelectedListener() to register a selection listener, etc.

For example, here is a XML layout from the Grid sample project, showing a GridView configuration:

```
<?xml version="1.0" encoding="utf-8"?>
<LinearLayout
  xmlns:android="http://schemas.android.com/apk/res/android"
  android:orientation="vertical"
  android:layout_width="fill_parent"
  android:layout_height="fill_parent"
  >
  <TextView
    android:id="@+id/selection"
    android:layout_width="fill_parent"
    android:layout_height="wrap_content"
    />
  <GridView
    android:id="@+id/grid"
    android:layout_width="fill_parent"
    android:layout_height="fill_parent"
    android:verticalSpacing="35"
    android:horizontalSpacing="5"
    android:numColumns="auto_fit"
    android:columnWidth="100"
    android:stretchMode="columnWidth"
    android:gravity="center"
    />
</LinearLayout>
```

For this grid, we take up the entire screen except for what our selection label requires. The number of columns is computed by Android (android:numColumns = "auto_fit") based on 5-pixel horizontal spacing (android:horizontalSpacing = "5"), 100-pixel columns (android:columnWidth = "100"), with the columns absorbing any "slop" width left over (android:stretchMode = "columnWidth").

The Java code to configure the GridView is:

```
public class GridDemo extends Activity
  implements AdapterView.OnItemSelectedListener {
  TextView selection;
  String[] items={"lorem", "ipsum", "dolor", "sit", "amet",
          "consectetuer", "adipiscing", "elit", "morbi", "vel",
```

```
            "ligula", "vitae", "arcu", "aliquet", "mollis",
            "etiam", "vel", "erat", "placerat", "ante",
            "porttitor", "sodales", "pellentesque", "augue", "purus"};

@Override
public void onCreate(Bundle icicle) {
  super.onCreate(icicle);
  setContentView(R.layout.main);
  selection=(TextView)findViewById(R.id.selection);

  GridView g=(GridView) findViewById(R.id.grid);
  g.setAdapter(new FunnyLookingAdapter(this,
                      android.R.layout.simple_list_item_1,
                      items));
  g.setOnItemSelectedListener(this);
}

public void onItemSelected(AdapterView parent, View v,
                            int position, long id) {
  selection.setText(items[position]);
}

public void onNothingSelected(AdapterView parent) {
  selection.setText("");
}

private class FunnyLookingAdapter extends ArrayAdapter {
  Context ctxt;

  FunnyLookingAdapter(Context ctxt, int resource,
                      String[] items) {
    super(ctxt, resource, items);

    this.ctxt=ctxt;
  }

  public View getView(int position, View convertView,
                      ViewGroup parent) {
    TextView label=(TextView)convertView;

    if (convertView==null) {
      convertView=new TextView(ctxt);
      label=(TextView)convertView;
    }

    label.setText(items[position]);

    return(convertView);
  }
}
}
```

For the grid cells, rather than using auto-generated `TextView` widgets as in the previous sections, we create our own views, by subclassing `ArrayAdapter` and overriding `getView()`. In this case, we wrap the funny-looking strings in our own `TextView` widgets, just to be different. If `getView()` receives a `TextView`, we just reset its text; otherwise, we create a new `TextView` instance and populate it.

With the 35-pixel vertical spacing from the XML layout (`android:verticalSpacing = "35"`), the grid overflows the boundaries of the emulator's screen:

Figure 20. The GridDemo sample application, as initially launched

Figure 21. The same application, scrolled to the bottom of the grid

Fields: Now With 35% Less Typing!

The AutoCompleteTextView is sort of a hybrid between the EditView (field) and the Spinner. With auto-completion, as the user types, the text is treated as a prefix filter, comparing the entered text as a prefix against a list of candidates. Matches are shown in a selection list that, like with Spinner, folds down from the field. The user can either type out an entry (e.g., something not in the list) or choose an entry from the list to be the value of the field.

AutoCompleteTextView subclasses EditView, so you can configure all the standard look-and-feel aspects, such as font face and color.

In addition, AutoCompleteTextView has a android:completionThreshold property, to indicate the minimum number of characters a user must enter before the list filtering begins.

You can give AutoCompleteTextView an adapter containing the list of candidate values via setAdapter(). However, since the user could type something not in the list, AutoCompleteTextView does not support selection listeners. Instead, you can register a TextWatcher, like you can with any EditView, to be notified when the text changes. These events will occur either because of manual typing or from a selection from the drop-down list.

Below we have a familiar-looking XML layout, this time containing an AutoCompleteTextView (pulled from the AutoComplete sample application):

```xml
<?xml version="1.0" encoding="utf-8"?>
<LinearLayout
  xmlns:android="http://schemas.android.com/apk/res/android"
  android:orientation="vertical"
  android:layout_width="fill_parent"
  android:layout_height="fill_parent"
  >
  <TextView
    android:id="@+id/selection"
    android:layout_width="fill_parent"
    android:layout_height="wrap_content"
    />
  <AutoCompleteTextView android:id="@+id/edit"
      android:layout_width="fill_parent"
      android:layout_height="wrap_content"
      android:completionThreshold="3"/>
</LinearLayout>
```

The corresponding Java code is:

```java
public class AutoCompleteDemo extends Activity
  implements TextWatcher {
  TextView selection;
  AutoCompleteTextView edit;
  String[] items={"lorem", "ipsum", "dolor", "sit", "amet",
          "consectetuer", "adipiscing", "elit", "morbi", "vel",
          "ligula", "vitae", "arcu", "aliquet", "mollis",
          "etiam", "vel", "erat", "placerat", "ante",
          "porttitor", "sodales", "pellentesque", "augue", "purus"};

  @Override
  public void onCreate(Bundle icicle) {
    super.onCreate(icicle);
    setContentView(R.layout.main);
    selection=(TextView)findViewById(R.id.selection);
    edit=(AutoCompleteTextView)findViewById(R.id.edit);
    edit.addTextChangedListener(this);

    edit.setAdapter(new ArrayAdapter<String>(this,
```

```
                              android.R.layout.simple_list_item_1,
                              items));
    }

    public void onTextChanged(CharSequence s, int start, int before,
                              int count) {
      selection.setText(edit.getText());
    }

    public void beforeTextChanged(CharSequence s, int start,
                              int count, int after) {
      // needed for interface, but not used
    }
}
```

This time, our activity implements TextWatcher, which means our callbacks are onTextChanged() and beforeTextChanged(). In this case, we are only interested in the former, and we update the selection label to match the AutoCompleteTextView's current contents.

Here we have the results:

Figure 22. The AutoCompleteDemo sample application, as initially launched

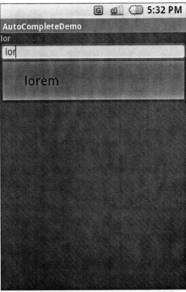

Figure 23. The same application, after a few matching letters were entered, showing the auto-complete drop-down

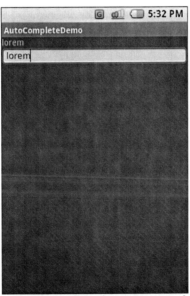

Figure 24. The same application, after the auto-complete value was selected

Galleries, Give Or Take The Art

The Gallery widget is not one ordinarily found in GUI toolkits. It is, in effect, a horizontally-laid-out listbox. One choice follows the next across the horizontal plane, with the currently-selected item highlighted. On an Android device, one rotates through the options through the left and right D-pad buttons.

Compared to the ListView, the Gallery takes up less screen space while still showing multiple choices at one time (assuming they are short enough). Compared to the Spinner, the Gallery always shows more than one choice at a time.

The quintessential example use for the Gallery is image preview – given a collection of photos or icons, the Gallery lets people preview the pictures in the process of choosing one.

Code-wise, the Gallery works much like a Spinner or GridView. In your XML layout, you have a few properties at your disposal:

- android:spacing controls the number of pixels between entries in the list

- android:spinnerSelector controls what is used to indicate a selection – this can either be a reference to a Drawable (see the resources chapter) or an RGB value in #AARRGGBB or similar notation

- android:drawSelectorOnTop indicates if the selection bar (or Drawable) should be drawn before (false) or after (true) drawing the selected child – if you choose true, be sure that your selector has sufficient transparency to show the child through the selector, otherwise users will not be able to read the selection

CHAPTER 9

Employing Fancy Widgets and Containers

The widgets and containers covered to date are not only found in many GUI toolkits (in one form or fashion), but also are widely used in building GUI applications, whether Web-based, desktop, or mobile. The widgets and containers in this chapter are a little less widely used, though you will likely find many to be quite useful.

Pick and Choose

With limited-input devices like phones, having widgets and dialogs that are aware of the type of stuff somebody is supposed to be entering is very helpful. It minimizes keystrokes and screen taps, plus reduces the chance of making some sort of error (e.g., entering a letter someplace where only numbers are expected).

As shown previously, `EditView` has content-aware flavors for entering in numbers, phone numbers, etc. Android also supports widgets (`DatePicker`, `TimePicker`) and dialogs (`DatePickerDialog`, `TimePickerDialog`) for helping users enter dates and times.

The `DatePicker` and `DatePickerDialog` allow you to set the starting date for the selection, in the form of a year, month, and day of month value. Note that the month runs from `0` for January through `11` for December. You can also choose the day on which a week "begins" – the traditional US calendar has weeks beginning on a Sunday (SUNDAY). Most importantly, each let you provide a callback object (OnDateSetListener) where you are informed of a new date selected by the user. It is up to you to store that date someplace, particularly if you are using the dialog, since there is no other way for you to get at the chosen date later on.

Similarly, TimePicker and TimePickerDialog let you:

- set the initial time the user can adjust, in the form of an hour (0 through 23) and a minute (0 through 59)

- indicate if the selection should be in 12-hour mode with an AM/PM toggle, or in 24-hour mode (what in the US is thought of as "military time" and in the rest of the world is thought of as "the way times are supposed to be")

- provide a callback object (OnTimeSetListener) to be notified of when the user has chosen a new time, which is supplied to you in the form of an hour and minute

For example, from the Chrono sample project, here's a trivial layout containing a label and two buttons – the buttons will pop up the dialog flavors of the date and time pickers:

```xml
<?xml version="1.0" encoding="utf-8"?>
<LinearLayout
  xmlns:android="http://schemas.android.com/apk/res/android"
  android:orientation="vertical"
  android:layout_width="fill_parent"
  android:layout_height="fill_parent"
  >
  <TextView android:id="@+id/dateAndTime"
    android:layout_width="fill_parent"
    android:layout_height="wrap_content"
    />
  <Button android:id="@+id/dateBtn"
    android:layout_width="fill_parent"
    android:layout_height="wrap_content"
    android:text="Set the Date"
    />
  <Button android:id="@+id/timeBtn"
    android:layout_width="fill_parent"
    android:layout_height="wrap_content"
    android:text="Set the Time"
```

```
      />
</LinearLayout>
```

The more interesting stuff comes in the Java source:

```
public class ChronoDemo extends Activity {
  DateFormat fmtDateAndTime=DateFormat.getDateTimeInstance();
  TextView dateAndTimeLabel;
  Calendar dateAndTime=Calendar.getInstance();
  DatePicker.OnDateSetListener d=new DatePicker.OnDateSetListener() {
    public void dateSet(DatePicker view, int year, int monthOfYear,
                int dayOfMonth) {
      dateAndTime.set(Calendar.YEAR, year);
      dateAndTime.set(Calendar.MONTH, monthOfYear);
      dateAndTime.set(Calendar.DAY_OF_MONTH, dayOfMonth);
      updateLabel();
    }
  };
  TimePicker.OnTimeSetListener t=new TimePicker.OnTimeSetListener() {
    public void timeSet(TimePicker view, int hourOfDay,
                        int minute) {
      dateAndTime.set(Calendar.HOUR, hourOfDay);
      dateAndTime.set(Calendar.MINUTE, minute);
      updateLabel();
    }
  };

  @Override
  public void onCreate(Bundle icicle) {
    super.onCreate(icicle);
    setContentView(R.layout.main);

    Button btn=(Button)findViewById(R.id.dateBtn);

    btn.setOnClickListener(new View.OnClickListener() {
      public void onClick(View v) {
        new DatePickerDialog(ChronoDemo.this,
              d,
              dateAndTime.get(Calendar.YEAR),
              dateAndTime.get(Calendar.MONTH),
              dateAndTime.get(Calendar.DAY_OF_MONTH),
                    Calendar.SUNDAY).show();
      }
    });

    btn=(Button)findViewById(R.id.timeBtn);

    btn.setOnClickListener(new View.OnClickListener() {
      public void onClick(View v) {
        new TimePickerDialog(ChronoDemo.this,
                    t, "Set the time",
                    dateAndTime.get(Calendar.HOUR),
                    dateAndTime.get(Calendar.MINUTE),
```

```
                        true).show();
      }
    });

    dateAndTimeLabel=(TextView)findViewById(R.id.dateAndTime);

    updateLabel();
  }

  private void updateLabel() {
    dateAndTimeLabel.setText(fmtDateAndTime
                        .format(dateAndTime.getTime()));
  }
}
```

The "model" for this activity is just a Calendar instance, initially set to be the current date and time. We pour it into the view via a DateFormat formatter. In the updateLabel() method, we take the current Calendar, format it, and put it in the TextView.

Each button is given a OnClickListener callback object. When the button is clicked, either a DatePickerDialog or a TimePickerDialog is shown. In the case of the DatePickerDialog, we give it a OnDateSetListener callback that updates the Calendar with the new date (year, month, day of month). We also give the dialog the last-selected date, getting the values out of the Calendar. In the case of the TimePickerDialog, it gets a OnTimeSetListener callback to update the time portion of the Calendar, the last-selected time, and a true indicating we want 24-hour mode on the time selector.

With all this wired together, the resulting activity looks like this:

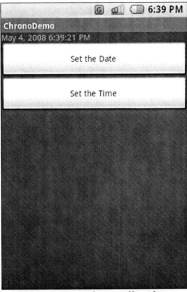

Figure 25. The ChronoDemo sample application, as initially launched

Figure 26. The same application, showing the date picker dialog

Figure 27. The same application, showing the time picker dialog

Time Keeps Flowing Like a River

If you want to display the time, rather than have users enter the time, you may wish to use the DigitalClock or AnalogClock widgets. These are extremely easy to use, as they automatically update with the passage of time. All you need to do it put them in your layout and let them do their thing.

For example, from the Clocks sample application, here is an XML layout containing both DigitalClock and AnalogClock:

```
<?xml version="1.0" encoding="utf-8"?>
<RelativeLayout xmlns:android="http://schemas.android.com/apk/res/android"
  android:orientation="vertical"
  android:layout_width="fill_parent"
  android:layout_height="fill_parent"
  >
  <AnalogClock android:id="@+id/analog"
    android:layout_width="fill_parent"
    android:layout_height="wrap_content"
    android:layout_centerHorizontal="true"
    android:layout_alignParentTop="true"
    />
  <DigitalClock android:id="@+id/digital"
```

```
    android:layout_width="wrap_content"
    android:layout_height="wrap_content"
    android:layout_centerHorizontal="true"
    android:layout_below="@id/analog"
    />
</RelativeLayout>
```

Without any Java code other than the generated stub, we can build this project and get the following activity:

Figure 28. The ClocksDemo sample application

Making Progress

If you need to be doing something for a long period of time, you owe it to your users to do two things:

- Use a background thread, which will be covered in a later chapter
- Keep them apprised of your progress, lest they think your activity has wandered away and will never come back

The typical approach to keeping users informed of progress is some form of progress bar or "throbber" (think the animated graphic towards the upper-right corner of many Web browsers). Android supports this through the ProgressBar widget.

A ProgressBar keeps track of progress, defined as an integer, with 0 indicating no progress has been made. You can define the maximum end of the range – what value indicates progress is complete – via the android:max property. By default, a ProgressBar starts with a progress of 0, though you can start from some other position via the android:progress property.

If you prefer your progress bar to be indeterminate, use the android:indeterminate property, setting it to true. You probably should also set the android:indeterminateBehavior property to either repeat (to loop endlessly until stopped in Java code) or cycle to reverse course and head back to 0.

In your Java code, you can either positively set the amount of progress that has been made (via setProgress()) or increment the progress from its current amount (via incrementProgressBy()). You can find out how much progress has been made via getProgress().

Since the ProgressBar is tied closely to the use of threads – a background thread doing work, updating the UI thread with new progress information – we will hold off demonstrating the use of ProgressBar to a later chapter.

Putting It On My Tab

The general Android philosophy is to keep activities short and sweet. If there is more information than can reasonably fit on one screen, albeit perhaps with scrolling, then it perhaps belongs in another activity kicked off via an Intent, as will be described later in this book. However, that can be complicated to set up. Moreover, sometimes there legitimately is a lot of information that needs to be collected to be processed as an atomic operation.

In a traditional UI, you might use tabs to accomplish this end, such as a JTabbedPane in Java/Swing. In Android, you now have an option of using a

TabHost container in much the same way – a portion of your activity's screen is taken up with tabs which, when clicked, swap out part of the view and replace it with something else. For example, you might have an activity with a tab for entering a location and a second tab for showing a map of that location.

Some GUI toolkits refer to "tabs" as being just the things a user clicks on to toggle from one view to another. Some toolkits refer to "tabs" as being the combination of the clickable button-ish element and the content that appears when that tab is chosen. Android treats the tab buttons and contents as discrete entities, so we will call them "tab buttons" and "tab contents" in this section.

The Pieces

There are a few widgets and containers you need to use in order to set up a tabbed portion of a view:

- TabHost is the overarching container for the tab buttons and tab contents
- TabWidget implements the row of tab buttons, which contain text labels and optionally contain icons
- FrameLayout is the container for the tab contents; each tab content is a child of the FrameLayout

This is similar to the approach that Mozilla's XUL takes. In XUL's case, the tabbox element corresponds to Android's TabHost, the tabs element corresponds to TabWidget, and tabpanels corresponds to the FrameLayout.

The Idiosyncrasies

There are a few rules to follow, at least in this milestone edition of the Android toolkit, in order to make these three work together:

- You must give the TabWidget an android:id of @android:id/tabs

- You must set aside some padding in the FrameLayout for the tab buttons (more on this below)

- If you wish to use the TabActivity, you must give the TabHost an android:id of @android:id/tabhost

TabActivity, like ListActivity, wraps a common UI pattern (activity made up entirely of tabs) into a pattern-aware activity subclass. You do not necessarily have to use TabActivity – a plain activity can use tabs as well.

With respect to the FrameLayout padding issue, for whatever reason, the TabWidget does not seem to allocate its own space inside the TabHost container. In other words, no matter what you specify for android:layout_height for the TabWidget, the FrameLayout ignores it and draws at the top of the overall TabHost. Your tab contents obscure your tab buttons. Hence, you need to leave enough padding (via android:paddingTop) in FrameLayout to "shove" the actual tab contents down beneath the tab buttons. This is likely a bug, so this behavior may well change in future versions of the toolkit.

In addition, the TabWidget seems to always draw itself with room for icons, even if you do not supply icons. Hence, for this version of the toolkit, you need to supply at least 62 pixels of padding, perhaps more depending on the icons you supply.

For example, here is a layout definition for a tabbed activity, from Tab:

```
<?xml version="1.0" encoding="utf-8"?>
<LinearLayout xmlns:android="http://schemas.android.com/apk/res/android"
  android:orientation="vertical"
  android:layout_width="fill_parent"
  android:layout_height="fill_parent">
  <TabHost android:id="@+id/tabhost"
    android:layout_width="fill_parent"
    android:layout_height="fill_parent">
    <TabWidget android:id="@android:id/tabs"
      android:layout_width="fill_parent"
      android:layout_height="wrap_content"
    />
    <FrameLayout android:id="@android:id/tabcontent"
      android:layout_width="fill_parent"
      android:layout_height="fill_parent"
```

```
      android:paddingTop="62px">
      <AnalogClock android:id="@+id/tab1"
        android:layout_width="fill_parent"
        android:layout_height="fill_parent"
        android:layout_centerHorizontal="true"
      />
      <Button android:id="@+id/tab2"
        android:layout_width="fill_parent"
        android:layout_height="fill_parent"
        android:text="A semi-random button"
      />
    </FrameLayout>
  </TabHost>
</LinearLayout>
```

Note that the TabWidget and FrameLayout are immediate children of the TabHost, and the FrameLayout itself has children representing the various tabs. In this case, there are two tabs: a clock and a button. In a more complicated scenario, the tabs are probably some form of container (e.g., LinearLayout) with their own contents.

Wiring It Together

The Java code needs to tell the TabHost what views represent the tab contents and what the tab buttons should look like. This is all wrapped up in TabSpec objects. You get a TabSpec instance from the host via newTabSpec(), fill it out, then add it to the host in the proper sequence.

The two key methods on TabSpec are:

- setContent(), where you indicate what goes in the tab content for this tab, typically the android:id of the view you want shown when this tab is selected

- setIndicator(), where you provide the caption for the tab button and, in some flavors of this method, supply a Drawable to represent the icon for the tab

Note that tab "indicators" can actually be views in their own right, if you need more control than a simple label and optional icon.

Also note that you must call setup() on the TabHost before configuring any of these TabSpec objects. The call to setup() is not needed if you are using the TabActivity base class for your activity.

For example, here is the Java code to wire together the tabs from the preceding layout example:

```
package com.commonsware.android.fancy;

import android.app.Activity;
import android.os.Bundle;
import android.widget.TabHost;

public class TabDemo extends Activity {
  @Override
  public void onCreate(Bundle icicle) {
    super.onCreate(icicle);
    setContentView(R.layout.main);

    TabHost tabs=(TabHost)findViewById(R.id.tabhost);

    tabs.setup();

    TabHost.TabSpec spec=tabs.newTabSpec("tag1");

    spec.setContent(R.id.tab1);
    spec.setIndicator("Clock");
    tabs.addTab(spec);

    spec=tabs.newTabSpec("tag2");
    spec.setContent(R.id.tab2);
    spec.setIndicator("Button");
    tabs.addTab(spec);

    tabs.setCurrentTab(0);
  }
}
```

We find our TabHost via the familiar findViewById() method, then have it setup(). After that, we get a TabSpec via newTabSpec(), supplying a tag whose purpose is unknown at this time. Given the spec, you call setContent() and setIndicator(), then call addTab() back on the TabHost to register the tab as available for use. Finally, you can choose which tab is the one to show via setCurrentTab(), providing the 0-based index of the tab.

The result?

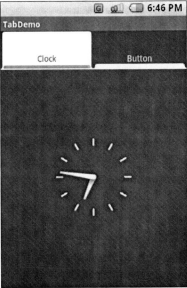

Figure 29. The TabDemo sample application, showing the first tab

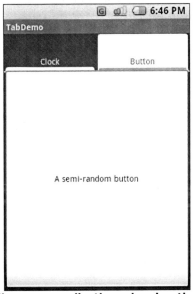

Figure 30. The same application, showing the second tab

Other Containers of Note

Android offers AbsoluteLayout, where the contents are laid out based on specific coordinate positions. You tell AbsoluteLayout where to place a child in precise X,Y coordinates, and Android puts it there, no questions asked. On the plus side, this gives you precise positioning. On the minus side, it means your views will only look "right" on screens of a certain dimension, or it requires you to write a bunch of code to adjust the coordinates based on screen size. Since Android screens might run the gamut of sizes, plus have new sizes crop up periodically, using AbsoluteLayout could get quite annoying.

Android also has a new flavor of list, the ExpandableListView. This provides a simplified tree representation, supporting two levels of depth: groups and children. Groups contain children; children are "leaves" of the tree. This requires a new set of adapters, since the ListAdapter family does not provide any sort of group information for the items in the list. This view feels like it is a work-in-progress and so is not covered here, but should appear in a future edition of this book.

CHAPTER 10

Applying Menus

Like applications for the desktop and some mobile operating systems, such as PalmOS and Windows Mobile, Android supports activities with "application" menus. Some Android phones will have a dedicated menu key for popping up the menu; others will offer alternate means for triggering the menu to appear.

Also, as with many GUI toolkits, you can create "context menus". On a traditional GUI, this might be triggered by the right-mouse button. On mobile devices, context menus typically appear when the user "taps-and-holds" over a particular widget. For example, if a TextView had a context menu, and the device was designed for finger-based touch input, you could push the TextView with your finger, hold it for a second or two, and a pop-up menu will appear for the user to choose from.

Where Android differs from most other GUI toolkits is in terms of menu construction. While you can add items to the menu, you do not have full control over the menu's contents, nor the timing of when the menu is built. Part of the menu is system-defined, and that portion is managed by the Android framework itself.

Flavors of Menu

Android considers the two types of menu described above as being the "options menu" and "context menu". The options menu is triggered by pressing the hardware "Menu" button on the device, while the context menu is raised by a tap-and-hold on the widget sporting the menu.

In addition, the options menu operates in one of two modes: icon and expanded. When the user first presses the "Menu" button, the icon mode will appear, showing up to the first five menu choices as large, finger-friendly buttons in a grid at the bottom of the screen. If the menu has more than five choices, a sixth button will appear, labeled "More" – clicking that option will bring up the expanded mode, showing all available choices. Notably, the selection bar will not be on the first menu choice, but rather the sixth, figuring that the user probably wants something lower down on the menu, since they passed on the first five choices already. The menu is scrollable, so the user can get to any of the menu choices.

Menus of Options

Rather than building your activity's options menu during onCreate(), the way you wire up the rest of your UI, you instead need to implement onCreateOptionsMenu(). This callback receives an instance of Menu.

The first thing you should do is chain upward to the superclass (super.onCreateOptionsMenu(menu)), so the Android framework can add in any menu choices it feels are necessary. Then, you can go about adding your own options, described below.

If you will need to adjust the menu during your activity's use (e.g., disable a now-invalid menu choice), just hold onto the Menu instance you receive in onCreateOptionsMenu().

Given that you have received a Menu object via onCreateOptionsMenu(), you add menu choices by calling add(). There are many flavors of this method, but all require the following parameters:

- A group identifier (int), which should be 0 unless you are creating a specific grouped set of menu choices for use with setGroupCheckable() (see below)

- A choice identifier (also an `int`), for use in identifying this choice in the `onOptionsItemSelected()` callback when a menu choice is chosen

You must also provide an icon (by its resource ID) or the text of the menu choice (as a `String` or by its resource ID) – these provide the "face" of the menu choice. Some flavors of `add()` also allow you to supply a `Runnable` to be called when the menu choice is chosen.

If you provide a `Runnable`, your choice identifier (second parameter) can be `0`. Otherwise, you should make your choice identifiers be an increment over `FIRST` (e.g., `FIRST+1`), so you do not collide with any Android system menu choices put on the same menu.

The `add()` family of methods all return an instance of `Menu.Item`, where you can adjust any of the menu item settings you have already set (e.g., the text of the menu choice). You can also set the shortcuts for the menu choice – single-character mnemonics that choose that menu choice when the menu is visible. Android supports both an alphabetic (or "qwerty") set of shortcuts and a numeric set of shortcuts. These are set individually by calling `setAlphabeticShortcut()` and `setNumericShortcut()` respectively. The menu is placed into alphabetic shortcut mode by calling `setQwertyMode()` on the menu with a `true` parameter.

The choice and group identifiers are keys used to unlock additional menu features, such as:

- Calling `setItemCheckable()` with a choice identifier, to control if the menu choice has a two-state checkbox alongside the title, where the checkbox value gets toggled when the user chooses that menu choice

- Calling `setGroupCheckable()` with a group identifier, to turn a set of menu choices into ones with a mutual-exclusion radio button between them, so one out of the group can be in the "checked" state at any time

You can also call:

- addSeparator() to add a separator line between already-defined and upcoming menu choices

- addIntentOptions() to populate the menu with menu choices corresponding to the available activities for an intent (see the chapter on launching activities)

Finally, you can create fly-out sub-menus by calling addSubMenu(), supplying the same parameters as addMenu() except the Runnable callback. Android will eventually call onCreatePanelMenu(), passing it the choice identifier of your sub-menu, along with another Menu instance representing the sub-menu itself. As with onCreateOptionsMenu(), you should chain upward to the superclass, then add menu choices to the sub-menu. One limitation is that you cannot indefinitely nest sub-menus – a menu can have a sub-menu, but a sub-menu cannot itself have a sub-sub-menu.

NOTE: Separators and sub-menus only work when the options menu is in "expanded" mode, not when it is in "icon" mode. You should only use these features if you have a really long menu, and then only starting with the sixth menu choice.

If the user makes a menu choice, and that choice came with a Runnable instance attached, your Runnable will be invoked. Otherwise, your activity will be notified via the onOptionsItemSelected() callback that a menu choice was selected. You are given the Menu.Item object corresponding to the selected menu choice. A typical pattern is to switch() on the menu ID (item.getId()) and take appropriate behavior. Note that onOptionsItemSelected() is used regardless of whether the chosen menu item was in the base menu or in a submenu.

Menus in Context

By and large, context menus use the same guts as option menus – the ContextMenu class extends the regular Menu class, offering only the means to set a "header" or caption for the popup menu via setHeader(). The two main differences are how you populate the menu and how you are informed of menu choices.

Since context menus are per-widget, rather than per-activity, there is no callback in the Activity to populate the context menu the way there is onCreateOptionsMenu() to populate the options menu. Instead, each widget itself is told when to populate the context menu. To save you the total headache of subclassing a bunch of widgets just to set up your context menus, though, Android offers a setOnPopulateContextMenuListener() method on all widgets. This takes an instance of the OnPopulateContextMenuListener callback interface. Your implementation of that interface – specifically, your implementation of onPopulateContextMenu() – is where you set up the contents of the context menu.

The onPopulateContextMenu() method gets the ContextMenu itself, the View the context menu is associated with, and an opaque Object representing "extra information" about the menu being built. If the context menu is for a selection widget that inherits from AdapterView, this object is supposed to be an instance of ContextMenuInfo, which tells you which item in the list the user did the tap-and-hold over, in case you want to customize the context menu based on that information. For example, you could toggle a checkable menu choice based upon the current state of the item. Note that you only get this "extra information" when the menu is built, not when a choice is made.

It is also important to note that onPopulateContextMenu() gets called for each time the context menu is requested. Unlike the options menu (which is only built once per activity), context menus are discarded once they are used or dismissed. Hence, you do not want to hold onto the supplied ContextMenu object; just rely on getting the chance to rebuild the menu to suit your activity's needs on an on-demand basis based on user actions.

To find out when a context menu choice was chosen, implement onContextItemSelected() on the activity. Note that you only get the Menu.Item instance that was chosen in this callback. As a result, if your activity has two or more context menus, you may want to ensure they have unique menu item identifiers for all their choices, so you can tell them apart in this callback. Otherwise, this callback behaves the same as onOptionsItemSelected() as is described above.

Taking a Peek

In the sample project Menus, you will find an amended version of the ListView sample (List) with an associated menu. Since the menus are defined in Java code, the XML layout need not change and is not reprinted here.

However, the Java code has a few new behaviors:

```
package com.commonsware.android.menus;

import android.app.Activity;
import android.os.Bundle;
import android.app.ListActivity;
import android.view.ContextMenu;
import android.view.Menu;
import android.view.View;
import android.widget.AdapterView;
import android.widget.ArrayAdapter;
import android.widget.ListView;
import android.widget.TextView;

public class MenuDemo extends ListActivity {
  TextView selection;
  String[] items={"lorem", "ipsum", "dolor", "sit", "amet",
        "consectetuer", "adipiscing", "elit", "morbi", "vel",
        "ligula", "vitae", "arcu", "aliquet", "mollis",
        "etiam", "vel", "erat", "placerat", "ante",
        "porttitor", "sodales", "pellentesque", "augue", "purus"};
  public static final int EIGHT_ID = Menu.FIRST+1;
  public static final int SIXTEEN_ID = Menu.FIRST+2;
  public static final int TWENTY_FOUR_ID = Menu.FIRST+3;
  public static final int TWO_ID = Menu.FIRST+4;

  @Override
  public void onCreate(Bundle icicle) {
  super.onCreate(icicle);
  setContentView(R.layout.main);
    setListAdapter(new ArrayAdapter<String>(this,
              android.R.layout.simple_list_item_1, items));
    selection=(TextView)findViewById(R.id.selection);

    getListView()
      .setOnPopulateContextMenuListener(new View.OnPopulateContextMenuListener() {
      public void onPopulateContextMenu(ContextMenu menu, View v, Object menuInfo) {
        populateMenu(menu);
        menu.setHeader("Divider Height");
      }
    });
  }

  public void onListItemClick(ListView parent, View v, int position,
                long id) {
    selection.setText(items[position]);
```

```
    }

    @Override
    public boolean onCreateOptionsMenu(Menu menu) {
      populateMenu(menu);

      return(super.onCreateOptionsMenu(menu));
    }

    @Override
    public boolean onOptionsItemSelected(Menu.Item item) {
      applyMenuChoice(item);

      return(applyMenuChoice(item) || super.onOptionsItemSelected(item));
    }

    @Override
    public boolean onContextItemSelected(Menu.Item item) {
      return(applyMenuChoice(item) || super.onContextItemSelected(item));
    }

    private void populateMenu(Menu menu) {
      menu.add(0, TWO_ID, "2 Pixels");
      menu.add(0, EIGHT_ID, "8 Pixels");
      menu.add(0, SIXTEEN_ID, "16 Pixels");
      menu.add(0, TWENTY_FOUR_ID, "24 Pixels");
    }

    private boolean applyMenuChoice(Menu.Item item) {
      switch (item.getId()) {
        case EIGHT_ID:
          getListView().setDividerHeight(8);
          return(true);

        case SIXTEEN_ID:
          getListView().setDividerHeight(16);
          return(true);

        case TWENTY_FOUR_ID:
          getListView().setDividerHeight(24);
          return(true);

        case TWO_ID:
          getListView().setDividerHeight(2);
          return(true);
      }

      return(false);
    }
}
```

In onCreate(), we register a OnPopulateContextMenuListener object with the list widget, so it will get a context menu, which we fill in via our populateMenu() private method. We also set the header of the menu (menu.setHeader("Divider Height")).

We also implement the onCreateOptionsMenu() callback, indicating that our activity also has an options menu. Once again, we delegate to populateMenu() to fill in the menu.

Our implementations of onOptionsItemSelected() (for options menu selections) and onContextItemSelected() (for context menu selections) both delegate to a private applyMenuChoice() method, plus chaining upwards to the superclass if none of our menu choices was the one selected by the user.

In populateMenu(), we add four menu choices, each with a unique identifier. Being lazy, we eschew the icons.

In applyMenuChoice(), we see if any of our menu choices were chosen; if so, we set the list's background color to be the user-selected hue.

Initially, the activity looks the same in the emulator as it did for ListDemo:

Figure 31. The MenuDemo sample application, as initially launched

But, if you press the Menu button, you will get our options menu:

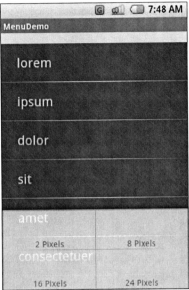

Figure 32. The same application, showing the options menu

Choosing a height (say, 16 pixels) then changes the divider height of the list to something garish:

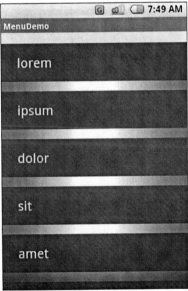

Figure 33. The same application, made ugly

You can trigger the context menu by doing a tap-and-hold on any item in the list:

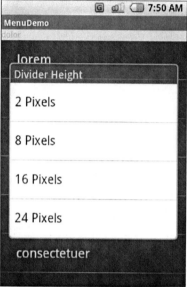

Figure 34. The same application, showing a context menu

Once again, choosing an option sets the divider height.

CHAPTER 11

Embedding the WebKit Browser

Other GUI toolkits let you use HTML for presenting information, from limited HTML renderers (e.g., Java/Swing, wxWidgets) to embedding Internet Explorer into .NET applications. Android is much the same, in that you can embed the built-in Web browser as a widget in your own activities, for displaying HTML or full-fledged browsing. The Android browser is based on WebKit, the same engine that powers Apple's Safari Web browser.

The Android browser is sufficiently complex that it gets its own Java package (android.webkit), though using the WebView widget itself can be simple or powerful, based upon your requirements.

A Browser, Writ Small

For simple stuff, WebView is not significantly different than any other widget in Android – pop it into a layout, tell it what URL to navigate to via Java code, and you're done.

For example (Browser1), here is a simple layout with a WebView:

```
<?xml version="1.0" encoding="utf-8"?>
<LinearLayout xmlns:android="http://schemas.android.com/apk/res/android"
  android:orientation="vertical"
  android:layout_width="fill_parent"
  android:layout_height="fill_parent"
  >
  <WebView android:id="@+id/webkit"
```

```
    android:layout_width="fill_parent"
    android:layout_height="fill_parent"
  />
</LinearLayout>
```

As with any other widget, you need to tell it how it should fill up the space in the layout (in this case, it fills all remaining space).

The Java code is equally simple:

```
package com.commonsware.android.webkit;

import android.app.Activity;
import android.os.Bundle;
import android.webkit.WebView;

public class BrowserDemo1 extends Activity {
  WebView browser;

  @Override
  public void onCreate(Bundle icicle) {
    super.onCreate(icicle);
    setContentView(R.layout.main);
    browser=(WebView)findViewById(R.id.webkit);

    browser.loadUrl("http://commonsware.com");
  }
}
```

The only bit unusual with this edition of onCreate() is that we invoke loadUrl() on the WebView widget, to tell it to load a Web page (in this case, the home page of some random firm).

The resulting activity looks like a Web browser, just with hidden scrollbars:

Figure 35. The Browser1 sample application

As with the regular Android browser, you can pan around the page by dragging it, while the directional pad moves you around all the focusable elements on the page.

What is missing is all the extra accouterments that make up a Web browser, such as a navigational toolbar.

Loading It Up

There are two main ways to get content into the WebView. One, shown above, is to provide the browser with a URL and have the browser display that page via loadUrl(). The browser will access the Internet through whatever means are available to that specific device at the present time (WiFi, cellular network, Bluetooth-tethered phone, well-trained tiny carrier pigeons, etc.).

The alternative is to use loadData(). Here, you supply the HTML for the browser to view. You might use this to:

- display a manual that was installed as a file with your application package

- display snippets of HTML you retrieved as part of other processing, such as the description of an entry in an Atom feed

- generate a whole user interface using HTML, instead of using the Android widget set

There are two flavors of loadData(). The simpler one allows you to provide the content, the MIME type, and the encoding, all as strings. Typically, your MIME type will be text/html and your encoding will be UTF-8 for ordinary HTML.

For example, if you replace the loadUrl() invocation in the previous example with the following:

```
browser.loadData("<html><body>Hello, world!</body></html>",
                "text/html", "UTF-8");
```

You get:

Figure 36. The Browser2 sample application

This is also available as a fully-buildable sample, as Browser2.

Navigating the Waters

As was mentioned above, there is no navigation toolbar with the WebView widget. This allows you to use it in places where such a toolbar would be pointless and a waste of screen real estate. That being said, if you want to offer navigational capabilities, you can, but you have to supply the UI.

WebView offers ways to perform garden-variety browser navigation, including:

- reload() to refresh the currently-viewed Web page
- goBack() to go back one step in the browser history, and canGoBack() to determine if there is any history to go back to
- goForward() to go forward one step in the browser history, and canGoForward() to determine if there is any history to go forward to
- goBackOrForward() to go backwards or forwards in the browser history, where negative numbers represent a count of steps to go backwards, and positive numbers represent how many steps to go forwards
- canGoBackOrForward() to see if the browser can go backwards or forwards the stated number of steps (following the same positive/negative convention as goBackOrForward())
- clearCache() to clear the browser resource cache and clearHistory() to clear the browsing history

Entertaining the Client

Particularly if you are going to use the WebView as a local user interface (vs. browsing the Web), you will want to be able to get control at key times, particularly when users click on links. You will want to make sure those links are handled properly, either by loading your own content back into the WebView, by submitting an Intent to Android to open the URL in a full browser, or by some other means (see the chapter on launching activities).

Your hook into WebView activity is via setWebViewClient(), which takes an instance of a WebViewClient implementation as a parameter. The supplied callback object will be notified of a wide range of activities, ranging from when parts of a page have been retrieved (onPageStarted(), etc.) to when you, as the host application, need to handle certain user- or circumstance-initiated events, such as:

- onTooManyRedirects()

- onReceivedHttpAuthRequest()

- etc.

A common hook will be shouldOverrideUrlLoading(), where your callback is passed a URL (plus the WebView itself) and you return true if you will handle the request or false if you want default handling (e.g., actually fetch the Web page referenced by the URL). In the case of a feed reader application, for example, you will probably not have a full browser with navigation built into your reader, so if the user clicks a URL, you probably want to use an Intent to ask Android to load that page in a full browser. But, if you have inserted a "fake" URL into the HTML, representing a link to some activity-provided content, you can update the WebView yourself.

For example, let's amend the first browser example to be a browser-based equivalent of our original example: an application that, upon a click, shows the current time.

From Browser3, here is the revised Java:

```
package com.commonsware.android.webkit;

import android.app.Activity;
import android.os.Bundle;
import android.webkit.WebView;
import android.webkit.WebViewClient;
import java.util.Date;

public class BrowserDemo3 extends Activity {
  WebView browser;

  @Override
  public void onCreate(Bundle icicle) {
    super.onCreate(icicle);
```

```
    setContentView(R.layout.main);
    browser=(WebView)findViewById(R.id.webkit);

    loadTime();
    browser.setWebViewClient(new Callback());
  }

  void loadTime() {
    String page="<html><body><a href=\"/clock\">"
            +new Date().toString()
            +"</a></body></html>";

    browser.loadData(page, "text/html", "UTF-8");
  }

  private class Callback extends WebViewClient {
    public boolean shouldOverrideUrlLoading(WebView view, String url) {
      loadTime();

      return(true);
    }
  }
}
```

Here, we load a simple Web page into the browser (loadTime()) that consists of the current time, made into a hyperlink to the /clock URL. We also attach an instance of a WebViewClient subclass, providing our implementation of shouldOverrideUrlLoading(). In this case, no matter what the URL, we want to just reload the WebView via loadTime().

Running this activity gives us:

Figure 37. The Browser3 sample application

Selecting the link and clicking the D-pad center button will "click" the link, causing us to rebuild the page with the new time.

Settings, Preferences, and Options (Oh, My!)

With your favorite desktop Web browser, you have some sort of "settings" or "preferences" or "options" window. Between that and the toolbar controls, you can tweak and twiddle the behavior of your browser, from preferred fonts to the behavior of Javascript.

Similarly, you can adjust the settings of your WebView widget as you see fit, via the WebSettings instance returned from calling the widget's getSettings() method.

There are lots of options on WebSettings to play with. Most appear fairly esoteric (e.g., setFantasyFontFamily()). However, here are some that you may find more useful:

- Control the font sizing via setDefaultFontSize() (to use a point size) or setTextSize() (to use constants indicating relative sizes like LARGER and SMALLEST)

- Control Javascript via setJavaScriptEnabled() (to disable it outright) and setJavaScriptCanOpenWindowsAutomatically() (to merely stop it from opening pop-up windows)

- Control Web site rendering via setUseDesktopUserAgent() — false means the WebView gives the Web site a user-agent string that indicates it is a mobile browser, while true results in a user-agent string that suggests it is a desktop browser

The settings you change are not persistent, so you should store them somewhere (such as via the Android preferences engine) if you are allowing your users to determine the settings, versus hard-wiring the settings in your application.

CHAPTER 12

Showing Pop-Up Messages

Sometimes, your activity (or other piece of Android code) will need to speak up.

Not every interaction with Android users will be neat, tidy, and containable in activities composed of views. Errors will crop up. Background tasks may take way longer than expected. Something asynchronous may occur, such as an incoming message. In these and other cases, you may need to communicate with the user outside the bounds of the traditional user interface.

Of course, this is nothing new. Error messages in the form of dialog boxes have been around for a very long time. More subtle indicators also exist, from task tray icons to bouncing dock icons to a vibrating cell phone.

Android has quite a few systems for letting you alert your users outside the bounds of an Activity-based UI. One, notifications, is tied heavily into intents and services and, as such, is covered in a later chapter. In this chapter, you will see two means of raising pop-up messages: toasts and alerts.

Raising Toasts

A Toast is a transient message, meaning that it displays and disappears on its own without user interaction. Moreover, it does not take focus away from the currently-active Activity, so if the user is busy writing the next Great American Programming Guide, they will not have keystrokes be "eaten" by the message.

Since a Toast is transient, you have no way of knowing if the user even notices it. You get no acknowledgment from them, nor does the message stick around for a long time to pester the user. Hence, the Toast is mostly for advisory messages, such as indicating a long-running background task is completed, the battery has dropped to a low-but-not-too-low level, etc.

Making a Toast is fairly easy. The Toast class offers a static makeText() that accepts a String (or string resource ID) and returns a Toast instance. The makeText() method also needs the Activity (or other Context) plus a duration. The duration is expressed in the form of the LENGTH_SHORT or LENGTH_LONG constants to indicate, on a relative basis, how long the message should remain visible.

If you would prefer your Toast be made out of some other View, rather that be a boring old piece of text, simply create a new Toast instance via the constructor (which takes a Context), then call setView() to supply it with the view to use and setDuration() to set the duration.

Once your Toast is configured, call its show() method, and the message will be displayed.

Alert! Alert!

If you would prefer something in the more classic dialog box style, what you want is an AlertDialog. As with any other modal dialog box, an AlertDialog pops up, grabs the focus, and stays there until closed by the user. You might use this for a critical error, a validation message that cannot be effectively displayed in the base activity UI, or something else where you are sure that the user needs to see the message and needs to see it now.

The simplest way to construct an AlertDialog is to use the Builder class. Following in true builder style, Builder offers a series of methods to configure an `AlertDialog`, each method returning the `Builder` for easy chaining. At the end, you call `show()` on the builder to display the dialog box.

Commonly-used configuration methods on `Builder` include:

- `setMessage()` if you want the "body" of the dialog to be a simple textual message, from either a supplied `String` or a supplied string resource ID

- `setTitle()` and `setIcon()`, to configure the text and/or icon to appear in the title bar of the dialog box

- `setPositiveButton()`, `setNeutralButton()`, and `setNegativeButton()`, to indicate which button(s) should appear across the bottom of the dialog, where they should be positioned (left, center, or right, respectively), what their captions should be, and what logic should be invoked when the button is clicked (besides dismissing the dialog).

If you need to configure the `AlertDialog` beyond what the builder allows, instead of calling `show()`, call `create()` to get the partially-built `AlertDialog` instance, configure it the rest of the way, then call one of the flavors of `show()` on the `AlertDialog` itself.

Once `show()` is called, the dialog box will appear and await user input.

Checking Them Out

To see how these work in practice, take a peek at `Message`, containing the following layout...:

```xml
<?xml version="1.0" encoding="utf-8"?>
<LinearLayout xmlns:android="http://schemas.android.com/apk/res/android"
  android:orientation="vertical"
  android:layout_width="fill_parent"
  android:layout_height="fill_parent" >
  <Button
    android:id="@+id/alert"
    android:text="Raise an alert"
    android:layout_width="fill_parent"
    android:layout_height="wrap_content"/>
```

```
  <Button
    android:id="@+id/toast"
    android:text="Make a toast"
    android:layout_width="fill_parent"
    android:layout_height="wrap_content"/>
</LinearLayout>
```

...and Java code:

```
public class MessageDemo extends Activity implements View.OnClickListener {
  Button alert;
  Button toast;

  @Override
  public void onCreate(Bundle icicle) {
    super.onCreate(icicle);

    setContentView(R.layout.main);

    alert=(Button)findViewById(R.id.alert);
    alert.setOnClickListener(this);
    toast=(Button)findViewById(R.id.toast);
    toast.setOnClickListener(this);
  }

  public void onClick(View view) {
    if (view==alert) {
      new AlertDialog.Builder(this)
        .setTitle("MessageDemo")
        .setMessage("eek!")
        .setNeutralButton("Close", new DialogInterface.OnClickListener() {
          public void onClick(DialogInterface dlg, int sumthin) {
            // do nothing - it will close on its own
          }
        })
        .show();
    }
    else {
      Toast
        .makeText(this, "<clink, clink>", Toast.LENGTH_SHORT)
        .show();
    }
  }
}
```

The layout is unremarkable – just a pair of buttons to trigger the alert and the toast.

When you click the alert button, we use a builder (new Builder(this)) to set the title (setTitle("MessageDemo")), message (setMessage("eek!")), and "neutral button" (setNeutralButton("Close", new OnClickListener() ...) before showing the dialog. When the button is clicked, the OnClickListener callback does nothing – the mere fact the button was pressed causes the dialog to be dismissed. However, you could update information in your activity based upon the user action, particularly if you have multiple buttons for the user to choose from. The result is a typical dialog box:

Figure 38. The MessageDemo sample application, after clicking the "Raise an alert" button

When you click the toast button, the Toast class makes us a text-based toast (makeText(this, "<clink, clink>", LENGTH_SHORT)), which we then show(). The result is a short-lived, non-interrupting message:

Figure 39. The same application, after clicking the "Make a toast" button

CHAPTER 13

Dealing with Threads

Ideally, you want your activities to be downright snappy, so your users don't feel that your application is sluggish. Responding to user input quickly (e.g., 200ms) is a fine goal. At minimum, though, you need to make sure you respond within 5 seconds, lest the ActivityManager decide to play the role of the Grim Reaper and kill off your activity as being non-responsive.

Of course, your activity might have real work to do, which takes non-negligible amounts of time. There are two ways of dealing with this:

1. Do expensive operations in a background service, relying on notifications to prompt users to go back to your activity

2. Do expensive work in a background thread

Android provides a veritable cornucopia of means to set up background threads yet allow them to safely interact with the UI on the UI thread. These include Handler objects, posting Runnable objects to the View, and using UIThreadUtilities.

Getting Through the Handlers

The most flexible means of making an Android-friendly background thread is to create an instance of a Handler subclass. You only need one Handler object per activity, and you do not need to manually register it or anything –

merely creating the instance is sufficient to register it with the Android threading subsystem.

Your background thread can communicate with the Handler, which will do all of its work on the activity UI thread. This is important, as UI changes, such as updating widgets, should only occur on the activity UI thread.

You have two options for communicating with the Handler: messages and Runnable objects.

Messages

To send a Message to a Handler, first invoke obtainMessage() to get the Message object out of the pool. There are a few flavors of obtainMessage(), allowing you to just create empty Message objects, or ones populated with message identifiers and arguments. The more complicated your Handler processing needs to be, the more likely it is you will need to put data into the Message to help the Handler distinguish different events.

Then, you send the Message to the Handler via its message queue, using one of the sendMessage...() family of methods:

- sendMessage() puts the message on the queue immediately

- sendMessageAtFrontOfQueue() puts the message on the queue immediately, and moreover puts it at the front of the message queue (versus the back, as is the default), so your message takes priority over all others

- sendMessageAtTime() puts the message on the queue at the stated time, expressed in the form of milliseconds based on system uptime (SystemClock.uptimeMillis())

- sendMessageDelayed() puts the message on the queue after a delay, expressed in milliseconds

To process these messages, your Handler needs to implement handleMessage(), which will be called with each message that appears on the message queue. There, the handler can update the UI as needed. However, it should still do that work quickly, as other UI work is suspended until the Handler is done.

For example, let's create a ProgressBar and update it via a Handler. Here is the layout from Handler:

```xml
<?xml version="1.0" encoding="utf-8"?>
<LinearLayout xmlns:android="http://schemas.android.com/apk/res/android"
  android:orientation="vertical"
  android:layout_width="fill_parent"
  android:layout_height="fill_parent"
  >
  <ProgressBar android:id="@+id/progress"
    style="?android:attr/progressBarStyleHorizontal"
    android:layout_width="fill_parent"
    android:layout_height="wrap_content"
    android:max="100" />
</LinearLayout>
```

The ProgressBar, in addition to setting the width and height as normal, also employs two other properties of note:

- style, which will be covered in greater detail in some future edition of this book. For now, suffice it to say that it indicates this ProgressBar should be drawn as the traditional horizontal bar showing the amount of work that has been completed.

- android:max, which indicates the maximum value for the ProgressBar (i.e., at what value is the work "done" and the progress bar completed). A value of 100 means the ProgressBar works on a simple percentage system.

And here is the Java:

```java
package com.commonsware.android.threads;

import android.app.Activity;
import android.os.Bundle;
import android.os.Handler;
import android.os.Message;
import android.widget.ProgressBar;

public class HandlerDemo extends Activity {
  ProgressBar bar;
```

```
Handler handler=new Handler() {
  @Override
  public void handleMessage(Message msg) {
    bar.incrementProgressBy(5);
  }
};
boolean isRunning=false;

@Override
public void onCreate(Bundle icicle) {
  super.onCreate(icicle);
  setContentView(R.layout.main);
  bar=(ProgressBar)findViewById(R.id.progress);
}

public void onStart() {
  super.onStart();
  bar.setProgress(0);

  Thread background=new Thread(new Runnable() {
    public void run() {
      try {
        for (int i=0;i<20 && isRunning;i++) {
          Thread.sleep(1000);
          handler.sendMessage(handler.obtainMessage());
        }
      }
      catch (Throwable t) {
        // just end the background thread
      }
    }
  });

  isRunning=true;
  background.start();
}

public void onStop() {
  super.onStop();
  isRunning=false;
}
}
```

As part of constructing the Activity, we create an instance of Handler, with our implementation of handleMessage(). Basically, for any message received, we update the ProgressBar by 5 points, then exit the message handler.

In onStart(), we set up a background thread. In a real system, this thread would do something meaningful. Here, we just sleep one second, post a Message to the Handler, and repeat for a total of 20 passes.

Note that we then *leave* onStart(). This is crucial. The onStart() method is invoked on the activity UI thread, so it can update widgets and such. However, that means we need to get out of onStart(), both to let the Handler get its work done, and also so Android does not think our activity is stuck.

The resulting activity is simply a horizontal progress bar:

Figure 40. The HandlerDemo sample application

Runnables

If you would rather not fuss with Message objects, you can also pass Runnable objects to the Handler, which will run those Runnable objects on the activity UI thread. Handler offers a set of post...() methods for passing Runnable objects in for eventual processing.

Running In Place

Just as Handler supports post() and postDelayed() to add Runnable objects to the event queue, you can use those same methods on View. This lightly simplifies your code, in that you can then skip the Handler object. However, you lose a bit of flexibility, and the Handler has been around longer in the Android toolkit and may be more tested.

Utilities (And I Don't Mean Water Works)

Yet another option is to use the UIThreadUtilities helper class, which offers a set of static methods to assist in working with the UI thread.

First, it offers isUIThread(), which will tell you if you are presently executing on the UI thread of the supplied View. In the Handler sample shown above, this method would be superfluous – you pretty much can always tell by "eyeballing" the code whether it will be executing on the UI thread or not. But, if you package some of your code in a JAR for others to reuse, you might not know whether your code is being executed on the UI thread or from a background thread. Therefore, for safety, you can invoke isUIThread() to find out and take appropriate action if you are not on the UI thread.

Such "appropriate action" might be to use runOnUIThread(). This works similar to the post() methods on Handler and View, in that it queues up a Runnable to run on the UI thread...if you are not on the UI thread right now. If you already are on the UI thread, it invokes the Runnable immediately. To identify the proper UI thread, you must supply an Activity, Dialog, or View.

And Now, The Caveats

Background threads, while eminently possible using the Android Handler system, are not all happiness and warm puppies. Background threads not only add complexity, but they have real-world costs in terms of available memory, CPU, and battery life.

To that end, there are a wide range of scenarios you need to account for with your background thread, including:

- The possibility that users will interact with your activity's UI while the background thread is chugging along. If the work that the background thread is doing is altered or invalidated by the user input, you will need to communicate this to the background thread. Android includes many classes in the java.util.concurrent package that will help you communicate safely with your background thread.

- The possibility that the activity will be killed off while background work is going on. For example, after starting your activity, the user might have a call come in, followed by a text message, followed by a need to look up a contact...all of which might be sufficient to kick your activity out of memory. The next chapter will cover the various events Android will take your activity through; hook the proper ones and be sure to shut down your background thread cleanly when you have the chance.

- The possibility that your user will get irritated if you chew up a lot of CPU time and battery life without giving any payback. Tactically, this means using ProgressBar or other means of letting the user know that something is happening. Strategically, this means you still need to be efficient at what you do – background threads are no panacea for sluggish or pointless code.

- The possibility that you will encounter an error during background processing. For example, if you are gathering information off the Internet, the device might lose connectivity. Alerting the user of the problem via a Notification and shutting down the background thread may be your best option.

CHAPTER 14

Handling Activity Lifecycle Events

While this may sound like a broken record...please remember that Android devices, by and large, are phones. As such, some activities are more important that others – taking a call is probably more important to users than is playing Sudoku. And, since it is a phone, it probably has less RAM than does your current desktop or notebook.

As a result, your activity may find itself being killed off because other activities are going on and the system needs your activity's memory. Think of it as the Android equivalent of the "circle of life" – your activity dies so others may live, and so on. You cannot assume that your activity will run until you think it is complete, or even until the user thinks it is complete.

This is one example – perhaps the most important example – of how an activity's lifecycle will affect your own application logic. This chapter covers the various states and callbacks that make up an activity's lifecycle and how you can hook into them appropriately.

Schroedinger's Activity

An activity, generally speaking, is in one of four states at any point in time:

- **Active**: the activity was started by the user, is running, and is in the foreground. This is what you're used to thinking of in terms of your activity's operation.

- **Paused**: the activity was started by the user, is running, and is visible, but a notification or something is overlaying part of the screen. During this time, the user can see your activity but may not be able to interact with it. For example, if a call comes in, the user will get the opportunity to take the call or ignore it.

- **Stopped**: the activity was started by the user, is running, but it is hidden by other activities that have been launched or switched to. Your application will not be able to present anything meaningful to the user directly, only by way of a Notification.

- **Dead**: either the activity was never started (e.g., just after a phone reset) or the activity was terminated, perhaps due to lack of available memory.

Life, Death, and Your Activity

Android will call into your activity as the activity transitions between the four states listed above. Some transitions may result in multiple calls to your activity, and sometimes Android will kill your application without calling it. This whole area is rather murky and probably subject to change, so pay close attention to the official Android documentation as well as this section when deciding which events to pay attention to and which you can safely ignore.

Note that for all of these, you should chain upward and invoke the superclass' edition of the method, or Android may raise an exception.

onCreate() and onCompleteThaw()

We have been implementing onCreate() in all of our Activity subclasses in all the examples. This will get called in two situations:

1. When the activity is first started (e.g., since a system restart), onCreate() will be invoked with a null parameter.

2. If the activity had been running, had onFreeze() invoked, then sometime later was killed off, onCreate() will be invoked with the Bundle from onFreeze() as a parameter. Dealing with freezing and restoring state is covered later in this chapter.

Here is where you initialize your user interface and set up anything that needs to be done once, regardless of how the activity gets used.

If the activity is being restored from a frozen state (second scenario above), then onCompleteThaw() is also called, and is passed the same Bundle as was the preceding onCreate(). If you want, you can isolate your un-freezing logic here.

onStart(), onRestart(), and onResume()

These are invoked as your activity is brought to the foreground and made available to the user. The Android documentation is contradictory as to under what circumstances and in what order these are called. It is fairly safe to say that:

- onResume() will be called more commonly than the others, and should be called if the activity was paused (onPause()) and then brought back to the foreground relatively quickly. In fact, onResume() should be called just before the activity is brought to the foreground in all circumstances.

- onStart() may be called if the activity was stopped (onStop()) then started up again without the process being terminated

Generally speaking, in these methods you will wish to do things that only make sense when a user is looking at your activity, particularly things that might have changed since the last time your activity was looked at. For example, if you are polling a service for changes to some information (e.g., new entries for a feed), onResume() is a fine time to both refresh the current view and, if applicable, kick off a background thread to update the view (e.g., via a Handler).

onPause(), onFreeze(), onStop(), and onDestroy()

The onFreeze() event is triggered if Android thinks that it may have to kill off your activity in the not-too-distant future. You are passed a Bundle object, which works similar to a Map, where you can persist the current state of your UI (e.g., field values, checkbox states). That Bundle will be re-supplied to you in onCreate() and onCompleteThaw() if, indeed, your activity was killed off. However, it is possible that onFreeze() will be called several times without your activity actually being killed off, so do not assume that just because your onFreeze() handler is called that "the end is near".

Anything that steals your user away from your activity – mostly, the activation of another activity – will result in your onPause() being called. Here, you should undo anything you did in onResume(), such as stopping background threads, releasing any exclusive-access resources you may have acquired (e.g., camera), and the like.

Once onPause() is called, Android reserves the right to kill off your activity's process at any point. Hence, you should not be relying upon receiving any further events.

The onStop() event is the counterpart to onRestart(). However, since it might not get called, it is unclear what specifically you might want to do in this method.

Similarly, onDestroy() may or may not be called before your process ends. However, there is no question that, after onDestroy(), your process is ending, and so the next line of code of yours that will be invoked for this activity will be onCreate().

PART III – Data Stores, Network Services, and APIs

CHAPTER 15

Using Preferences

Android has many different ways for you to store data for long-term use by your activity. The simplest to use is the preferences system.

Android allows activities and applications to keep preferences, in the form of key/value pairs (akin to a Map), that will hang around between invocations of an activity. As the name suggests, the primary purpose is for you to store user-specified configuration details, such as the last feed the user looked at in your feed reader, or what sort order to use by default on a list, or whatever. Of course, you can store in the preferences whatever you like, so long as it is keyed by a String and has a primitive value (boolean, String, etc.)

Preferences can either be for a single activity or shared among all activities in an application. Eventually, preferences might be shareable across applications, but that is not supported as of the time of this writing.

Getting What You Want

To get access to the preferences, you have two APIs to choose from:

1. getPreferences() from within your Activity, to access activity-specific preferences

2. getSharedPreferences() from within your Activity (or other application Context), to access application-level preferences

Both take a security mode parameter – for now, pass in 0. The getSharedPreferences() method also takes a name of a set of preferences – getPreferences() effectively calls getSharedPreferences() with the activity's class name as the preference set name.

Both of those methods return an instance of SharedPreferences, which offers a series of getters to access named preferences, returning a suitably-typed result (e.g., getBoolean() to return a boolean preference). The getters also take a default value, which is returned if there is no preference set under the specified key.

Stating Your Preference

Given the appropriate SharedPreferences object, you can use edit() to get an "editor" for the preferences. This object has a set of setters that mirror the getters on the parent SharedPreferences object. It also has:

- remove() to get rid of a single named preference
- clear() to get rid of all preferences
- commit() to persist your changes made via the editor

The last one is important – if you modify preferences via the editor and fail to commit() the changes, those changes will evaporate once the editor goes out of scope.

Conversely, since the preferences object supports live changes, if one part of your application (say, an activity) modifies shared preferences, another part of your application (say, a service) will have access to the changed value immediately.

A Preference For Action

To demonstrate preferences, we need an activity that gives the user something to input (so we can persist it as a preference)...and that we know will go through a likely activity lifecycle event for us to persist the change.

The first criterion is easy: just use a checkbox. In fact, this example (Prefs) is based off of our earlier checkbox demo:

```xml
<?xml version="1.0" encoding="utf-8"?>
<LinearLayout xmlns:android="http://schemas.android.com/apk/res/android"
  android:layout_width="fill_parent"
  android:layout_height="fill_parent">
  <CheckBox android:id="@+id/check"
    android:layout_width="wrap_content"
    android:layout_height="wrap_content"
    android:text="This checkbox is: unchecked" />
  <Button android:id="@+id/close"
    android:layout_width="wrap_content"
    android:layout_height="wrap_content"
    android:text="Close" />
</LinearLayout>
```

Here, we have a row of two widgets: our checkbox, and a button labeled "Close".

The Java is a bit more involved:

```java
package com.commonsware.android.prefs;

import android.app.Activity;
import android.content.SharedPreferences;
import android.os.Bundle;
import android.view.View;
import android.widget.Button;
import android.widget.CheckBox;
import android.widget.CompoundButton;

public class PrefsDemo extends Activity
  implements CompoundButton.OnCheckedChangeListener {
  CheckBox cb;

  @Override
  public void onCreate(Bundle icicle) {
    super.onCreate(icicle);
    setContentView(R.layout.main);

    cb=(CheckBox)findViewById(R.id.check);
    cb.setOnCheckedChangeListener(this);

    Button btn=(Button)findViewById(R.id.close);

    btn.setOnClickListener(new Button.OnClickListener() {
      public void onClick(View v) {
        finish();
      }
```

```
    });
  }

  public void onCheckedChanged(CompoundButton buttonView, boolean isChecked) {
    if (isChecked) {
      cb.setText("This checkbox is: checked");
    }
    else {
      cb.setText("This checkbox is: unchecked");
    }
  }

  public void onResume() {
    super.onResume();

    SharedPreferences settings=getPreferences(0);

    cb.setChecked(settings.getBoolean("cb_checked", false));
  }

  public void onPause() {
    super.onPause();

    SharedPreferences settings=getPreferences(0);
    SharedPreferences.Editor editor=settings.edit();

    editor.putBoolean("cb_checked", cb.isChecked());
    editor.commit();
  }
}
```

In onCreate(), we do the same setup as before, tying our activity in as the OnCheckedChangeListener for the checkbox. We also tie an anonymous OnClickListener to the button, which calls finish() on the activity. This proactively closes the activity, causing Android to go through the full chain of onPause(), onStop(), and onDestroy() as it closes out the activity. This way, we can be sure that, for our test, we get a likely spot to persist the preferences.

Unlike in the original example, we also hook into onResume() and onPause(). In onResume(), we access the activity's preferences and retrieve a cb_checked boolean preference, and set the checkbox to that value. By default, if the preference is not found, it will be set to false. Conversely, in onPause(), we get the activity's preferences, store the cb_checked preference as the checkbox's current state, and commit the change.

When we first launch the activity, the checkbox is unchecked:

Figure 41. The PrefsDemo sample application, as initially launched

If you check the checkbox, then click the Close button, then re-open the activity, you will see that it opens with the checkbox already checked:

Figure 42. The same application, after checking the checkbox

Notice that the label for the checkbox is also correct, in that it says the checkbox is checked. This means that our onCheckedChanged() implementation is being called, even though we are manually setting the checkbox state via setChecked().

CHAPTER 16

Accessing Files

While Android offers structured storage, via preferences and databases, sometimes a simple file will suffice. Android offers two models for accessing files: one for files pre-packaged with your application, and one for files created on-device by your application.

You And The Horse You Rode In On

Let's suppose you have some static data you want to ship with the application, such as a list of words for a spell-checker. The easiest way to deploy that is to put the file in the res/raw directory, so it gets put in the Android application .apk file as part of the packaging process.

To access this file, you need to get yourself a Resources object. From an activity, that is as simple as calling getResources(). A Resources object offers openRawResource() to get an InputStream on the file you specify. Rather than a path, openRawResource() expects an integer identifier for the file as packaged. This works just like accessing widgets via findViewById() – if you put a file named words.xml in res/raw, the identifier is accessible in Java as R.raw.words.

Since you can only get an InputStream, you have no means of modifying this file. Hence, it is really only useful for static reference data. Moreover, since it is unchanging until the user installs an updated version of your application package, either the reference data has to be valid for the foreseeable future, or you will need to provide some means of updating the data. The simplest way to handle that is to use the reference data to bootstrap some other modifiable form of storage (e.g., a database), but this makes for two copies of the data in storage. An alternative is to keep the reference data as-is but keep modifications in a file or database, and merge them together when you need a complete picture of the information. For example, if your application ships a file of URLs, you could have a second file that tracks URLs added by the user or reference URLs that were deleted by the user.

In the static sample project, you will find a reworking of the listbox example from earlier, this time using a static XML file instead of a hardwired array in Java. The layout is the same:

```xml
<?xml version="1.0" encoding="utf-8"?>
<LinearLayout xmlns:android="http://schemas.android.com/apk/res/android"
  android:orientation="vertical"
  android:layout_width="fill_parent"
  android:layout_height="fill_parent" >
  <TextView
    android:id="@+id/selection"
    android:layout_width="fill_parent"
    android:layout_height="wrap_content"
  />
  <ListView
    android:id="@android:id/list"
    android:layout_width="fill_parent"
    android:layout_height="fill_parent"
    android:drawSelectorOnTop="false"
  />
</LinearLayout>
```

In addition to that XML file, you also need an XML file with the words to show in the list:

```xml
<words>
  <word value="lorem" />
  <word value="ipsum" />
  <word value="dolor" />
  <word value="sit" />
  <word value="amet" />
  <word value="consectetuer" />
  <word value="adipiscing" />
  <word value="elit" />
  <word value="morbi" />
  <word value="vel" />
  <word value="ligula" />
```

```
<word value="vitae" />
<word value="arcu" />
<word value="aliquet" />
<word value="mollis" />
<word value="etiam" />
<word value="vel" />
<word value="erat" />
<word value="placerat" />
<word value="ante" />
<word value="porttitor" />
<word value="sodales" />
<word value="pellentesque" />
<word value="augue" />
<word value="purus" />
</words>
```

While this XML structure is not exactly a model of space efficiency, it will suffice for a demo.

The Java code now must read in that XML file, parse out the words, and put them someplace for the list to pick up:

```
public class StaticFileDemo extends ListActivity {
  TextView selection;
  ArrayList items=new ArrayList();

  @Override
  public void onCreate(Bundle icicle) {
    super.onCreate(icicle);
    setContentView(R.layout.main);
    selection=(TextView)findViewById(R.id.selection);

    try {
      InputStream in=getResources().openRawResource(R.raw.words);
      DocumentBuilder builder=DocumentBuilderFactory
                              .newInstance()
                              .newDocumentBuilder();
      Document doc=builder.parse(in, null);
      NodeList words=doc.getElementsByTagName("word");

      for (int i=0;i<words.getLength();i++) {
        items.add(((Element)words.item(i)).getAttribute("value"));
      }

      in.close();
    }
    catch (Throwable t) {
      showAlert("Exception!", 0, t.toString(), "Cancel", true);
    }

    setListAdapter(new ArrayAdapter<String>(this,
```

```
                        android.R.layout.simple_list_item_1,
                        items));
  }

  public void onListItemClick(ListView parent, View v, int position,
                        long id) {
    selection.setText(items.get(position).toString());
  }
}
```

The differences mostly lie within onCreate(). We get an InputStream for the XML file (getResources().openRawResource(R.raw.words)), then use the built-in XML parsing logic to parse the file into a DOM Document, pick out the word elements, then pour the value attributes into an ArrayList for use by the ArrayAdapter.

The resulting activity looks the same as before, since the list of words is the same, just relocated:

Figure 43. The StaticFileDemo sample application

Of course, there are even easier ways to have XML files available to you as pre-packaged files – using an XML resource. That is covered in the next chapter. However, while this example used XML, the file could just as easily have been a simple one-word-per-line list, or in some other format not handled natively by the Android resource system.

Readin' 'n Writin'

Reading and writing your own, application-specific data files is nearly identical to what you might do in a desktop Java application. The key is to use openFileInput() and openFileOutput() on your Activity or other Context to get an InputStream and OutputStream, respectively. From that point forward, it is not much different than regular Java I/O logic:

- Wrap those streams as needed, such as using an InputStreamReader or OutputStreamWriter for text-based I/O

- Read or write the data

- Use close() to release the stream when done

Relative paths (i.e., those without leading slashes) are local to the application. If two applications both try reading a notes.txt file via openFileInput(), they will each access their own edition of the file. If you need to have one file accessible from many places, you probably want to create a content provider, as will be described an upcoming chapter.

Below you will see the layout for the world's most trivial text editor, pulled from the ReadWrite sample application:

```xml
<?xml version="1.0" encoding="utf-8"?>
<LinearLayout xmlns:android="http://schemas.android.com/apk/res/android"
  android:layout_width="fill_parent"
  android:layout_height="fill_parent"
  android:orientation="vertical">
  <Button android:id="@+id/close"
    android:layout_width="wrap_content"
    android:layout_height="wrap_content"
    android:text="Close" />
  <EditText
    android:id="@+id/editor"
    android:layout_width="fill_parent"
    android:layout_height="fill_parent"
    android:singleLine="false"
    />
</LinearLayout>
```

All we have here is a large text-editing widget, with a "Close" button above it.

The Java is only slightly more complicated:

```java
package com.commonsware.android.files;

import android.app.Activity;
import android.os.Bundle;
import android.view.View;
import android.widget.Button;
import android.widget.EditText;
import java.io.BufferedReader;
import java.io.InputStream;
import java.io.InputStreamReader;
import java.io.InputStream;
import java.io.OutputStream;
import java.io.OutputStreamWriter;

public class ReadWriteFileDemo extends Activity {
  EditText editor;

  @Override
  public void onCreate(Bundle icicle) {
    super.onCreate(icicle);
    setContentView(R.layout.main);
    editor=(EditText)findViewById(R.id.editor);

    Button btn=(Button)findViewById(R.id.close);

    btn.setOnClickListener(new Button.OnClickListener() {
      public void onClick(View v) {
        finish();
      }
    });
  }

  public void onResume() {
    super.onResume();

    try {
      InputStream in=openFileInput("notes.txt");

      if (in!=null) {
        BufferedReader reader=new BufferedReader(new InputStreamReader(in));
        String str;
        StringBuffer buf=new StringBuffer();

        while ((str = reader.readLine()) != null) {
          buf.append(str+"\n");
        }

        in.close();
        editor.setText(buf.toString());
      }
    }
    catch (java.io.FileNotFoundException e) {
      // that's OK, we probably haven't created it yet
    }
```

```
    catch (Throwable t) {
      showAlert("Exception!", 0, t.toString(), "Cancel", true);
    }
  }

public void onPause() {
  super.onPause();

  try {
    OutputStreamWriter out=new OutputStreamWriter(openFileOutput("notes.txt", 0));

    out.write(editor.getText().toString());
    out.close();
  }
  catch (Throwable t) {
    showAlert("Exception!", 0, t.toString(), "Cancel", true);
  }
  }
}
```

First, we wire up the button to close out our activity when clicked by using
setOnClickListener() to invoke finish() on the activity.

Next, we hook into onResume(), so we get control when our editor is coming
back to life, from a fresh launch or after having been frozen. We use
openFileInput() to read in notes.txt and pour the contents into the text
editor. If the file is not found, we assume this is the first time the activity
was run (or the file was deleted by other means), and we just leave the editor
empty.

Finally, we hook into onPause(), so we get control as our activity gets hidden
by other user activity or is closed, such as via our "Close" button. Here, we
use openFileOutput() to open notes.txt, into which we pour the contents of
the text editor.

The net result is that we have a persistent notepad: whatever is typed in will
remain until deleted, surviving our activity being closed, the phone being
turned off, or similar situations. Of course, it doesn't look like much:

Figure 44. The ReadWriteFileDemo sample application, as initially launched

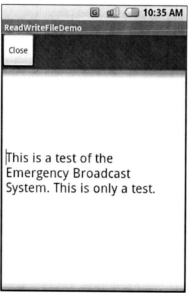

Figure 45. The same application, after entering some text

CHAPTER 17

Working with Resources

Resources are static bits of information held outside the Java source code. You have seen one type of resource – the layout – frequently in the examples in this book. There are many other types of resource, such as images and strings, that you can take advantage of in your Android applications.

The Resource Lineup

Resources are stored as files under the res/ directory in your Android project layout. With the exception of raw resources (res/raw/), all the other types of resources are parsed for you, either by the Android packaging system or by the Android system on the device or emulator. So, for example, when you lay out an activity's UI via a layout resource (res/layout/), you do not have to parse the layout XML yourself – Android handles that for you.

In addition to layout resources (first seen in an earlier chapter) and raw resources (introduced in another earlier chapter), there are several other types of resource available to you, including:

- Animations (res/anim/), designed for short clips as part of a user interface, such as an animation suggesting the turning of a page when a button is clicked

- Images (res/drawable), for putting static icons or other pictures in a user interface

- Strings, colors, arrays, and dimensions (res/values/), to both give these sorts of constants symbolic names and to keep them separate from the rest of the code (e.g., for internationalization and localization)

- XML (res/xml/), for static XML files containing your own data and structure

String Theory

Keeping your labels and other bits of text outside the main source code of your application is generally considered to be a very good idea. In particular, it helps with internationalization (I18N) and localization (L10N), covered later in this chapter. Even if you are not going to translate your strings to other languages, it is easier to make corrections if all the strings are in one spot instead of scattered throughout your source code.

Android supports regular externalized strings, along with "string formats", where the string has placeholders for dynamically-inserted information. On top of that, Android supports simple text formatting, called "styled text", so you can make your words be bold or italic intermingled with normal text.

Plain Strings

Generally speaking, all you need to do is have an XML file in the res/values directory (typically named res/values/strings.xml), with a resources root element, and one child string element for each string you wish to encode as a resource. The string element takes a name attribute, which is the unique name for this string, and a single text element containing the text of the string:

```
<resources>
  <string name="quick">The quick brown fox...</string>
  <string name="laughs">He who laughs last...</string>
</resources>
```

The only tricky part is if the string value contains a quote (") or an apostrophe ('). In those cases, you will want to escape those values, by preceding them with a backslash (e.g., These are the times that try men\'s souls). Or, if it is just an apostrophe, you could enclose the value in quotes (e.g., "These are the times that try men's souls.").

You can then reference this string from a layout file (as @string/..., where the ellipsis is the unique name – e.g., @string/laughs). Or you can get the string from your Java code by calling getString() with the resource ID of the string resource, that being the unique name prefixed with R.string. (e.g., getString(R.string.quick)).

String Formats

As with other implementations of the Java language, Android's Dalvik VM supports string formats. Here, the string contains placeholders representing data to be replaced at runtime by variable information (e.g., My name is %1$s). Plain strings stored as resources can be used as string formats:

```
String strFormat=getString(R.string.my_name);
String strResult=String.format(strFormat, "Tim");
((TextView)findViewById(R.layout.some_label))
  .setText(strResult);
```

Styled Text

If you want really rich text, you should have raw resources containing HTML, then pour those into a WebKit widget. However, for light HTML formatting, using <b>, <i>, and <u>, you can just use a string resource:

```
<resources>
  <string name="b">This has <b>bold</b> in it.</string>
  <string name="i">Whereas this has <i>italics</i>!</string>
</resources>
```

You can access these the same as with plain strings, with the exception that the result of the getString() call is really a Spanned:

```
((TextView)findViewById(R.layout.another_label))
        .setText(getString(R.string.laughs));
```

Styled Formats

Where styled text gets tricky is with styled string formats, as `String.format()` works on `String` objects, not `Spanned` objects with formatting instructions. If you really want to have styled string formats, here is the workaround:

1. Entity-escape the angle brackets in the string resource (e.g., `this is` `&lt;b&gt;%1$s&lt;/b&gt;`)

2. Retrieve the string resource as normal, though it will not be styled at this point (e.g., `getString(R.string.funky_format)`)

3. Generate the format results, being sure to escape any string values you substitute in, in case they contain angle brackets or ampersands

```
String.format(getString(R.string.funky_format),
              TextUtils.htmlEncode(strName));
```

4. Convert the entity-escaped HTML into a `Spanned` object via `Html.fromHtml()`

```
someTextView.setText(Html
                     .fromHtml(resultFromStringFormat));
```

To see this in action, let's look at the `Strings` demo. Here is the layout file:

```xml
<?xml version="1.0" encoding="utf-8"?>
<LinearLayout xmlns:android="http://schemas.android.com/apk/res/android"
  android:orientation="vertical"
  android:layout_width="fill_parent"
  android:layout_height="fill_parent"
  >
  <LinearLayout xmlns:android="http://schemas.android.com/apk/res/android"
    android:orientation="horizontal"
    android:layout_width="fill_parent"
    android:layout_height="wrap_content"
    >
    <Button android:id="@+id/format"
      android:layout_width="wrap_content"
      android:layout_height="wrap_content"
      android:text="@string/btn_name"
      />
    <EditText android:id="@+id/name"
      android:layout_width="fill_parent"
      android:layout_height="wrap_content"
      />
  </LinearLayout>
  <TextView android:id="@+id/result"
```

```
     android:layout_width="fill_parent"
     android:layout_height="wrap_content"
     />
</LinearLayout>
```

As you can see, it is just a button, a field, and a label. The intent is for somebody to enter their name in the field, then click the button to cause the label to be updated with a formatted message containing their name.

The Button in the layout file references a string resource (@string/btn_name), so we need a string resource file (res/values/strings.xml):

```
<?xml version="1.0" encoding="utf-8"?>
<resources>
  <string name="app_name">StringsDemo</string>
  <string name="btn_name">Name:</string>
  <string name="funky_format">My name is &lt;b&gt;%1$s&lt;/b&gt;</string>
</resources>
```

The app_name resource is automatically created by the activityCreator script. The btn_name string is the caption of the Button, while our styled string format is in funky_format.

Finally, to hook all this together, we need a pinch of Java:

```
package com.commonsware.android.resources;

import android.app.Activity;
import android.os.Bundle;
import android.text.TextUtils;
import android.text.Html;
import android.view.View;
import android.widget.Button;
import android.widget.EditText;
import android.widget.TextView;

public class StringsDemo extends Activity {
  EditText name;
  TextView result;

  @Override
  public void onCreate(Bundle icicle) {
    super.onCreate(icicle);
    setContentView(R.layout.main);

    name=(EditText)findViewById(R.id.name);
```

```
  result=(TextView)findViewById(R.id.result);

  Button btn=(Button)findViewById(R.id.format);

  btn.setOnClickListener(new Button.OnClickListener() {
    public void onClick(View v) {
      applyFormat();
    }
  });
}

private void applyFormat() {
  String format=getString(R.string.funky_format);
  String simpleResult=String.format(format,
                 TextUtils.htmlEncode(name.getText().toString()));
  result.setText(Html.fromHtml(simpleResult));
}
}
```

The string resource manipulation can be found in applyFormat(), which is called when the button is clicked. First, we get our format via getString() – something we could have done at onCreate() time for efficiency. Next, we format the value in the field using this format, getting a String back, since the string resource is in entity-encoded HTML. Note the use of TextUtils.htmlEncode() to entity-encode the entered name, in case somebody decides to use an ampersand or something. Finally, we convert the simple HTML into a styled text object via Html.fromHtml() and update our label.

When the activity is first launched, we have an empty label:

Figure 46. The StringsDemo sample application, as initially launched

but if we fill in a name and click the button, we get:

Figure 47. The same application, after filling in some heroic figure's name

Got the Picture?

Android supports images in the PNG, JPEG, and GIF formats. GIF is officially discouraged, however; PNG is the overall preferred format. Images can be used anywhere that requires a Drawable, such as the image and background of an ImageView.

Using images is simply a matter of putting your image files in res/drawable/ and then referencing them as a resource. Within layout files, images are referenced as @drawable/... where the ellipsis is the base name of the file (e.g., for res/drawable/foo.png, the resource name is @drawable/foo). In Java, where you need an image resource ID, use R.drawable. plus the base name (e.g., R.drawable.foo).

If you need a Uri to an image resource, you can use one of two different string formats for the path:

1. android.resource://com.example.app/..., where com.example.app is the name of the Java package used by your application in AndroidManifest.xml and ... is the numeric resource ID for the resource in question (e.g., the value of R.drawable.foo)

2. android.resource://com.example.app/raw/..., where com.example.app is the name of the Java package used by your application in AndroidManifest.xml and ... is the textual name of the raw resource (e.g., foo for res/drawable/foo.png)

Note that Android ships with some image resources built in. Those are addressed in Java with an android.R.drawable prefix to distinguish them from application-specific resources (e.g., android.R.drawable.picture_frame).

So, let's update the previous example to use an icon for the button instead of the string resource. This can be found as Images. First, we slightly adjust the layout file, using an ImageButton and referencing a drawable named @drawable/icon:

```
<?xml version="1.0" encoding="utf-8"?>
<LinearLayout xmlns:android="http://schemas.android.com/apk/res/android"
```

```
  android:orientation="vertical"
  android:layout_width="fill_parent"
  android:layout_height="fill_parent"
  >
  <LinearLayout xmlns:android="http://schemas.android.com/apk/res/android"
    android:orientation="horizontal"
    android:layout_width="fill_parent"
    android:layout_height="wrap_content"
    >
    <ImageButton android:id="@+id/format"
      android:layout_width="wrap_content"
      android:layout_height="wrap_content"
      android:src="@drawable/icon"
      />
    <EditText android:id="@+id/name"
      android:layout_width="fill_parent"
      android:layout_height="wrap_content"
      />
  </LinearLayout>
  <TextView android:id="@+id/result"
    android:layout_width="fill_parent"
    android:layout_height="wrap_content"
    />
</LinearLayout>
```

Next, we need to put an image file in `res/drawable` with a base name of icon. In this case, we use a 32x32 PNG file from the Nuvola[14] icon set. Finally, we twiddle the Java source, replacing our `Button` with an `ImageButton`:

```
package com.commonsware.android.resources;

import android.app.Activity;
import android.os.Bundle;
import android.text.TextUtils;
import android.text.Html;
import android.view.View;
import android.widget.Button;
import android.widget.ImageButton;
import android.widget.EditText;
import android.widget.TextView;

public class ImagesDemo extends Activity {
  EditText name;
  TextView result;

  @Override
  public void onCreate(Bundle icicle) {
    super.onCreate(icicle);
    setContentView(R.layout.main);
```

---

14   http://en.wikipedia.org/wiki/Nuvola

```
    name=(EditText)findViewById(R.id.name);
    result=(TextView)findViewById(R.id.result);

  ImageButton btn=(ImageButton)findViewById(R.id.format);

  btn.setOnClickListener(new Button.OnClickListener() {
    public void onClick(View v) {
      applyFormat();
    }
  });
}

private void applyFormat() {
  String format=getString(R.string.funky_format);
  String simpleResult=String.format(format,
              TextUtils.htmlEncode(name.getText().toString()));
  result.setText(Html.fromHtml(simpleResult));
}
```

Now, our button has the desired icon:

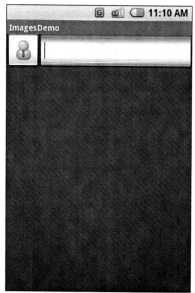

Figure 48. The ImagesDemo sample application

XML: The Resource Way

In a previous chapter, we showed how you can package XML files as raw resources and get access to them for parsing and usage. There is another way of packaging static XML with your application: the XML resource.

Simply put the XML file in res/xml/, and you can access it by getXml() on a Resources object, supplying it a resource ID of R.xml. plus the base name of your XML file. So, in an activity, with an XML file of words.xml, you could call getResources().getXml(R.xml.words).

This returns an instance of the presently-undocumented XmlPullParser, found in the org.xmlpull.v1 Java namespace. Documentation for this library can be found at at the parser's site[15] as of this writing.

An XML pull parser is event-driven: you keep calling next() on the parser to get the next event, which could be START_TAG, END_TAG, END_DOCUMENT, etc. On a START_TAG event, you can access the tag's name and attributes; a single TEXT event represents the concatenation of all text nodes that are direct children of this element. By looping, testing, and invoking per-element logic, you parse the file.

To see this in action, let's rewrite the Java code for the Static sample project to use an XML resource. This new project, XML, requires that you place the words.xml file from Static not in res/raw/, but in res/xml/. The layout stays the same, so all that needs replacing is the Java source:

```
package com.commonsware.android.resources;

import android.app.Activity;
import android.os.Bundle;
import android.app.ListActivity;
import android.view.View;
import android.widget.AdapterView;
import android.widget.ArrayAdapter;
import android.widget.ListView;
import android.widget.TextView;
import java.io.InputStream;
import java.util.ArrayList;
```

---

15   http://www.xmlpull.org/v1/doc/api/org/xmlpull/v1/package-summary.html

```
import org.xmlpull.v1.XmlPullParser;
import org.xmlpull.v1.XmlPullParserException;

public class XMLResourceDemo extends ListActivity {
  TextView selection;
  ArrayList items=new ArrayList();

  @Override
  public void onCreate(Bundle icicle) {
    super.onCreate(icicle);
    setContentView(R.layout.main);
    selection=(TextView)findViewById(R.id.selection);

    try {
      XmlPullParser xpp=getResources().getXml(R.xml.words);

      while (xpp.getEventType()!=XmlPullParser.END_DOCUMENT) {
        if (xpp.getEventType()==XmlPullParser.START_TAG) {
          if (xpp.getName().equals("word")) {
            items.add(xpp.getAttributeValue(0));
          }
        }

        xpp.next();
      }
    }
    catch (Throwable t) {
      showAlert("Exception!", 0, t.toString(), "Cancel", true);
    }

    setListAdapter(new ArrayAdapter<String>(this,
                         android.R.layout.simple_list_item_1,
                         items));
  }

  public void onListItemClick(ListView parent, View v, int position,
                  long id) {
    selection.setText(items.get(position).toString());
  }
}
```

Now, inside our try...catch block, we get our XmlPullParser and loop until the end of the document. If the current event is START_TAG and the name of the element is word (xpp.getName().equals("word")), then we get the one-and-only attribute and pop that into our list of items for the selection widget. Since we're in complete control over the XML file, it is safe enough to assume there is exactly one attribute. But, if you were not as comfortable that the XML is properly defined, you might consider checking the attribute count   (getAttributeCount())   and   the   name   of   the   attribute (getAttributeName()) before blindly assuming the 0-index attribute is what you think it is.

The result looks the same as before, albeit with a different name in the title bar:

Figure 49. The XMLResourceDemo sample application

Miscellaneous Values

In the res/values/ directory, you can place one (or more) XML files describing simple resources: dimensions, colors, and arrays. We have already seen uses of dimensions and colors in previous examples, where they were passed as simple strings (e.g., "10px") as parameters to calls. You can, of course, set these up as Java static final objects and use their symbolic names...but this only works inside Java source, not in layout XML files. By putting these values in resource XML files, you can reference them from both Java and layouts, plus have them centrally located for easy editing.

Resource XML files have a root element of resources; everything else is a child of that root.

Dimensions

Dimensions are used in several places in Android to describe distances, such a widget's padding. While this book usually uses pixels (e.g., 10px for ten pixels), there are several different units of measurement available to you:

- in and mm for inches and millimeters, respectively, based on the actual size of the screen

- pt for points, which in publishing terms is 1/72nd of an inch (again, based on the actual physical size of the screen)

- dp and sp for device-independent pixels and scale-independent pixels – one pixel equals one dp for a 160dpi resolution screen, with the ratio scaling based on the actual screen pixel density (scale-independent pixels also take into account the user's preferred font size)

To encode a dimension as a resource, add a dimen element, with a name attribute for your unique name for this resource, and a single child text element representing the value:

```
<resources>
  <dimen name="thin">10px</dimen>
  <dimen name="fat">1in</dimen>
</resources>
```

In a layout, you can reference dimensions as @dimen/..., where the ellipsis is a placeholder for your unique name for the resource (e.g., thin and fat from the sample above). In Java, you reference dimension resources by the unique name prefixed with R.dimen. (e.g., Resources.getDimen(R.dimen.thin)).

Colors

Colors in Android are hexadecimal RGB values, also optionally specifying an alpha channel. You have your choice of single-character hex values or double-character hex values, leaving you with four styles:

- #RGB

- #ARGB

- #RRGGBB

- #AARRGGBB

These work similarly to their counterparts in Cascading Style Sheets (CSS).

You can, of course, put these RGB values as string literals in Java source or layout resources. If you wish to turn them into resources, though, all you need to do is add `color` elements to the resources file, with a `name` attribute for your unique name for this color, and a single text element containing the RGB value itself:

```
<resources>
  <color name="yellow_orange">#FFD555</color>
  <color name="forest_green">#005500</color>
  <color name="burnt_umber">#8A3324</color>
</resources>
```

In a layout, you can reference colors as `@color/...`, replacing the ellipsis with your unique name for the color (e.g., `burnt_umber`). In Java, you reference color resources by the unique name prefixed with `R.color.` (e.g., `Resources.getColor(R.dimen.forest_green)`).

Arrays

Array resources are designed to hold lists of simple strings, such as a list of honorifics (Mr., Mrs., Ms., Dr., etc.).

In the resource file, you need one `array` element per array, with a `name` attribute for the unique name you are giving the array. Then, add one or more child `item` elements, each of which having a single text element with the value for that entry in the array:

```
<resources>
  <array name="honorifics">
    <item>Dr.</item>
    <item>Mr.</item>
    <item>Mrs.</item>
    <item>Ms.</item>
  </array>
</resources>
```

From your Java code, you can then use `Resources.getStringArray()` to get a `String[]` of the items in the list. The parameter to `getStringArray()` is your unique name for the array, prefixed with `R.array`. (e.g., `Resources.getStringArray(R.array.honorifics)`).

Different Strokes for Different Folks

One set of resources may not fit all situations where your application may be used. One obvious area comes with string resources and dealing with internationalization (I18N) and localization (L10N). Putting strings all in one language works fine – probably at least for the developer – but only covers one language.

That is not the only scenario where resources might need to differ, though. Here are others:

- **Screen orientation**: is the screen in a portrait orientation? Landscape? Is the screen square and, therefore, does not really have an orientation?

- **Screen size**: how many pixels does the screen have, so you can size your resources accordingly (e.g., large versus small icons)?

- **Touchscreen**: does the device have a touchscreen? If so, is the touchscreen set up to be used with a stylus or a finger?

- **Keyboard**: what keyboard does the user have (QWERTY, numeric, neither), either now or as an option?

- **Other input**: does the device have some other form of input, like a directional pad or click-wheel?

The way Android presently handles this is by having multiple resource directories, with the criteria for each embedded in their names.

Suppose, for example, you want to support strings in both English and Spanish. Normally, for a single-language setup, you would put your strings in a file named `res/values/strings.xml`. To support both English and Spanish, you would create two folders, `res/values-en` and `res/values-es`, where the value after the hyphen is the ISO 639-1[16] two-letter code for the language you want. Your English-language strings would go in `res/values-en/strings.xml` and the Spanish ones in `res/values-es/strings.xml`. Android will choose the proper file based on the user's device settings.

Seems easy, right?

Where things start to get complicated is when you need to use multiple disparate criteria for your resources. This may come most frequently with layouts, as you might want one layout for portrait and small screens, one layout for larger screens in landscape mode, and variations of each for finger-input versus other types of input (keyboard, stylus). This will allow you to make the best use of the available screen "real estate", without any coding changes to your activity using the layout.

Once you get into these sorts of situations, though, all sorts of rules come into play, such as:

- The configuration options (e.g., -en) have a particular order of precedence, and they must appear in the directory name in that order. The Android documentation[17] outlines the specific order in which these options can appear. For the purposes of this example, screen orientation must precede touchscreen type, which must precede screen size.

- There can only be one value of each configuration option category per directory. You cannot, for example, consider portrait and square screens to be the same – each will require its own named `res/layout...` folder.

- Options are case sensitive

So, for the scenario described above, in theory, we would need the following directories:

- `res/layout-port-finger`

- `res/layout-square-finger`

---

16 http://en.wikipedia.org/wiki/ISO_639-1
17 http://code.google.com/android/devel/resources-i18n.html#AlternateResources

- `res/layout-landscape-finger-640x480`

- `res/layout-port-notouch`

- `res/layout-square-notouch`

- `res/layout-landscape-notouch-640x480`

- `res/layout-port-stylus`

- `res/layout-square-stylus`

- `res/layout-landscape-stylus-640x480`

Note that for some of these, the actual layout files will be identical. For example, we only care about finger layouts being different than the other two, but since we cannot combine those two, we would theoretically have to have separate directories with identical contents for notouch and stylus.

Also note that there is nothing preventing you from also having a directory with the unadorned base name (res/layout). In fact, this is probably a good idea, in case future editions of the Android runtime introduce other configuration options you did not consider – having a default layout might make the difference between your application working or failing on that new device.

Now, we can "cheat" a bit, by decoding the rules Android uses for determining which, among a set of candidates, is the "right" resource directory to use:

1. First up, Android tosses out ones that are specifically invalid. So, for example, if the screen size of the device is 320x240, the 640x480 directories would be dropped as candidates, since they specifically call for some other size.

2. Next, Android counts the number of matches for each folder, and only pays attention to those with the most matches.

3. Finally, Android goes in the order of precedence of the options – in other words, it goes from left to right in the directory name.

So we could skate by with only the following configurations:

- `res/layout-landscape-finger-640x480`

- `res/layout-landscape-640x480`
- `res/layout-finger`
- `res/layout`

If the device is in portrait or square mode, or does not have a 640x480 screen size, the first two candidates will be skipped, and the layout will be chosen based on whether the device supports finger input or not. Otherwise, one of the two landscape 640x480 layouts will be chosen, as they would be a "stronger" match than the others, with the final determination being on whether the device supports finger input or not.

CHAPTER 18

Managing and Accessing Local Databases

SQLite[18] is a very popular embedded database, as it combines a clean SQL interface with a very small memory footprint and decent speed. Moreover, it is public domain, so everyone can use it. Lots of firms (Adobe, Apple, Google, Sun, Symbian) and open source projects (Mozilla, PHP, Python) all ship products with SQLite.

For Android, SQLite is "baked into" the Android runtime, so every Android application can create SQLite databases. Since SQLite uses a SQL interface, it is fairly straightforward to use for people with experience in other SQL-based databases. However, its native API is not JDBC, and JDBC might be too much overhead for a memory-limited device like a phone, anyway. Hence, Android programmers have a different API to learn – the good news being is that it is not that difficult.

This chapter will cover the basics of SQLite use in the context of working on Android. It by no means is a thorough coverage of SQLite as a whole. If you want to learn more about SQLite and how to use it in other environment than Android, a fine book is The Definitive Guide to SQLite[19] by Michael Owens.

---

18 http://www.sqlite.org
19 http://www.amazon.com/Definitive-Guide-SQLite/dp/1590596730

Activities will typically access a database via a content provider or service. As such, this chapter does not have a full example. You will find a full example of a content provider that accesses a database in the Building a Content Provider chapter.

A Quick SQLite Primer

SQLite, as the name suggests, uses a dialect of SQL for queries (SELECT), data manipulation (INSERT, et. al.), and data definition (CREATE TABLE, et. al.). SQLite has a few places where it deviates from the SQL-92 standard, no different than most SQL databases. The good news is that SQLite is so space-efficient that the Android runtime can include all of SQLite, not some arbitrary subset to trim it down to size.

The biggest difference from other SQL databases you will encounter is probably the data typing. While you can specify the data types for columns in a CREATE TABLE statement, and while SQLite will use those as a hint, that is as far as it goes. You can put whatever data you want in whatever column you want. Put a string in an INTEGER column? Sure! No problem! Vice versa? Works too! SQLite refers to this as "manifest typing", as described in the documentation[20]:

> *In manifest typing, the datatype is a property of the value it-self, not of the column in which the value is stored. SQLite thus allows the user to store any value of any datatype into any column regardless of the declared type of that column.*

In addition, there are a handful of standard SQL features not supported in SQLite, notably FOREIGN KEY constraints, nested transactions, RIGHT OUTER JOIN and FULL OUTER JOIN, and some flavors of ALTER TABLE.

Beyond that, though, you get a full SQL system, complete with triggers, transactions, and the like. Stock SQL statements, like SELECT, work pretty much as you might expect.

---

20 http://www.sqlite.org/different.html

If you are used to working with a major database, like Oracle, you may look upon SQLite as being a "toy" database. Please bear in mind that Oracle and SQLite are meant to solve different problems, and that you will not be seeing a full copy of Oracle on a phone any time real soon, in all likelihood.

Start at the Beginning

No databases are automatically supplied to you by Android. If you want to use SQLite, you have to create your own database, then populate it with your own tables, indexes, and data.

To create a database, your `Activity`, `ContentProvider`, or other `Context` subclass can call `createDatabase()`, providing four parameters:

- The name of the database – any class in your application can access this database under this name (though nothing outside your application can access it)

- An integer version number for the database (see below)

- The security mode for accessing this database – for now, use `0`

- An optional instance of a `CursorFactory` subclass that should be used in conjunction with this database, covered in greater detail in the section on querying the database, later in this chapter

The version number is for your own bookkeeping. When somebody upgrades your application to a new version, if your new version uses a different database schema, you can compare the version you want to use with the version of the database that is already installed. That will help your application figure out what needs to be changed in the table structures. This is covered in greater detail in the chapter on creating a content provider.

The result of the `createDatabase()` call is an instance of `SQLiteDatabase`, which you can use for creating tables and the like, described later in this chapter.

You also get a SQLiteDatabase instance when you call openDatabase() to access a database you already created. This takes the name of the database and, optionally, the CursorFactory used when querying the database.

When you are done with the database (e.g., your activity is being closed), simply call close() on the SQLiteDatabase to release your connection. If you wish to get rid of the database entirely, your Activity, ContentProvider, or other Context subclass can call deleteDatabase() with the database's name.

Setting the Table

For creating your tables and indexes, you will need to call execSQL() on your SQLiteDatabase, providing the DDL statement you wish to apply against the database. Barring a database error, this method returns nothing.

So, for example, you can:

```
db.execSQL("CREATE TABLE widgets "+
           "(ID INTEGER PRIMARY KEY AUTOINCREMENT, "+
           "name TEXT, inventory INTEGER)");
db.execSQL("CREATE INDEX widgetsByNameIdx "+
           "ON widgets (name)");
```

This will create a table, named widgets, with a primary key column named ID that is an auto-incremented integer (i.e., SQLite will assign the value for you when you insert rows), plus two data columns: name (text) and inventory (integer). SQLite will automatically create an index for you on your primary key column, so the second statement adds another index on the table, by name.

Most likely, you will create tables and indexes when you first create the database, or possibly when the database needs upgrading to accommodate a new release of your application. If you do not change your table schemas, you might never drop your tables or indexes, but if you do, just use execSQL() to invoke DROP INDEX and DROP TABLE statements as needed.

Makin' Data

Given that you have a database and one or more tables, you probably want to put some data in them and such. You have two major approaches for doing this.

You can always use execSQL(), just like you did for creating the tables. The execSQL() method works for any SQL that does not return results, so it can handle INSERT, UPDATE, DELETE, etc. just fine. So, for example:

```
db.execSQL("INSERT INTO widgets (name, inventory)"+
        "VALUES ('Sprocket', 5)");
```

Your alternative is to use the insert(), update(), and delete() methods on the SQLiteDatabase object. These are "builder" sorts of methods, in that the break down the SQL statements into discrete chunks, then take those chunks as parameters.

These methods make use of ContentValues objects, which implement a Map-esque interface, albeit one that has additional methods for working with SQLite types. For example, in addition to get() to retrieve a value by its key, you have getAsInteger(), getAsString(), and so forth.

The insert() method takes the name of the table, the name of one column as the "null column hack", and a ContentValues with the initial values you want put into this row. The "null column hack" is for the case where the ContentValues instance is empty – the column named as the "null column hack" will be explicitly assigned the value NULL in the SQL INSERT statement generated by insert().

The update() method takes the name of the table, a ContentValues representing the columns and replacement values to use, an optional WHERE clause, and an optional list of parameters to fill into the WHERE clause, to replace any embedded question marks (?). Since update() only replaces columns with fixed values, versus ones computed based on other information, you may need to use execSQL() to accomplish some ends.

The WHERE clause and parameter list works akin to the positional SQL parameters you may be used to from other SQL APIs. For example:

```
// replacements is a ContentValues instance
String[] parms=new String[] {"snicklefritz"};
db.update("widgets", replacements, "name=?", parms);
```

The delete() method works akin to update(), taking the name of the table, the optional WHERE clause, and the corresponding parameters to fill into the WHERE clause.

What Goes Around, Comes Around

As with INSERT, UPDATE, and DELETE, you have two main options for retrieving data from a SQLite database using SELECT:

1.   You can use rawQuery() to invoke a SELECT statement directly, or

2.   You can use query() to build up a query from its component parts

Confounding matters further is the SQLiteQueryBuilder class and the issue of cursors and cursor factories. Let's take all of this one piece at a time.

Raw Queries

The simplest solution, at least in terms of the API, is rawQuery(). Simply call it with your SQL SELECT statement. The SELECT statement can include positional parameters; the array of these forms your second parameter to rawQuery(). So, we wind up with:

```
String[] parms={"snicklefritz"};
Cursor result=
  db.rawQuery("SELECT ID,inventory FROM widgets WHERE name=?",
            parms);
```

If your queries are pretty much "baked into" your application, this is a very straightforward way to use them. However, it gets complicated if parts of the query are dynamic, beyond what positional parameters can really handle. For example, if the set of columns you need to retrieve is not known at compile time, puttering around concatenating column names into a comma-delimited list can be annoying...which is where query() comes in.

Regular Queries

The query() method takes the discrete pieces of a SELECT statement and builds the query from them. The pieces, in order that they appear as parameters to query(), are:

- The name of the table to query against
- The list of columns to retrieve
- The WHERE clause, optionally including positional parameters
- The list of values to substitute in for those positional parameters
- The GROUP BY clause, if any
- The ORDER BY clause, if any

These can be null when they are not needed (except the table name, of course). So, our previous snippet converts into:

```
String[] columns={"ID", "inventory"};
String[] parms={"snicklefritz"};
Cursor result=db.query("widgets", columns, "name=?",
                       parms, null, null, null);
```

Building with Builders

Yet another option is to use SQLiteQueryBuilder, which offers much richer query-building options, particularly for nasty queries involving things like the union of multiple sub-query results. More importantly, the SQLiteQueryBuilder interface dovetails nicely with the ContentProvider interface for executing queries. Hence, a common pattern for your content provider's query() implementation is to create a SQLiteQueryBuilder, fill in some defaults, then allow it to build up (and optionally execute) the full query combining the defaults with what is provided to the content provider on the query request.

For example, here is a snippet of code from a content provider using `SQLiteQueryBuilder`:

```
SQLiteQueryBuilder qb=new SQLiteQueryBuilder();

qb.setTables(getTableName());

if (isCollectionUri(url)) {
  qb.setProjectionMap(getDefaultProjection());
}
else {
  qb.appendWhere(getIdColumnName()+"=" + url.getPathSegments().get(1));
}

String orderBy;

if (TextUtils.isEmpty(sort)) {
  orderBy=getDefaultSortOrder();
} else {
  orderBy=sort;
}

Cursor c=qb.query(db, projection, selection, selectionArgs, null, null,
orderBy);
c.setNotificationUri(getContext().getContentResolver(), url);
```

Content providers are explained in greater detail later in the book, so some of this you will have to take on faith until then. Here, we see:

- A `SQLiteQueryBuilder` is constructed
- It is told the table to use for the query (`setTables(getTableName())`)
- It is either told the default set of columns to return (`setProjectionMap()`), or is given a piece of a WHERE clause to identify a particular row in the table by an identifier extracted from the `Uri` supplied to the `query()` call (`appendWhere()`)
- Finally, it is told to execute the query, blending the pre-set values with those supplied on the call to `query()` (`qb.query(db, projection, selection, selectionArgs, null, null, orderBy)`)

Instead of having the `SQLiteQueryBuilder` execute the query directly, we could have called `buildQuery()` to have it generate and return the SQL SELECT statement we needed, which we could then execute ourselves.

Using Cursors

No matter how you execute the query, you get a Cursor back. This is the Android/SQLite edition of the database cursor, a concept used in many database systems. With the cursor, you can:

- Find out how many rows are in the result set via count()

- Iterate over the rows via first(), next(), and isAfterLast()

- Find out the names of the columns via getColumnNames(), convert those into column numbers via getColumnIndex(), and get values for the current row for a given column via methods like getString(), getInt(), etc.

- Re-execute the query that created the cursor via requery()

- Release the cursor's resources via close()

For example, here we iterate over the widgets table entries from the previous snippets:

```
Cursor result=
  db.rawQuery("SELECT ID, name, inventory FROM widgets");

while (!result.isAfterLast()) {
int id=result.getInt(0);
String name=result.getString(1);
int inventory=result.getInt(2);

// do something useful with these

result.next();
}

result.close();
```

Change for the Sake of Change

For a simple SELECT, and in some other situations, the cursor will support updates (supportUpdates()). This means not only can you read data using the cursor, but you can modify the data and commit those changes back to the database. You do this by:

- Updating values for particular columns in the current row via methods like updateInt() and updateString(), or deleting the current row via deleteRow()

- Committing those changes back to the database via commitUpdates()

- Invoking requery() to refresh the cursor based on the results of your changes, if you want to continue using the cursor

And, of course, you should close() the cursor when done.

Making Your Own Cursors

There may be circumstances in which you want to use your own Cursor subclass, rather than the stock implementation provided by Android. In those cases, you can use flavors of query() and rawQuery() that take a CursorFactory instance as a parameter. The factory, as one might expect, is responsible for creating new cursors via its newCursor() implementation.

Finding and implementing a valid use for this facility is left as an exercise for the reader. Suffice it to say that you should not need to create your own cursor classes much, if at all, in ordinary Android development.

Data, Data, Everywhere

If you are used to developing for other databases, you are also probably used to having tools to inspect and manipulate the contents of the database, beyond merely the database's API. With Android's emulator, you have two main options for this.

First, the emulator bundles in the sqlite3 console program and makes it available from the adb shell command. Once you are in the emulator's shell, just execute sqlite3, providing it the path to your database file. Your database file can be found at:

```
/data/data/your.app.package/databases/your-db-name.db
```

Here your.app.package is the Java package for your application (e.g., com.commonsware.android) and your-db-name is the name of your database, as supplied to createDatabase().

The sqlite3 program works, and if you are used to poking around your tables using a console interface, you are welcome to use it. If you prefer something a little bit friendlier, you can always copy the SQLite database off the device onto your development machine, then use a SQLite-aware client program to putter around. Note, though, that you are working off a copy of the database; if you want your changes to go back to the device, you will need to transfer the database back over.

To get the database off the device, you can use the adb pull command (or the equivalent in your IDE), which takes the path to the on-device database and the local destination as parameters. To store a modified database on the device, use adb push, which takes the local path to the database and the on-device destination as parameters.

One of the most-accessible SQLite clients is the SQLite Manager[21] extension for Firefox, as it works across all platforms.

---

21 https://addons.mozilla.org/en-US/firefox/addon/5817

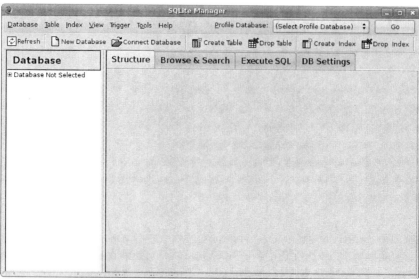

Figure 50. the SQLite Manager Firefox extension

You can find dozens of others on the SQLite Web site[22].

---

22 http://www.sqlite.org

CHAPTER 19

Leveraging Java Libraries

Java has as many, if not more, third-party libraries than any other modern programming language. Here, "third-party libraries" refer to the innumerable JARs that you can include in a server or desktop Java application – the things that the Java SDKs themselves do not provide.

In the case of Android, the Dalvik VM at its heart is not precisely Java, and what it provides in its SDK is not precisely the same as any traditional Java SDK. That being said, many Java third-party libraries still provide capabilities that Android lacks natively and therefore may be of use to you in your project, for the ones you can get working with Android's flavor of Java.

This chapter explains what it will take for you to leverage such libraries and the limitations on Android's support for arbitrary third-party code.

The Outer Limits

Not all available Java code, of course, will work well with Android. There are a number of factors to consider, including:

- **Expected Platform APIs**: Does the code assume a newer JVM than the one Android is based on? Or, does the code assume the existence of Java APIs that ship with J2SE but not with Android, such as Swing?

- **Size**: Existing Java code designed for use on desktops or servers need not worry too much about on-disk size, or, to some extent, even in-RAM size. Android, of course, is short on both. Using third-party Java code, particularly when pre-packaged as JARs, may balloon the size of your application.

- **Performance**: Does the Java code effectively assume a much more powerful CPU than what you may find on many Android devices? Just because a desktop can run it without issue doesn't mean your average mobile phone will handle it well.

- **Interface**: Does the Java code assume a console interface? Or is it a pure API that you can wrap your own interface around?

One trick for addressing some of these concerns is to use open source Java code, and actually work with the code to make it more Android-friendly. For example, if you're only using 10% of the third-party library, maybe it's worthwhile to recompile the subset of the project to be only what you need, or at least removing the unnecessary classes from the JAR. The former approach is safer, in that you get compiler help to make sure you're not discarding some essential piece of code, though it may be more tedious to do.

Ants and Jars

You have two choices for integrating third-party code into your project: use source code, or use pre-packaged JARs.

If you choose to use their source code, all you need to do is copy it into your own source tree (under src/ in your project), so it can sit alongside your existing code, then let the compiler perform its magic.

If you choose to use an existing JAR, perhaps one for which you do not have the source code, you will need to teach your build chain how to use the JAR. If you are using an IDE, that's a matter of telling it to reference the JAR. If, on the other hand, you are not using an IDE and are relying upon the build.xml Ant script, you will need to make some changes. Here's a pattern that works:

1. Copy the third-party JAR(s) into a `lib/` directory you add to your project, as a peer of `src/`, `bin/`, etc.

2. Add a `classpath` element to the `javac` task in the `compile` target of your `build.xml` script, pointing it to your new `lib/` directory

3. Add new `arg` elements to your `exec` task in the `dex` target of the `build.xml` script, pointing it to the specific JARs to translate to Dalvik instructions and package

For example, here are the two aforementioned Ant tasks from the `build.xml` for `MailBuzz`, a project we will examine in greater detail in the chapters on services:

```
<!-- Compile this project's .java files into .class files. -->
<target name="compile" depends="dirs, resource-src, aidl">
  <javac encoding="ascii" target="1.5" debug="true" extdirs=""
      srcdir="."
      destdir="${outdir-classes}"
      bootclasspath="${android-jar}">
    <classpath>
      <fileset dir="lib">
        <include name="**/*.jar"/>
      </fileset>
    </classpath>
  </javac>
</target>

<!-- Convert this project's .class files into .dex files. -->
<target name="dex" depends="compile">
  <exec executable="${dx}" failonerror="true">
    <arg value="-JXmx384M" />
    <arg value="--dex" />
    <arg value="--output=${basedir}/${intermediate-dex}" />
    <arg value="--locals=full" />
    <arg value="--positions=lines" />
    <arg path="${basedir}/${outdir-classes}" />
    <arg path="${basedir}/lib/activation-1.1.jar"/>
    <arg path="${basedir}/lib/mail-1.4.jar"/>
  </exec>
</target>
```

MailBuzz, as the name suggests, deals with email. To accomplish that end, MailBuzz leverages the JavaMail APIs and needs two JavaMail JARs: `mail-1.4.jar` and `activation-1.1.jar`. With both of those in the `lib/` directory, the `classpath` tells `javac` to link against those JARs, so any JavaMail references in the MailBuzz code can be correctly resolved. Then, those JARs are listed, along with the MailBuzz compiled classes, in the task that invokes the dex tool to convert the Java code into Dalvik VM instructions. Without this step, even though your code may compile, it won't find the JavaMail classes at runtime and will fail with an exception.

As noted above, using JARs can make your project portly – MailBuzz is about 250KB thanks to the JavaMail classes.

Of course, it is entirely possible that JavaMail would require features in Java that the Dalvik VM simply doesn't offer. This wouldn't necessarily be discovered at compile time, though, so your testing will need to ensure that you exercise all relevant uses of the third-party API, so you know that it will run without incident.

CHAPTER 20

Communicating via the Internet

The expectation is that most, if not all, Android devices will have built-in Internet access. That could be WiFi, cellular data services (EDGE, 3G, etc.), or possibly something else entirely. Regardless, most people – or at least those with a data plan or WiFi access – will be able to get to the Internet from their Android phone.

Not surprisingly, the Android platform gives developers a wide range of ways to make use of this Internet access. Some offer high-level access, such as the integrated WebKit browser component we saw in an earlier chapter. If you want, you can drop all the way down to using raw sockets. Or, in between, you can leverage APIs – both on-device and from 3rd-party JARs – that give you access to specific protocols: HTTP, XMPP, SMTP, and so on.

The emphasis of this book is on the higher-level forms of access: the WebKit component and Internet-access APIs, as busy coders should be trying to reuse existing components versus rolling one's own on-the-wire protocol wherever possible.

REST and Relaxation

Android does not have built-in SOAP or XML-RPC client APIs. However, it does have the Apache Jakarta Commons HttpClient library baked in. You can either layer a SOAP/XML-RPC layer atop this library, or use it "straight" for accessing REST-style Web services. For the purposes of this book, "REST-style Web services" is defined as "simple HTTP requests for ordinary URLs over the full range of HTTP verbs, with formatted payloads (XML, JSON, etc.) as responses".

More expansive tutorials, FAQs, and HOWTOs can be found at the HttpClient Web site[23]. Here, we'll cover the basics, while checking the weather.

HTTP Operations via Apache Commons

The first step to using HttpClient is, not surprisingly, to create an HttpClient object. The client object handles all HTTP requests upon your behalf.

Those requests are bundled up into HttpMethod instances, with different HttpMethod subclasses for each different HTTP verb (e.g., GetMethod for HTTP GET requests). You create an HttpMethod subclass instance, fill in the URL to retrieve and other configuration data (e.g., form values if you are doing an HTTP POST via PostMethod), then pass the method to the client to actually make the HTTP request.

The request will, at minimum, give you an HTTP response code (e.g., 200 for OK) and various HTTP headers (e.g., Set-Cookie). In many cases, you will also be given the body of the response, which you can obtain as a byte array, a String, or an InputStream for later processing.

When you are done with the request, close the InputStream (if that's how you got the response body), then invoke releaseConnection() on the method object, to drop the HTTP connection.

For example, let's take a look at the Weather sample project. This implements an activity that retrieves weather data for your current location from the National Weather Service (**NOTE**: this probably only works in the US). That data is converted into an HTML page, which is poured into a WebKit widget for display. Rebuilding this demo using a ListView is left as an exercise for the reader. Also, since this sample is relatively long, we will only show

---

23 http://hc.apache.org/httpclient-3.x/

relevant pieces of the Java code here in this chapter, though you can always download the full source from the CommonsWare Web site[24].

We retrieve the National Weather Service data every time the activity pops back to the foreground by implementing onResume() in the activity:

```
@Override
public void onResume() {
  super.onResume();

  Location loc=getLocation();
  String url=String.format(format, loc.getLatitude(), loc.getLongitude());
  GetMethod method=new GetMethod(url);

  try {
    int statusCode=client.executeMethod(method);

    if (statusCode!=HttpStatus.SC_OK) {
      Toast
        .makeText(this,
              "Request failed: "+method.getStatusLine(),
              2000)
        .show();
    }
    else {
      buildForecasts(method.getResponseBodyAsStream());
      browser.loadData(generatePage(), "text/html", "UTF-8");
    }
  }
  catch (Throwable t) {
    Toast
      .makeText(this, "Request failed: "+t.toString(), 2000)
      .show();
  }
  finally {
    method.releaseConnection();
  }
}
```

First, we retrieve our location using a private getLocation() method, which uses Android's built-in location services – more on this in a later chapter. For now, all you need to know is that Location sports getLatitude() and getLongitude() methods that return the latitude and longitude of the device's position, respectively.

---

24 http://commonsware.com/Android/

We hold the URL to the National Weather Service XML in a string resource, and pour in the latitude and longitude at runtime. Given our HttpClient instance created in onCreate(), we populate a GetMethod with that customized URL, then execute that method. If we get 200 as the result code, we build the forecast HTML page (see below) and pour that into the WebKit widget. If we get some other response back, or if the HttpClient blows up with an exception, we provide that error as a Toast, before eventually releasing our HTTP connection for this request.

Parsing Responses

The response you get will be formatted using some system – HTML, XML, JSON, whatever. It is up to you, of course, to pick out what information you need and do something useful with it. In the case of the WeatherDemo, we need to extract the forecast time, temperature, and icon (indicating sky conditions and precipitation) and generate an HTML page from it.

Android includes:

- Three XML parsers: the traditional W3C DOM (org.w3c.dom), a SAX parser (org.xml.sax), and the XML pull parser discussed in the chapter on resources
- A JSON parser (org.json)

You are also welcome to use third-party Java code, where possible, to handle other formats, such as a dedicated RSS/Atom parser for a feed reader. The use of third-party Java code is discussed in a separate chapter.

For WeatherDemo, we use the W3C DOM parser in our buildForecasts() method:

```
void buildForecasts(InputStream in) throws Exception {
  DocumentBuilder builder=DocumentBuilderFactory
                      .newInstance()
                      .newDocumentBuilder();
  Document doc=builder.parse(in, null);
  NodeList times=doc.getElementsByTagName("start-valid-time");

  for (int i=0;i<times.getLength();i++) {
```

```
      Element time=(Element)times.item(i);
      Forecast forecast=new Forecast();

      forecasts.add(forecast);
      forecast.setTime(time.getFirstChild().getNodeValue());
   }

   NodeList temps=doc.getElementsByTagName("value");

   for (int i=0;i<temps.getLength();i++) {
     Element temp=(Element)temps.item(i);
     Forecast forecast=forecasts.get(i);

      forecast.setTemp(new Integer(temp.getFirstChild().getNodeValue()));
   }

   NodeList icons=doc.getElementsByTagName("icon-link");

   for (int i=0;i<icons.getLength();i++) {
     Element icon=(Element)icons.item(i);
     Forecast forecast=forecasts.get(i);

      forecast.setIcon(icon.getFirstChild().getNodeValue());
   }
```

The National Weather Service XML format is...curiously structured, relying heavily on sequential position in lists versus the more object-oriented style you find in formats like RSS or Atom. That being said, we can take a few liberties and simplify the parsing somewhat, taking advantage of the fact that the elements we want (start-valid-time for the forecast time, value for the temperature, and icon-link for the icon URL) are all unique within the document.

The HTML comes in as an InputStream and is fed into the DOM parser. From there, we scan for the start-valid-time elements and populate a set of Forecast models using those start times. Then, we find the temperature value elements and icon-link URLs and fill those in to the Forecast objects.

In turn, the generatePage() method creates a rudimentary HTML table with the forecasts:

```
String generatePage() {
  StringBuffer bufResult=new StringBuffer("<html><body><table>");

  bufResult.append("<tr><th width=\"50%\">Time</th>"+
                "<th>Temperature</th><th>Forecast</th></tr>");
```

```
for (Forecast forecast : forecasts) {
  bufResult.append("<tr><td align=\"center\">");
  bufResult.append(forecast.getTime());
  bufResult.append("</td><td align=\"center\">");
  bufResult.append(forecast.getTemp());
  bufResult.append("</td><td><img src=\"");
  bufResult.append(forecast.getIcon());
  bufResult.append("\"></td></tr>");
}

bufResult.append("</table></body></html>");

return(bufResult.toString());
}
```

The result looks like this:

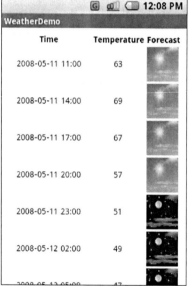

Figure 51. The WeatherDemo sample application

Stuff To Consider

If you need to use SSL, bear in mind that the default HttpClient setup does not include SSL support. Mostly, this is because you need to decide how to handle SSL certificate presentation – do you blindly accept all certificates, even self-signed or expired ones? Or do you want to ask the user if they really want to use some strange certificates? The HttpClient Web site has instructions[25] for adding SSL support with various certificate policies to your project.

Similarly, HttpClient, by default, is designed for single-threaded use. If you will be using HttpClient from a service or some other place where multiple threads might be an issue, you can readily set up HttpClient to support multiple threads – again, the HttpClient Web site has the instructions[26].

Email over Java

Android has no built-in facility to sending or receiving emails. This doesn't preclude you from doing so yourself, but you will need to either roll your own SMTP, POP3, or IMAP client code, or use one from a third-party, like JavaMail. As described in the chapter on integrating third-party Java code, there are caveats to going this route, such as bloating the size of your application. Eventually, "lean and mean" editions of these libraries will spring up, focused on Android-style deployments. And, eventually, Android-style devices will expand their storage, memory, and CPU capacities.

In the meantime, though, we can still use APIs like JavaMail, so long as we live with the limitations.

Case in point is the MailBuzz project, first mentioned in the preceding chapter. This application combines an activity and a service, designed to monitor an email account for new messages. This isn't a full email client, but it is a feature you might find in full email client, and it shows off integrating JavaMail nicely, plus the use of services. In this chapter, though, we'll focus on the JavaMail side, for accessing POP3 and IMAP on your Android device. This is not meant to be a thorough JavaMail tutorial, of course.

For the purposes of MailBuzz, what we want is to connect to a mail server, grab the messages, extract the Message-Id headers, and hold onto the IDs.

---

25 http://hc.apache.org/httpclient-3.x/sslguide.html
26 http://hc.apache.org/httpclient-3.x/threading.html

Every time we check for new messages, we see if the last set of message IDs is missing any from the just-retrieved set of IDs – if so, we have a new message and can pop up a "new mail!" Notification. While we could use JavaMail's MessageCountListener to more directly detect new messages, that assumes a constant Internet connection, and that's far from assured with a mobile device. While this implementation is decidedly more clunky, it should handle a greater range of real-world situations.

The IMAP and POP3 logic is encapsulated in the MailClient class:

```
package com.commonsware.android.service;

import java.security.Security;
import javax.mail.Folder;
import javax.mail.Message;
import javax.mail.MessagingException;
import javax.mail.Session;
import javax.mail.Store;

public class MailClient {
  public static String[] getPOP3MessageIds(String server, String user,
                        String pw)
    throws MessagingException {
    return(getMessageIds("pop3", server, user, pw));
  }

  public static String[] getIMAPMessageIds(String server, String user,
                        String pw)
    throws MessagingException {
    return(getMessageIds("imap", server, user, pw));
  }

  private static String[] getMessageIds(String type, String server,
                        String user, String pw)
    throws MessagingException {
    String[] result=null;

    Session session=Session.getDefaultInstance(System.getProperties());
    Store store=session.getStore(type);

    store.connect(server, user, pw);

    try {
      Folder folder=store.getFolder("INBOX");

      folder.open(Folder.READ_ONLY);

      try {
        Message[] msgs=folder.getMessages();
```

```
        result=new String[msgs.length];

      for (int i=0;i<msgs.length;i++) {
        String[] headers=msgs[i].getHeader("Message-Id");

        if (headers==null) {
          result[i]=null;
        }
        else {
          result[i]=headers[0];
        }
      }
    }
    finally {
      folder.close(false);
    }
  }
  finally {
    store.close();
  }

  return(result);
}
}
```

JavaMail does a nice job of abstracting out the differences between the protocols, so while the public APIs are getPOP3MessageIds() and getIMAPMessageIds(), the guts are contained in a common getMessageIds() static method, which takes the type (POP3 or IMAP), server, user, and password as parameters.

The JavaMail pattern is:

1. Get a Session

2. Get a Store of the specific type and connect to the server

3. Get access to the proper mail Folder, typically INBOX for new messages

4. Open the Folder for read operations

5. Get the messages in the folder

6. Iterate over the messages and get the Message-Id header, if any, pouring the results into a String[] which is returned to the overall caller

7. Close the folder and store on the way back out, or in case an exception is raised

This code, combined with the hooks to the JavaMail JARs described in the preceding chapter, gives MailBuzz access to the message IDs of the messages in the inbox of the user-supplied mail account.

PART IV – Intents

CHAPTER 21

Creating Intent Filters

Up to now, the focus of this book has been on activities opened directly by the user from the device's launcher. This, of course, is the most obvious case for getting your activity up and visible to the user. And, in many cases it is the primary way the user will start using your application.

However, remember that the Android system is based upon lots of loosely-coupled components. What you might accomplish in a desktop GUI via dialog boxes, child windows, and the like are mostly supposed to be independent activities. While one activity will be "special", in that it shows up in the launcher, the other activities all need to be reached...somehow.

The "how" is via intents.

An intent is basically a message that you pass to Android saying, "Yo! I want to do...er...something! Yeah!" How specific the "something" is depends on the situation – sometimes you know exactly what you want to do (e.g., open up one of your other activities), and sometimes you don't.

In the abstract, Android is all about intents and receivers of those intents. So, now that we are well-versed in creating activities, let's dive into intents, so we can create more complex applications while simultaneously being "good Android citizens".

What's Your Intent?

When Sir Tim Berners-Lee cooked up the Hypertext Transfer Protocol – HTTP – he set up a system of verbs plus addresses in the form of URLs. The address indicated a resource, such as a Web page, graphic, or server-side program. The verb indicated what should be done: GET to retrieve it, POST to send form data to it for processing, etc.

Intents are similar, in that they represent an action plus context. There are more actions and more components to the context with Android intents than there are with HTTP verbs and resources, but the concept is still the same.

Just as a Web browser knows how to process a verb+URL pair, Android knows how to find activities or other application logic that will handle a given intent.

Pieces of Intents

The two most important pieces of an intent are the action and what Android refers to as the "data". These are almost exactly analogous to HTTP verbs and URLs – the action is the verb, and the "data" is a Uri, such as `content://contacts/people/1` representing a contact in the contacts database. Actions are constants, such as VIEW_ACTION (to bring up a viewer for the resource), EDIT_ACTION (to edit the resource), or PICK_ACTION (to choose an available item given a Uri representing a collection, such as `content://contacts/people`).

If you were to create an intent combining VIEW_ACTION with a content Uri of `content://contacts/people/1`, and pass that intent to Android, Android would know to find and open an activity capable of viewing that resource.

There are other criteria you can place inside an intent (represented as an Intent object), besides the action and "data" Uri, such as:

- A category. Your "main" activity will be in the LAUNCHER category, indicating it should show up on the launcher menu. Other activities will probably be in the DEFAULT or ALTERNATIVE categories.

- A MIME type, indicating the type of resource you want to operate on, if you don't know a collection Uri.

- A component, which is to say, the class of the activity that is supposed to receive this intent. Using components this way obviates the need for the other properties of the intent. However, it does make the intent more fragile, as it assumes specific implementations.

- "Extras", which is a Bundle of other information you want to pass along to the receiver with the intent, that the receiver might want to take advantage of. What pieces of information a given receiver can use is up to the receiver and (hopefully) is well-documented.

Stock Options

Some of the actions defined as part of Android for launching activities are:

- ANSWER_ACTION
- CALL_ACTION
- DELETE_ACTION
- DIAL_ACTION
- EDIT_ACTION
- FACTORY_TEST_ACTION
- GET_CONTENT_ACTION
- INSERT_ACTION
- MAIN_ACTION
- PICK_ACTION
- PICK_ACTIVITY_ACTION
- RUN_ACTION
- SEARCH_ACTION
- SENDTO_ACTION

- SEND_ACTION

- SYNC_ACTION

- VIEW_ACTION

- WEB_SEARCH_ACTION

The main ones you will use are MAIN_ACTION for the main entry point of your application, VIEW_ACTION and EDIT_ACTION for viewing and editing content, and PICK_ACTION to allow other applications to select an item from your content.

Note that there are also some actions specifically for "broadcast" intents – intents that can be picked up by many activities or listeners, not just one. Similarly, there are many other intent actions not aimed at starting activities, such as MEDIA_MOUNTED_ACTION, indicating that a media card has been mounted in the system.

Similarly, here are the standard available categories (with DEFAULT_CATEGORY and LAUNCHER_CATEGORY being the ones you will use most):

- ALTERNATIVE_CATEGORY

- BROWSABLE_CATEGORY

- DEFAULT_CATEGORY

- GADGET_CATEGORY

- HOME_CATEGORY

- LAUNCHER_CATEGORY

- PREFERENCE_CATEGORY

- SELECTED_ALTERNATIVE_CATEGORY

- TAB_CATEGORY

- TEST_CATEGORY

Intent Routing

As noted above, if you specify the target component in your intent, Android has no doubt where the intent is supposed to be routed to – it will launch the named activity. This might be OK if the target intent is in your application. It definitely is not recommended for sending intents to other applications. Component names, by and large, are considered private to the application and are subject to change. Content Uri templates and MIME types are the preferred ways of identifying services you wish third-party code to supply.

If you do not specify the target component, then Android has to figure out what activities (or other intent receivers) are eligible to receive the intent. Note the use of the plural "activities", as a broadly-written intent might well resolve to several activities. That is the...ummm...intent (pardon the pun), as you will see later in this chapter. This routing approach is referred to as implicit routing.

Basically, there are three rules, all of which must be true for a given activity to be eligible for a given intent:

1. The activity must support the specified action

2. The activity must support the stated MIME type (if supplied)

3. The activity must support all of the categories named in the intent

The upshot is that you want to make your intents specific enough to find the right receiver(s), and no more specific than that.

This will become clearer as we work through some examples later in this chapter.

Stating Your Intent(ions)

All Android components that wish to be notified via intents must declare intent filters, so Android knows which intents should go to that component. To do this, you need to add intent-filter elements to your AndroidManifest.xml file.

All of the example projects have intent filters defined, courtesy of the Android application-building script (activityCreator.py or the IDE equivalent). They look something like this:

```
<manifest xmlns:android="http://schemas.android.com/apk/res/android"
  package="com.commonsware.android.prefs">
  <application>
    <activity android:name=".PrefsDemo" android:label="PrefsDemo">
      <intent-filter>
        <action android:name="android.intent.action.MAIN" />
        <category android:name="android.intent.category.LAUNCHER" />
      </intent-filter>
    </activity>
  </application>
</manifest>
```

Note the intent-filter element under the activity element. Here, we declare that this activity:

- Is the main activity for this application
- It is in the LAUNCHER category, meaning it gets an icon in the Android main menu

Because this activity is the main one for the application, Android knows this is the component it should launch when somebody chooses the application from the main menu.

The intent filter also has a label (android:label = "PrefsDemo"). In this case, this controls the name associated with the application's icon in the main menu.

You are welcome to have more than one action or more than one category in your intent filters. That indicates that the associated component (e.g., activity) handles multiple different sorts of intents.

More than likely, you will also want to have your secondary (non-MAIN) activities specify the MIME type of data they work on. Then, if an intent is targeted for that MIME type – either directly, or indirectly by the Uri referencing something of that type – Android will know that the component handles such data.

For example, you could have an activity declared like this:

```
<activity android:name=".TourViewActivity">
    <intent-filter>
        <action android:name="android.intent.action.VIEW" />
        <category android:name="android.intent.category.DEFAULT" />
        <data android:mimeType="vnd.android.cursor.item/vnd.commonsware.tour" />
    </intent-filter>
</activity>
```

This activity will get launched by an intent requesting to view a Uri representing a vnd.android.cursor.item/vnd.commonsware.tour piece of content. That intent could come from another activity in the same application (e.g., the MAIN activity for this application) or from another activity in another Android application that happens to know a Uri that this activity handles.

Narrow Receivers

In the examples shown above, the intent filters were set up on activities. Sometimes, tying intents to activities is not exactly what we want:

- Some system events might cause us to want to trigger something in a service rather than an activity

- Some events might need to launch different activities in different circumstances, where the criteria are not solely based on the intent itself, but some other state (e.g., if we get intent X and the database has a Y, then launch activity M; if the database does not have a Y, then launch activity N)

For these cases, Android offers the intent receiver, defined as a class implementing the IntentReceiver interface. Intent receivers are disposable objects designed to receive intents – particularly broadcast intents – and take action, typically involving launching other intents to trigger logic in an activity, service, or other component.

The IntentReceiver interface has only one method: onReceiveIntent(). Intent receivers implement that method, where they do whatever it is they wish to do upon an incoming intent. To declare an intent receiver, add an receiver element to your `AndroidManifest.xml` file:

```
<receiver android:name=".MyIntentReceiverClassName" />
```

An intent receiver is only alive for as long as it takes to process `onReceiveIntent()` – as soon as that method returns, the receiver instance is subject to garbage collection and will not be reused. This means intent receivers are somewhat limited in what they can do, mostly to avoid anything that involves any sort of callback. For example, they cannot bind to a service, and they cannot open a dialog box.

The exception is if the `IntentReceiver` is implemented on some longer-lived component, such as an activity or service – in that case, the intent receiver lives as long as its "host" does (e.g., until the activity is frozen). However, in this case, you cannot declare the intent receiver via `AndroidManifest.xml`. Instead, you need to call `registerIntent()` on your `Activity`'s `onResume()` callback to declare interest in an intent, then call `unregisterIntent()` from your `Activity`'s `onPause()` when you no longer need those intents.

You can see an example of an intent receiver in action in the TourIt sample application.

CHAPTER 22

Launching Activities and Sub-Activities

As discussed previously, the theory behind the Android UI architecture is that developers should decompose their application into distinct activities, each implemented as an Activity, each reachable via intents, with one "main" activity being the one launched by the Android launcher. For example, a calendar application could have activities for viewing the calendar, viewing a single event, editing an event (including adding a new one), and so forth.

This, of course, implies that one of your activities has the means to start up another activity. For example, if somebody clicks on an event from the view-calendar activity, you might want to show the view-event activity for that event. This means that, somehow, you need to be able to cause the view-event activity to launch and show a specific event (the one the user clicked upon).

This can be further broken down into two scenarios:

1. You know what activity you want to launch, probably because it is another activity in your own application

2. You have a content Uri to...something, and you want your users to be able to do...something with it, but you do not know up front what the options are

This chapter covers the first scenario; the next chapter handles the second.

Peers and Subs

One key question you need to answer when you decide to launch an activity is: does your activity need to know when the launched activity ends?

For example, suppose you want to spawn an activity to collect authentication information for some Web service you are connecting to – maybe you need to authenticate with OpenID[27] in order to use an OAuth[28] service. In this case, your main activity will need to know when the authentication is complete so it can start to use the Web service.

On the other hand, imagine an email application in Android. When the user elects to view an attachment, neither you nor the user necessarily expect the main activity to know when the user is done viewing that attachment.

In the first scenario, the launched activity is clearly subordinate to the launching activity. In that case, you probably want to launch the child as a sub-activity, which means your activity will be notified when the child activity is complete.

In the second scenario, the launched activity is more a peer of your activity, so you probably want to launch the "child" just as a regular activity. Your activity will not be informed when the "child" is done, but, then again, your activity really doesn't need to know.

Start 'Em Up

The two pieces for starting an activity are an intent and your choice of how to start it up.

---

27 http://openid.net/
28 http://oauth.net/

Make an Intent

As discussed in a previous chapter, intents encapsulate a request, made to Android, for some activity or other intent receiver to do something.

If the activity you intend to launch is one of your own, you may find it simplest to create an explicit intent, naming the component you wish to launch. For example, from within your activity, you could create an intent like this:

```
new Intent(this, HelpActivity.class);
```

This would stipulate that you wanted to launch the HelpActivity. This activity would need to be named in your AndroidManifest.xml file, though not necessarily with any intent filter, since you are trying to request it directly.

Or, you could put together an intent for some Uri, requesting a particular action:

```
Uri uri=Uri.parse("geo:"+lat.toString()+
                  ","+lon.toString());
Intent i=new Intent(Intent.VIEW_ACTION, uri);
```

Here, given that we have the latitude and longitude of some position (lat and lon, respectively) of type Double, we construct a geo scheme Uri and create an intent requesting to view this Uri (VIEW_ACTION).

Make the Call

Once you have your intent, you need to pass it to Android and get the child activity to launch. You have four choices:

1. The simplest option is to call startActivity() with the intent – this will cause Android to find the best-match activity or intent receiver and pass the intent to it for handling. Your activity will not be informed when the "child" activity is complete.

2. You can call startSubActivity(), passing it the intent and a number (unique to the calling activity). Android will find the best-match handler and pass the intent over to it. However, your activity will be notified when the child activity is complete via the onActivityResult() callback (see below).

3. You can call broadcastIntent(). In this case, Android will pass the intent to all registered activities and intent receivers that could possibly want this intent, not just the best match.

4. You can call broadcastIntentSerialized(). Here, Android will pass the intent to all candidate activities and intent receivers one at a time – if any one "consumes" the intent, the rest of the the candidates are not notified.

Most of the time, you will wind up using startActivity() or startSubActivity() – broadcast intents are more typically raised by the Android system itself.

With startSubActivity(), as noted, you can implement the onActivityResult() callback to be notified when the child activity has completed its work. The callback receives the unique number supplied to startSubActivity(), so you can determine which child activity is the one that has completed. You also get:

- A result code, from the child activity calling setResult(). Typically this is RESULT_OK or RESULT_CANCELLED, though you can create your own return codes (pick a number starting with RESULT_FIRST_USER)

- An optional String containing some result data, possibly a URL to some internal or external resource – for example, a PICK_ACTION intent typically returns the selected bit of content via this data string

- An optional Bundle containing additional information beyond the result code and data string

To demonstrate launching a peer activity, take a peek at the Launch sample application. The XML layout is fairly straightforward: two fields for the latitude and longitude, plus a button:

```
<?xml version="1.0" encoding="utf-8"?>
<LinearLayout xmlns:android="http://schemas.android.com/apk/res/android"
  android:orientation="vertical"
  android:layout_width="fill_parent"
  android:layout_height="fill_parent"
  >
  <TableLayout
    android:layout_width="fill_parent"
    android:layout_height="wrap_content"
    android:stretchColumns="1,2"
  >
    <TableRow>
      <TextView
        android:layout_width="wrap_content"
        android:layout_height="wrap_content"
        android:paddingLeft="2dip"
        android:paddingRight="4dip"
        android:text="Location:"
      />
      <EditText android:id="@+id/lat"
        android:layout_width="fill_parent"
        android:layout_height="wrap_content"
        android:cursorVisible="true"
        android:editable="true"
        android:singleLine="true"
        android:layout_weight="1"
      />
      <EditText android:id="@+id/lon"
        android:layout_width="fill_parent"
        android:layout_height="wrap_content"
        android:cursorVisible="true"
        android:editable="true"
        android:singleLine="true"
        android:layout_weight="1"
      />
    </TableRow>
  </TableLayout>
  <Button android:id="@+id/map"
    android:layout_width="fill_parent"
    android:layout_height="wrap_content"
    android:text="Show Me!"
  />
</LinearLayout>
```

The button's OnClickListener simply takes the latitude and longitude, pours them into a geo scheme Uri, then starts the activity.

```
package com.commonsware.android.activities;

import android.app.Activity;
import android.content.Intent;
import android.net.Uri;
```

```
import android.os.Bundle;
import android.view.View;
import android.widget.Button;
import android.widget.EditText;

public class LaunchDemo extends Activity {
  private EditText lat;
  private EditText lon;

  @Override
  public void onCreate(Bundle icicle) {
    super.onCreate(icicle);
    setContentView(R.layout.main);

    Button btn=(Button)findViewById(R.id.map);
    lat=(EditText)findViewById(R.id.lat);
    lon=(EditText)findViewById(R.id.lon);

    btn.setOnClickListener(new View.OnClickListener() {
      public void onClick(View view) {
        String _lat=lat.getText().toString();
        String _lon=lon.getText().toString();
        Uri uri=Uri.parse("geo:"+_lat+","+_lon);

        startActivity(new Intent(Intent.VIEW_ACTION, uri));
      }
    });
  }
}
```

The activity is not much to look at:

Figure 52. The LaunchDemo sample application, as initially launched

If you fill in a location (e.g., 40.71167 latitude and -74.01333 longitude) and click the button, the resulting map is more interesting. Note that this is the built-in Android map activity – we did not create our own activity to display this map.

Figure 53. The map launched by Launch Demo, showing the region known as "Ground Zero" in New York City

In a later chapter, you will see how you can create maps in your own activities, in case you need greater control over how the map is displayed.

CHAPTER 23

Finding Available Actions via Introspection

Sometimes, you know just what you want to do, such as display one of your other activities.

Sometimes, you have a pretty good idea of what you want to do, such as view the content represented by a Uri, or have the user pick a piece of content of some MIME type.

Sometimes, you're lost. All you have is a content Uri, and you don't really know what you can do with it.

For example, suppose you were creating a common tagging subsystem for Android, where users could tag pieces of content – contacts, Web URLs, geographic locations, etc. Your subsystem would hold onto the Uri of the content plus the associated tags, so other subsystems could, say, ask for all pieces of content referencing some tag.

That's all well and good. However, you probably need some sort of maintenance activity, where users could view all their tags and the pieces of content so tagged. This might even serve as a quasi-bookmark service for items on their phone. The problem is, the user is going to expect to be able to do useful things with the content they find in your subsystem, such as dial a contact or show a map for a location.

The problem is, you have absolutely no idea what is all possible with any given content Uri. You probably can view any of them, but can you edit them? Can you dial them? Since new applications with new types of content could be added by any user at any time, you can't even assume you know all possible combinations just by looking at the stock applications shipped on all Android devices.

Fortunately, the Android developers thought of this.

Android offers various means by which you can present to your users a set of likely activities to spawn for a given content Uri...even if you have no idea what that content Uri really represents. This chapter explores some of these Uri action introspection tools.

Pick 'Em

Sometimes, you know your content Uri represents a collection of some type, such as content://contacts/people representing the list of contacts in the stock Android contacts list. In this case, you can let the user pick a contact that your activity can then use (e.g., tag it, dial it).

To do this, you need to create an intent for the PICK_ACTIVITY_ACTION on the target Uri, then start a sub activity (via startSubActivity()) to allow the user to pick a piece of content of the specified type. If your onActivityResult() callback for this request gets a RESULT_OK result code, your data string can be parsed into a Uri representing the chosen piece of content.

For example, take a look at Pick in the sample applications. This activity gives you a field for a collection Uri (with content://contacts/people pre-filled in for your convenience), plus a really big "Gimme!" button:

```
<?xml version="1.0" encoding="utf-8"?>
<LinearLayout xmlns:android="http://schemas.android.com/apk/res/android"
  android:orientation="vertical"
  android:layout_width="fill_parent"
  android:layout_height="fill_parent"
  >
  <EditText android:id="@+id/type"
```

```
      android:layout_width="fill_parent"
      android:layout_height="wrap_content"
      android:cursorVisible="true"
      android:editable="true"
      android:singleLine="true"
      android:text="content://contacts/people"
  />
  <Button
      android:id="@+id/pick"
      android:layout_width="fill_parent"
      android:layout_height="fill_parent"
      android:text="Gimme!"
      android:layout_weight="1"
  />
</LinearLayout>
```

Upon being clicked, the button creates the PICK_ACTIVITY_ACTION on the user-supplied collection Uri and starts the sub-activity. When that sub-activity completes with RESULT_OK, the VIEW_ACTION is invoked on the resulting content Uri.

```
package com.commonsware.android.introspection;

import android.app.Activity;
import android.content.Intent;
import android.net.Uri;
import android.os.Bundle;
import android.view.View;
import android.widget.Button;
import android.widget.EditText;


public class PickDemo extends Activity {
  static final int PICK_REQUEST = 1337;
  private EditText type;

  @Override
  public void onCreate(Bundle icicle) {
    super.onCreate(icicle);
    setContentView(R.layout.main);
    type=(EditText)findViewById(R.id.type);

    Button btn=(Button)findViewById(R.id.pick);

    btn.setOnClickListener(new View.OnClickListener() {
      public void onClick(View view) {
        Intent i=new Intent(Intent.PICK_ACTION,
                  Uri.parse(type.getText().toString()));

      startSubActivity(i, PICK_REQUEST);
    }
```

```
  });
}

protected void onActivityResult(int requestCode, int resultCode,
                String data, Bundle extras) {
  if (requestCode==PICK_REQUEST) {
    if (resultCode==RESULT_OK) {
      startActivity(new Intent(Intent.VIEW_ACTION,
                Uri.parse(data)));
    }
  }
}
}
```

The result: the user chooses a collection, picks a piece of content, and views it.

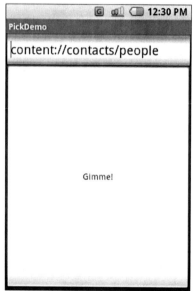

Figure 54. The PickDemo sample application, as initially launched

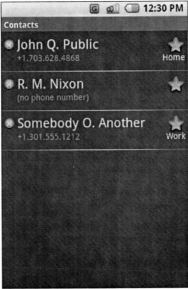

Figure 55. The same application, after clicking the "Gimme!" button, showing the list of available people

Figure 56. A view of a contact, launched by PickDemo after choosing one of the people from the pick list

One flaw in this application is that it may not have permission to view whatever content collection the user entered. For the sample, we had to specifically request permission to read the user's contacts, via a uses-permission element in AndroidManifest.xml. We'll cover more about requesting (and requiring) permissions later in this book.

Adaptable Adapters

One way to present your users with available actions to take on a piece of content is to use ActivityAdapter or ActivityIconAdapter. These are ListAdapter subclasses, meaning they supply child views to selection widgets like ListView and Spinner. In this case, they supply a list of available actions to take on the content – and for ActivityIconAdapter, it includes both a name (e.g., "Edit Contact") and an icon associated with the action.

Once a user has chosen an action – for example, by clicking on a list item – you can get the intent that combines the chosen action with the content Uri of the piece of content. That intent can be directly passed to startActivity() to take the user to the activity they requested.

All without you having to know anything about what the content is.

One confusing facet of ActivityAdapter and ActivityIconAdapter is that they take an Intent, not a Uri, on their constructor. This means you need to wrap the Uri for the content in an otherwise-empty Intent in order to satisfy the constructor's request:

```
Intent i=new Intent();
i.setData(Uri.parse(data));
ListAdapter adapter=new ActivityAdapter(this, i);
```

So, let's embellish the previous example – copied into Adapter – to give the user some choices for what to do with the picked piece of content, rather than always just viewing it as before.

The layout now adds a ListView, to show the available actions:

```xml
<?xml version="1.0" encoding="utf-8"?>
<LinearLayout xmlns:android="http://schemas.android.com/apk/res/android"
  android:orientation="vertical"
  android:layout_width="fill_parent"
  android:layout_height="fill_parent"
  >
  <EditText android:id="@+id/type"
    android:layout_width="fill_parent"
    android:layout_height="wrap_content"
    android:cursorVisible="true"
    android:editable="true"
    android:singleLine="true"
    android:text="content://contacts/people"
  />
  <Button
    android:id="@+id/pick"
    android:layout_width="fill_parent"
    android:layout_height="wrap_content"
    android:text="Gimme!"
  />
  <ListView
    android:id="@android:id/list"
    android:layout_width="fill_parent"
    android:layout_height="fill_parent"
    android:drawSelectorOnTop="false"
    android:layout_weight="1"
  />
</LinearLayout>
```

The resulting UI now shows the available actions:

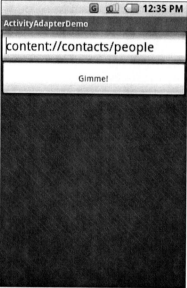

Figure 57. The ActivityAdapterDemo sample application, as initially launched

Figure 58. The same application, after clicking "Gimme!" and choosing a person

Note that, at the time of this writing, Android does not filter the available actions to only be the ones that are possible from the activity – it shows them all. Hence, the user is given action options that may not be allowed due to insufficient permissions. If you run the supplied sample code without modifications, you will be able to view a chosen contact, but not edit them, for example.

Would You Like to See the Menu?

Another way to give the user ways to take actions on a piece of content, without you knowing what actions are possible, is to inject a set of menu choices into the options menu via addIntentOptions(). This method, available on Menu, takes an Intent and other parameters and fills in a set of menu choices on the Menu instance, each representing one possible action. Choosing one of those menu choices spawns the associated activity.

The canonical example of using addIntentOptions() illustrates another flavor of having a piece of content and not knowing the actions that can be taken. In the previous example, showing ActivityAdapter, the content was from some other Android application, and we know nothing about it. It is also possible, though, that we know full well what the content is – it's ours. However, Android applications are perfectly capable of adding new actions to existing content types, so even though you wrote your application and know what you expect to be done with your content, there may be other options you are unaware of that are available to users.

For example, imagine the tagging subsystem mentioned in the introduction to this chapter. It would be very annoying to users if, every time they wanted to tag a piece of content, they had to go to a separate tagging tool, then turn around and pick the content they just had been working on (if that is even technically possible) before associating tags with it. Instead, they would probably prefer a menu choice in the content's own "home" activity where they can indicate they want to tag it, which leads them to the set-a-tag activity and tells that activity what content should get tagged.

To accomplish this, the tagging subsystem should set up an intent filter, supporting any piece of content, with their own action (e.g., TAG_ACTION) and a category of ALTERNATE_CATEGORY. The category ALTERNATE_CATEGORY is the convention for one application adding actions to another application's content.

If you want to write activities that are aware of possible add-ons like tagging, you should use addIntentOptions() to add those add-ons' actions to your options menu, such as the following:

```
Intent intent = new Intent(null, myContentUri);

intent.addCategory(Intent.ALTERNATIVE_CATEGORY);
menu.addIntentOptions(Menu.ALTERNATIVE, 0,
                new ComponentName(this,
                                    MyActivity.class),
                null, intent, 0, null);
```

Here, myContentUri is the content Uri of whatever is being viewed by the user in this activity, MyActivity is the name of the activity class, and menu is the menu being modified.

In this case, the Intent we are using to pick actions from requires that appropriate intent receivers support the ALTERNATIVE_CATEGORY. Then, we add the options to the menu with addIntentOptions() and the following parameters:

- The sort position for this set of menu choices, typically set to 0 (appear in the order added to the menu) or ALTERNATIVE (appear after other menu choices)

- A unique number for this set of menu choices, or 0 if you do not need a number

- A ComponentName instance representing the activity that is populating its menu – this is used to filter out the activity's own actions, so the activity can handle its own actions as it sees fit

- An array of Intent instances that are the "specific" matches – any actions matching those intents are shown first in the menu before any other possible actions

- The Intent for which you want the available actions

- A set of flags. The only one of likely relevance is represented as MATCH_DEFAULT_ONLY, which means matching actions must also implement the DEFAULT_CATEGORY category. If you do not need this, use a value of 0 for the flags.

- An array of Menu.Item, which will hold the menu items matching the array of Intent instances supplied as the "specifics", or null if you do not need those items (or are not using "specifics")

Asking Around

Both the ActivityAdapter family and addIntentOptions() use queryIntentActivityOptions() for the "heavy lifting" of finding possible actions. The queryIntentActivityOptions() method is implemented on PackageManager, which is available to your activity via getPackageManager().

The queryIntentActivityOptions() method takes some of the same parameters as does addIntentOptions(), notably the caller ComponentName, the "specifics" array of Intent instances, the overall Intent representing the actions you are seeking, and the set of flags. It returns a List of Intent instances matching the stated criteria, with the "specifics" ones first.

If you would like to offer alternative actions to users, but by means other than the ActivityAdapter and addIntentOptions() means, you could call queryIntentActivityOptions(), get the Intent instances, then use them to populate some other user interface (e.g., a toolbar).

PART V – Content Providers and Services

CHAPTER 24

Using a Content Provider

Any Uri in Android that begins with the content:// scheme represents a resource served up by a content provider. Content providers offer data encapsulation using Uri instances as handles – you neither know nor care where the data represented by the Uri comes from, so long as it is available to you when needed. The data could be stored in a SQLite database, or in flat files, or retrieved off a device, or be stored on some far-off server accessed over the Internet.

Given a Uri, you can perform basic CRUD (create, read, update, delete) operations using a content provider. Uri instances can represent either collections or individual pieces of content. Given a collection Uri, you can create new pieces of content via insert operations. Given an instance Uri, you can read data represented by the Uri, update that data, or delete the instance outright.

Android lets you use existing content providers, plus create your own. This chapter covers using content providers; the next chapter will explain how you can serve up your own data using the content provider framework.

Pieces of Me

The simplified model of the construction of a content Uri is the scheme, the namespace of data, and, optionally, the instance identifier, all separated by slashes in URL-style notation. The scheme of a content Uri is always `content://`.

So, a content `Uri` of `content://tours/5` represents the tours instance with an identifier of 5.

The combination of the scheme and the namespace is known as the "base Uri" of a content provider, or a set of data supported by a content provider. In the example above, `content://tours` is the base `Uri` for a content provider that serves up information about "tours" (in this case, bicycle tours from the TourIt sample application).

The base `Uri` can be more complicated. For example, the base `Uri` for contacts is `content://contacts/people`, as the contacts content provider may serve up other data using other base `Uri` values.

The base `Uri` represents a collection of instances. The base `Uri` combined with an instance identifier (e.g., 5) represents a single instance.

Most of the Android APIs expect these to be `Uri` objects, though in common discussion, it is simpler to think of them as strings. The `Uri.parse()` static method creates a `Uri` out of the string representation.

Getting a Handle

So, where do these `Uri` instances come from?

The most popular starting point, if you know the type of data you want to work with, is to get the base `Uri` from the content provider itself in code. For example, `android.provider.CONTENT_URI` is the base `Uri` for contacts represented as people – this maps to `content://contacts/people`. If you just need the collection, this `Uri` works as-is; if you need an instance and know its identifier, you can call `addId()` on the `Uri` to inject it, so you have a `Uri` for the instance.

You might also get Uri instances handed to you from other sources. In the preceding chapter, we saw how you got Uri handles for contacts via sub-activities responding to PICK_ACTION intents. In this case, the Uri is truly an opaque handle...unless you decide to pick it apart using the various getters on the Uri class.

You can also hard-wire literal String objects and convert them into Uri instances via Uri.parse(). For example, in the preceding chapter, the sample code used an EditView with content://contacts/people pre-filled in. This isn't an ideal solution, as the base Uri values could conceivably change over time.

Makin' Queries

Given a base Uri, you can run a query to return data out of the content provider related to that Uri. This has much of the feel of SQL: you specify the "columns" to return, the constraints to determine which "rows" to return, a sort order, etc. The difference is that this request is being made of a content provider, not directly of some database (e.g., SQLite).

The nexus of this is the managedQuery() method available to your activity. This method takes five parameters:

1. The base Uri of the content provider to query, or the instance Uri of a specific object to query

2. An array of properties of instances from that content provider that you want returned by the query

3. A constraint statement, functioning like a SQL WHERE clause

4. An optional set of parameters to bind into the constraint clause, replacing any ? that appear there

5. An optional sort statement, functioning like a SQL ORDER BY clause

This method returns a Cursor object, which you can use to retrieve the data returned by the query.

"Properties" is to content providers as columns are to databases. In other words, each instance (row) returned by a query consists of a set of properties (columns), each representing some piece of data.

This will hopefully make more sense given an example.

Our content provider examples come from the TourIt sample application, as described in Appendix A. Specifically, the following code fragment is from the TourViewActivity, which shows the cue sheet for a selected bicycle tour:

```
try {
  if (c==null) {
    c=managedQuery(getIntent().getData(), Tour.PROJECTION, null, null, null);
  }
  else {
    c.requery();
  }

  c.first();
  tour=new Tour(getIntent().getData(), c);

  int sel=getSelectedItemPosition();

  setListAdapter(new RouteAdapter(tour, this));
  setSelection(sel);
  setTitle("TourIt! - "+tour.getTitle());
}
catch (Throwable t) {
  android.util.Log.e("TourIt", "Exception creating tour", t);
}
```

In the call to managedQuery(), we provide:

- The Uri passed into the activity by the caller (getIntent().getData()), in this case representing a specific bicycle tour, provided to TourViewActivity from the invoking activity (TourListActivity)

- A list of properties to retrieve, supplied to us by our Tour model class (PROJECTION)

- Three null values, indicating that we do not need a constraint clause (the Uri represents the instance we need), nor parameters for the constraint, nor a sort order (we should only get one entry back)

The biggest "magic" here is the list of properties. The lineup of what properties are possible for a given content provider should be provided by the documentation (or source code) for the content provider itself. In this case, we delegate to the Tour model class the responsibility of telling us which properties it needs to fully represent the object:

```
class Tour {
  public static final String[] PROJECTION = new String[] {
    Provider.Tours.ID, Provider.Tours.TITLE,
    Provider.Tours.DESCRIPTION,
    Provider.Tours.CREATED_DATE,
    Provider.Tours.MODIFIED_DATE,
    Provider.Tours.ROUTE};
```

The projection is simply an array of strings, listing properties exposed by the tour content provider (Provider). The tour content provider, in turn, simply provides values for these symbolic names:

```
public static final String TITLE="title";
public static final String DESCRIPTION="desc";
public static final String CREATED_DATE="created";
public static final String MODIFIED_DATE="modified";
public static final String ROUTE="route";
```

So, when the TourViewActivity invokes the query and gets the Cursor, it has the data necessary to create the corresponding Tour model, via data it is retrieving from the tour content provider.

Adapting to the Circumstances

Now that we have a Cursor via managedQuery(), we have access to the query results and can do whatever we want with them. You might, for example, manually extract data from the Cursor to populate widgets or other objects – TourViewActivity does this by populating a Tour model object out of its Cursor.

However, if the goal of the query was to return a list from which the user should choose an item, you probably should consider using SimpleCursorAdapter. This class bridges between the Cursor and a selection widget, such as a ListView or Spinner. Pour the Cursor into a

SimpleCursorAdapter, hand the adapter off to the widget, and you're set –
your widget will show the available options.

For example, here is a fragment of the onCreate() method from
TourListActivity, which gives the user a list of tours to choose from:

```
toursCursor = managedQuery(getIntent().getData(), PROJECTION, null, null, null);

list=(ListView)findViewById(android.R.id.list);
list.setOnItemClickListener(this);

ListAdapter adapter = new SimpleCursorAdapter(this,
    R.layout.tourlist_item, toursCursor,
    new String[] {Provider.Tours.TITLE},
    new int[] {android.R.id.text1});
list.setAdapter(adapter);
```

After executing the managedQuery() and getting the Cursor, TourListActivity
creates a SimpleCursorAdapter with the following parameters:

- The activity (or other Context) creating the adapter; in this case, the
  TourListActivity itself

- The identifier for a layout to be used for rendering the list entries
  (R.layout.tourlist_item)

- The cursor (toursCursor)

- The properties to pull out of the cursor and use for configuring the
  list entry View instances (TITLE)

- The corresponding identifiers of TextView widgets in the list entry
  layout that those properties should go into (android.R.id.text1)

After that, we put the adapter into the ListView, and we get:

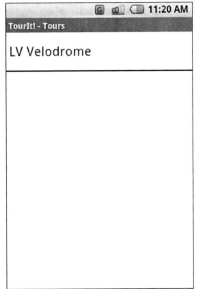

Figure 59. TourListActivity, showing a list of tours

If you need more control over the views than you can reasonably achieve with the stock view construction logic, subclass SimpleCursorAdapter and override getView() to create your own widgets to go into the list, as demonstrated earlier in this book.

Doing It By Hand

Of course, you can always do it the "hard way" – pulling data out of the Cursor by hand. The Cursor interface is similar in concept to other database access APIs offering cursors as objects, though, as always, the devil is in the details.

Position

Cursor instances have a built-in notion of position, akin to the Java Iterator interface. To get to the various rows, you can use:

- first() to move to the first row in the result set or last() to move to the last row in the result set

- next() to move to the next row and determine if there is yet another row to process (next() returns true if it points to another row after moving, false otherwise)

- prev() to move to the previous row, as the opposite to next()

- moveTo() to move to a specific index, or move() to move to a relative position plus or minus from your current position

- position() to return your current index

- a whole host of condition methods, including isFirst(), isLast(), isBeforeFirst(), and isAfterLast()

Getting Properties

Once you have the Cursor positioned at a row of interest, you have a variety of methods to retrieve properties from that row, with different methods supporting different types (getString(), getInt(), getFloat(), etc.). Each method takes the zero-based index of the property you want to retrieve.

If you want to see if a given property has a value, you can use isNull() to test it for null-ness.

So, as an example, let's examine how the Tour model class accesses its Cursor. The underlying assumption of the Tour is that it is provided a Cursor with only one row, and that Cursor will remain pointed to that row for the lifespan of the Tour instance. If this were a public interface, this approach would be scary, as Cursor objects are mutable. But, since the Tour model is used only within a fairly small application, the assumptions regarding the Tour's Cursor are probably safe.

That being said, here are some cursor-wrapping accessors from Tour:

```
String getTitle() {
  return(c.getString(1));
}

void setTitle(String title) {
  c.updateString(1, title);
}
```

Rather than copying properties into local fields, the Tour simply holds onto the Cursor. Hence, getTitle() retrieves the property value at index 1, and so forth. The exception is the route (waypoints and directions), which is represented in the database as a path to a file in JSON format – for this, the Tour parses the JSON and populates Waypoint and Direction model objects.

Setting Properties

Cursor instances not only let you read data, but change it as well. Simply use the setters (e.g., putString(), putInt()), supplying the index of the property to alter and the new value for that property.

Initially, those changes are just in the Cursor itself. To commit those changes to the content provider, you need to call commitUpdates(), which packages up the change(s) to your row(s).

At this point, though, your Cursor is stale – the content provider might alter the data you supplied to fit some content-specific conventions (e.g., rounding of floats, truncating strings). If you are going to continue using the Cursor, you should call requery() on the Cursor to re-execute the original query and thereby "refresh" the Cursor's rendition of the data.

So, to recap, the flow is:

- Call setters to make changes
- Call commitUpdates() to persist the changes
- Call requery() to refresh the Cursor if you will continue using it

You do not necessarily need a Cursor to make changes, though. You can also call update() on a ContentResolver (usually obtained by an activity via getContentResolver()). This works akin to a SQL UPDATE statement and takes four parameters:

- A Uri representing the collection (or instance) you wish to update
- A ContentValues (Map-like collection) instance representing the properties you wish to change

- A constraint statement, functioning like a SQL WHERE clause, to determine which rows should be updated

- An optional set of parameters to bind into the constraint clause, replacing any ? that appear there

As with a SQL UPDATE statement, update() could affect zero to several rows, as determined by the constraint statement and parameters.

Give and Take

Of course, content providers would be astonishingly weak if you couldn't add or remove data from them, only update what is there. Fortunately, content providers offer these abilities as well.

To insert data into a content provider, you have two options available on the ContentProvider interface (available through getContentProvider() to your activity):

1. Use insert() with a collection Uri and a ContentValues structure describing the initial set of data to put in the row

2. Use bulkInsert() with a collection Uri and an array of ContentValues structures to populate several rows at once

The insert() method returns a Uri for you to use for future operations on that new object. The bulkInsert() method returns the number of created rows; you would need to do a query to get back at the data you just inserted.

For example, here is a snippet of code from TourEditActivity to insert a new tour into the content provider:

```
if (tour==null) {
  ContentValues values=new ContentValues();

  values.put(Provider.Tours.TITLE, tour.getTitle());

  Uri url=getContentResolver().insert(Provider.Tours.CONTENT_URI, values);

  c=managedQuery(url, Tour.PROJECTION, null, null);
```

```
  c.first();

  try {
    tour=new Tour(url, c);
  }
  catch (Throwable t) {
    android.util.Log.e("TourIt", "Exception creating tour", t);
    Toast.makeText(this, R.string.save_failed, 2000).show();
    return;
  }
}
```

In this case, all we do is populate the title. Since we get a Uri back, we can turn around and get a Cursor on that Uri (via managedQuery(uri, PROJECTION, null, null)) and reuse our existing update logic to add in any additional data beyond the title itself.

To delete one or more rows from the content provider, use the delete() method on ContentResolver. This works akin to a SQL DELETE statement and takes three parameters:

1. A Uri representing the collection (or instance) you wish to update

2. A constraint statement, functioning like a SQL WHERE clause, to determine which rows should be updated

3. An optional set of parameters to bind into the constraint clause, replacing any ? that appear there

Beware of the BLOB!

Binary large objects – BLOBs – are supported in many databases, including SQLite. However, the Android model is more aimed at supporting such hunks of data via their own separate content Uri values. A content provider, therefore, does not provide direct access to binary data, like photos, via a Cursor. Rather, a property in the content provider will give you the content Uri for that particular BLOB. You can use getInputStream() and getOutputStream() on your ContentProvider to read and write the binary data.

Quite possibly, the rationale is to minimize unnecessary data copying. For example, the primary use of a photo in Android is to display it to the user.

The ImageView widget can do just that, via a content Uri to a JPEG. By storing the photo in a manner that has its own Uri, you do not need to copy data out of the content provider into some temporary holding area just to be able to display it – just use the Uri. The expectation, presumably, is that few Android applications will do much more than upload binary data and use widgets or built-in activities to display that data.

CHAPTER 25

Building a Content Provider

Building a content provider is probably the most complicated and tedious task in all of Android development. There are many requirements of a content provider, in terms of methods to implement and public data members to supply. And, until you try using it, you have no great way of telling if you did any of it correctly (versus, say, building an activity and getting validation errors from the resource compiler).

That being said, building a content provider is of huge importance if your application wishes to make data available to other applications. If your application is keeping its data solely to itself, you may be able to avoid creating a content provider, just accessing the data directly from your activities. But, if you want your data to possibly be used by others – for example, you are building a feed reader and you want other programs to be able to access the feeds you are downloading and caching – then a content provider is right for you.

First, Some Dissection

As was discussed in the previous chapter, the content Uri is the linchpin behind accessing data inside a content provider. When using a content provider, all you really need to know is the provider's base Uri; from there you can run queries as needed, or construct a Uri to a specific instance if you know the instance identifier.

When building a content provider, though, you need to know a bit more about the innards of the content Uri.

A content Uri has two to four pieces, depending on situation:

- It always has a scheme (content://), indicating it is a content Uri instead of a Uri to a Web resource (http://).

- It always has an authority, which is the first path segment after the scheme. The authority is a unique string identifying the content provider that handles the content associated with this Uri.

- It may have a data type path, which is the list of path segments after the authority and before the instance identifier (if any). The data type path can be empty, if the content provider only handles one type of content. It can be a single path segment (foo) or a chain of path segments (foo/bar/goo) as needed to handle whatever data access scenarios the content provider requires.

- It may have an instance identifier, which is an integer identifying a specific piece of content. A content Uri without an instance identifier refers to the collection of content represented by the authority (and, where provided, the data path).

For example, a content Uri could be as simple as content://sekrits, which would refer to the collection of content held by whatever content provider was tied to the sekrits authority (e.g., SecretsProvider). Or, it could be as complex as content://sekrits/card/pin/17, which would refer to a piece of content (identified as 17) managed by the sekrits content provider that is of the data type card/pin.

Next, Some Typing

Next, you need to come up with some MIME types corresponding with the content your content provider will provide.

Android uses both the content Uri and the MIME type as ways to identify content on the device. A collection content Uri – or, more accurately, the combination authority and data type path – should map to a pair of MIME types. One MIME type will represent the collection; the other will represent an instance. These map to the Uri patterns above for no-identifier and identifier, respectively. As you saw earlier in this book, you can fill in a MIME type into an Intent to route the Intent to the proper activity (e.g., PICK_ACTION on a collection MIME type to call up a selection activity to pick an instance out of that collection).

The collection MIME type should be of the form vnd.X.cursor.dir/Y, where X is the name of your firm, organization, or project, and Y is a dot-delimited type name. So, for example, you might use vnd.tlagency.cursor.dir/sekrits.card.pin as the MIME type for your collection of secrets.

The instance MIME type should be of the form vnd.X.cursor.item/Y, usually for the same values of X and Y as you used for the collection MIME type (though that is not strictly required).

Step #1: Create a Provider Class

Just as an activity and intent receiver are both Java classes, so is a content provider. So, the big step in creating a content provider is crafting its Java class, choosing as a base class either ContentProvider or DatabaseContentProvider. Not surprisingly, DatabaseContentProvider offers some extra hooks to help with content providers using SQLite databases for storage, whereas ContentProvider is more general-purpose.

Here's how you extend these base classes to make up your content provider.

ContentProvider

If you implement a subclass of ContentProvider, you are responsible for implementing six methods that, when combined, perform the services that a content provider is supposed to offer to activities wishing to create, read, update, or delete content.

onCreate()

As with an activity, the main entry point to a content provider is onCreate(). Here, you can do whatever initialization you want. In particular, here is where you should lazy-initialize your data store. For example, if you plan on storing your data in such-and-so directory on an SD card, with an XML file serving as a "table of contents", you should check and see if that directory and XML file are there and, if not, create them so the rest of your content provider knows they are out there and available for use.

Similarly, if you have rewritten your content provider sufficiently to cause the data store to shift structure, you should check to see what structure you have now and adjust it if what you have is out of date. You don't write your own "installer" program and so have no great way of determining if, when onCreate() is called, if this is the first time ever for the content provider, the first time for a new release of a content provider that was upgraded in-place, or if this is just a normal startup.

If your content provider uses SQLite for storage, and you are not using DatabaseContentProvider, you can detect to see if your tables exist by querying on the sqlite_master table. This is useful for lazy-creating a table your content provider will need.

For example, here is the onCreate() method for Provider, from the TourIt sample application:

```
@Override
public boolean onCreate() {
  db=(new DatabaseHelper()).openDatabase(getContext(), getDbName(), null,
                                         getDbVersion());

  return (db == null) ? false : true;
}
```

While that doesn't seem all that special, the "magic" is in the private DatabaseHelper object:

```
private class DatabaseHelper extends SQLiteOpenHelper {
  @Override
  public void onCreate(SQLiteDatabase db) {
```

```
    Cursor c=db.rawQuery("SELECT name FROM sqlite_master WHERE type='table' AND
name='tours'", null);

    try {
      if (c.count()==0) {
        db.execSQL("CREATE TABLE tours (_id INTEGER PRIMARY KEY AUTOINCREMENT, title TEXT,
desc TEXT DEFAULT '', created INTEGER, modified INTEGER, route TEXT DEFAULT '{}');");

        File sdcard=new File("/sdcard/tourit");

        if (sdcard.exists()) {
          for (File f : sdcard.listFiles()) {
            if (f.isDirectory()) {
              File tour=new File(f, "tour.js");

              if (tour.exists()) {
                long now=System.currentTimeMillis();
                ContentValues map=new ContentValues();

                map.put("title", f.getName());
                map.put("created", now);
                map.put("modified", now);
                map.put("route", tour.getPath());

                db.insert("tours", null, map);
              }
            }
          }
        }
      }
    }
    finally {
      c.close();
    }
  }

  @Override
  public void onUpgrade(SQLiteDatabase db, int oldVersion, int newVersion) {
    android.util.Log.w("TourIt", "Upgrading database, which will destroy all old data");
    db.execSQL("DROP TABLE IF EXISTS tours");
    onCreate(db);
  }
}
```

First, we query `sqlite_master` to see if our table is there – if it is, we're done. Otherwise, we execute some SQL to create the table, then scan the SD card to see if we can find any tours that need to be loaded. Those are poured into the table via `insert()` calls.

The method behind this madness is covered in greater detail in Appendix A, where we cover TourIt in more detail.

query()

As one might expect, the query() method is where your content provider gets details on a query some activity wants to perform. It is up to you to actually process said query.

The query method gets, as parameters:

- A Uri representing the collection or instance being queried
- A String[] representing the list of properties that should be returned
- A String representing what amounts to a SQL WHERE clause, constraining which instances should be considered for the query results
- A String[] representing values to "pour into" the WHERE clause, replacing any ? found there
- A String representing what amounts to a SQL ORDER BY clause

You are responsible for interpreting these parameters however they make sense and returning a Cursor that can be used to iterate over and access the data.

As you can imagine, these parameters are aimed towards people using a SQLite database for storage. You are welcome to ignore some of these parameters (e.g., you elect not to try to roll your own SQL WHERE clause parser), but you need to document that fact so activities only attempt to query you by instance Uri and not using parameters you elect not to handle.

For SQLite-backed storage providers, however, the query() method implementation should be largely boilerplate. Use a SQLiteQueryBuilder to convert the various parameters into a single SQL statement, then use query() on the builder to actually invoke the query and give you a Cursor back. The Cursor is what your query() method then returns.

For example, here is query() from Provider:

```
@Override
public Cursor query(Uri url, String[] projection, String selection,
                    String[] selectionArgs, String sort) {
  SQLiteQueryBuilder qb=new SQLiteQueryBuilder();

  qb.setTables(getTableName());

  if (isCollectionUri(url)) {
    qb.setProjectionMap(getDefaultProjection());
  }
  else {
    qb.appendWhere(getIdColumnName()+"=" + url.getPathSegments().get(1));
  }

  String orderBy;

  if (TextUtils.isEmpty(sort)) {
    orderBy=getDefaultSortOrder();
  } else {
    orderBy=sort;
  }

  Cursor c=qb.query(db, projection, selection, selectionArgs, null, null,
                    orderBy);
  c.setNotificationUri(getContext().getContentResolver(), url);
  return c;
}
```

We create a SQLiteQueryBuilder and pour the query details into the builder.
Note that the query could be based around either a collection or an instance
Uri – in the latter case, we need to add the instance ID to the query. When
done, we use the query() method on the builder to get a Cursor for the
results.

insert()

Your insert() method will receive a Uri representing the collection and a
ContentValues structure with the initial data for the new instance. You are
responsible for creating the new instance, filling in the supplied data, and
returning a Uri to the new instance.

If this is a SQLite-backed content provider, once again, the implementation
is mostly boilerplate: validate that all required values were supplied by the
activity, merge your own notion of default values with the supplied data, and
call insert() on the database to actually create the instance.

For example, here is insert() from Provider:

```
@Override
public Uri insert(Uri url, ContentValues initialValues) {
  long rowID;
  ContentValues values;

  if (initialValues!=null) {
    values=new ContentValues(initialValues);
  } else {
    values=new ContentValues();
  }

  if (!isCollectionUri(url)) {
    throw new IllegalArgumentException("Unknown URL " + url);
  }

  for (String colName : getRequiredColumns()) {
    if (values.containsKey(colName) == false) {
      throw new IllegalArgumentException("Missing column: "+colName);
    }
  }

  populateDefaultValues(values);

  rowID=db.insert(getTableName(), getNullColumnHack(), values);
  if (rowID > 0) {
    Uri uri=ContentUris.withAppendedId(getContentUri(), rowID);
    getContext().getContentResolver().notifyChange(uri, null);
    return uri;
  }

  throw new SQLException("Failed to insert row into " + url);
}
```

The pattern is the same as before: use the provider particulars plus the data to be inserted to actually do the insertion. Of note:

- You can only insert into a collection Uri, so we validate that by calling isCollectionUri()

- The provider also knows what columns are required (getRequiredColumns()), so we iterate over those and confirm our supplied values cover the requirements

- The provider is also responsible for filling in any default values (populateDefaultValues()) for columns not supplied in the insert() call and not automatically handled by the SQLite table definition

update()

Your update() method gets the Uri of the instance or collection to change, a ContentValues structure with the new values to apply, a String for a SQL WHERE clause, and a String[] with parameters to use to replace ? found in the WHERE clause. Your responsibility is to identify the instance(s) to be modified (based on the Uri and WHERE clause), then replace those instances' current property values with the ones supplied.

This will be annoying, unless you're using SQLite for storage. Then, you can pretty much pass all the parameters you received to the update() call to the database, though the update() call will vary slightly depending on whether you are updating one instance or several.

For example, here is update() from Provider:

```
@Override
public int update(Uri url, ContentValues values, String where,
                  String[] whereArgs) {
  int count;

  if (isCollectionUri(url)) {
    count=db.update(getTableName(), values, where, whereArgs);
  }
  else {
    String segment=url.getPathSegments().get(1);
    count=db
        .update(getTableName(), values, getIdColumnName()+"="
          + segment
          + (!TextUtils.isEmpty(where) ? " AND (" + where
            + ')' : ""), whereArgs);
  }

  getContext().getContentResolver().notifyChange(url, null);
  return count;
}
```

In this case, updates can either be to a specific instance or applied across the entire collection, so we check the Uri (isCollectionUri()) and, if it is an update for the collection, just perform the update. If we are updating a single instance, we need to add a constraint to the WHERE clause to only update for the requested row.

delete()

As with `update()`, `delete()` receives a `Uri` representing the instance or collection to work with and a WHERE clause and parameters. If the activity is deleting a single instance, the `Uri` should represent that instance and the WHERE clause may be null. But, the activity might be requesting to delete an open-ended set of instances, using the WHERE clause to constrain which ones to delete.

As with `update()`, though, this is simple if you are using SQLite for database storage (sense a theme?). You can let it handle the idiosyncrasies of parsing and applying the WHERE clause – all you have to do is call `delete()` on the database.

For example, here is `delete()` from `Provider`:

```
@Override
public int delete(Uri url, String where, String[] whereArgs) {
  int count;
  long rowId=0;

  if (isCollectionUri(url)) {
    count=db.delete(getTableName(), where, whereArgs);
  }
  else {
    String segment=url.getPathSegments().get(1);
    rowId=Long.parseLong(segment);
    count=db
        .delete(getTableName(), getIdColumnName()+"="
            + segment
            + (!TextUtils.isEmpty(where) ? " AND (" + where
              + ')' : ""), whereArgs);
  }

  getContext().getContentResolver().notifyChange(url, null);
  return count;
}
```

This is almost a clone of the `update()` implementation described above – either delete a subset of the entire collection or delete a single instance (if it also satisfies the supplied WHERE clause).

getType()

The last method you need to implement is getType(). This takes a Uri and returns the MIME type associated with that Uri. The Uri could be a collection or an instance Uri; you need to determine which was provided and return the corresponding MIME type.

For example, here is getType() from Provider:

```
@Override
public String getType(Uri url) {
  if (isCollectionUri(url)) {
    return(getCollectionType());
  }

  return(getSingleType());
}
```

As you can see, most of the logic delegates to private getCollectionType() and getSingleType() methods:

```
private String getCollectionType() {
  return("vnd.android.cursor.dir/vnd.commonsware.tour");
}

private String getSingleType() {
  return("vnd.android.cursor.item/vnd.commonsware.tour");
}
```

DatabaseContentProvider

If you want to use DatabaseContentProvider as a base class, here is what you need to do:

- You still need getType() as described in the preceding section

- You may elect to override onCreate() for your own initialization, but be sure to chain upward to the superclass (super.onCreate())

- You may elect to override upgradeDatabases() to rebuild your tables if your database schema has changed

- You need to implement queryInternal(), insertInternal(), updateInternal(), and deleteInternal() much as described above for query(), insert(), update(), and delete() respectively

Step #2: Supply a Uri

You also need to add a public static member...somewhere, containing the Uri for each collection your content provider supports. Typically, this is a public static final Uri put on the content provider class itself:

```
public static final Uri CONTENT_URI=
  Uri.parse("content://com.commonsware.android.tourit.Provider/tours");
```

You may wish to use the same namespace for the content Uri that you use for your Java classes, to reduce the chance of collision with others.

Step #3: Declare the Properties

Remember those properties you referenced when you were using a content provider, in the previous chapter? Well, you need to have those too for your own content provider.

Specifically, you want a public static class implementing BaseColumns that contains your property names, such as this example from Provider:

```
public static final class Tours implements BaseColumns {
  public static final Uri CONTENT_URI
      =Uri.parse("content://com.commonsware.android.tourit.Provider/tours");
  public static final String DEFAULT_SORT_ORDER="title";
  public static final String ID="_id";
  public static final String TITLE="title";
  public static final String DESCRIPTION="desc";
  public static final String CREATED_DATE="created";
  public static final String MODIFIED_DATE="modified";
  public static final String ROUTE="route";
}
```

If you are using SQLite as a data store, the values for the property name constants should be the corresponding column name in the table, so you can just pass the projection (array of properties) to SQLite on a query(), or pass the ContentValues on an insert() or update().

Note that nothing in here stipulates the types of the properties. They could be strings, integers, or whatever. The biggest limitation is what a Cursor can provide access to via its property getters. The fact that there is nothing in code that enforces type safety means you should document the property types well, so people attempting to use your content provider know what they can expect.

Step #4: Update the Manifest

The glue tying the content provider implementation to the rest of your application resides in your AndroidManifest.xml file. Simply add a <provider> element as a child of the <application> element:

```
<provider
  android:name=".Provider"
  android:authorities="com.commonsware.android.tourit.Provider" />
```

The android:name property is the name of the content provider class, with a leading dot to indicate it is in the stock namespace for this application's classes (just like you use with activities).

The android:authorities property should be a semicolon-delimited list of the authority values supported by the content provider. Recall, from earlier in this chapter, that each content Uri is made up of a scheme, authority, data type path, and instance identifier. Each authority from each CONTENT_URI value should be included in the android:authorities list.

Now, when Android encounters a content Uri, it can sift through the providers registered through manifests to find a matching authority. That tells Android which application and class implements the content provider, and from there Android can bridge between the calling activity and the content provider being called.

Notify-On-Change Support

An optional feature your content provider to its clients is notify-on-change support. This means that your content provider will let clients know if the data for a given content Uri changes.

For example, suppose you have created a content provider that retrieves RSS and Atom feeds from the Internet based on the user's feed subscriptions (via OPML, perhaps). The content provider offers read-only access to the contents of the feeds, with an eye towards several applications on the phone using those feeds versus everyone implementing their own feed poll-fetch-and-cache system. You have also implemented a service that will get updates to those feeds asynchronously, updating the underlying data store. Your content provider could alert applications using the feeds that such-and-so feed was updated, so applications using that specific feed can refresh and get the latest data.

On the content provider side, to do this, call notifyChange() on your ContentResolver instance (available in your content provider via getContext().getContentResolver()). This takes two parameters: the Uri of the piece of content that changed and the ContentObserver that initiated the change. In many cases, the latter will be null; a non-null value simply means that observer will not be notified of its own changes.

On the content consumer side, an activity can call registerContentObserver() on its ContentResolver (via getContentResolver()). This ties a ContentObserver instance to a supplied Uri – the observer will be notified whenever notifyChange() is called for that specific Uri. When the consumer is done with the Uri, unregisterContentObserver() releases the connection.

CHAPTER 26

Requesting and Requiring Permissions

In the late 1990's, a wave of viruses spread through the Internet, delivered via email, using contact information culled from Microsoft Outlook. A virus would simply email copies of itself to each of the Outlook contacts that had an email address. This was possible because, at the time, Outlook did not take any steps to protect data from programs using the Outlook API, since that API was designed for ordinary developers, not virus authors.

Nowadays, many applications that hold onto contact data secure that data by requiring that a user explicitly grant rights for other programs to access the contact information. Those rights could be granted on a case-by-case basis or a once at install time.

Android is no different, in that it requires permissions for applications to read or write contact data. Android's permission system is useful well beyond contact data, and for content providers and services beyond those supplied by the Android framework.

You, as an Android developer, will frequently need to ensure your applications have the appropriate permissions to do what you want to do with other applications' data. You may also elect to require permissions for other applications to use your data or services, if you make those available to other Android components. This chapter covers how to accomplish both these ends.

Mother, May I?

Requesting the use of other applications' data or services requires the uses-permission element to be added to your AndroidManifest.xml file. Your manifest may have zero or more uses-permission elements, all as direct children of the root manifest element.

The uses-permission element takes a single attribute, android:name, which is the name of the permission your application requires:

```
<uses-permission
    android:name="android.permission.ACCESS_LOCATION" />
```

The stock system permissions all begin with android.permission and are listed in the documentation for Manifest.permission in the online Android documentation. Third-party applications may have their own permissions, which hopefully they have documented for you.

Permissions are confirmed at the time the application is installed – the user will be prompted to confirm it is OK for your application to do what the permission calls for. This prompt is not available in the current emulator, however.

If you do not have the desired permission and try to do something that needs it, you may get a SecurityException informing you of the missing permission, but this is not a guarantee – failures may come in other forms, depending on if something else is catching and trying to handle that exception.

To see the effects of permissions, go back to the Pick example project. If you look at the AndroidManifest.xml file, you will see it requests the READ_CONTACTS permission. This is what allows you to view the contact information. Comment out the uses-permission element in the manifest, recompile, and try out the new version in the emulator. You should get a SecurityException. **NOTE**: you may need to restart the emulator, if you were using the PickDemo before during this same emulator session.

Figure 60. A security exception

Halt! Who Goes There?

The other side of the coin, of course, is to secure your own application. If your application is merely activities and intent receivers, security may be just an "outbound" thing, where you request permission to use resources of other applications. If, on the other hand, you put content providers or services in your application, you will want to implement "inbound" security to control which applications can do what with the data.

Note that the issue here is less about whether other applications might "mess up" your data, but rather about privacy of the user's information or use of services that might incur expense. That is where the stock permissions for built-in Android applications are focused – can you read or modify contacts, can you send SMS, etc. If your application does not store information that might be considered private – such as TourIt, which only stores bicycle tours – security is less an issue. If, on the other hand, your application stores private data, such as medical information, security is much more important.

The first step to securing your own application using permissions is to declare said permissions, once again in the AndroidManifest.xml file. In this case, instead of uses-permission, you add permission elements. Once again, you can have zero or more permission elements, all as direct children of the root manifest element.

Declaring a permission is slightly more complicated than using a permission. There are three pieces of information you need to supply:

1. The symbolic name of the permission. To keep your permissions from colliding with those from other applications, you should use your application's Java namespace as a prefix

2. A label for the permission: something short that would be understandable by users

3. A description for the permission: something a wee bit longer that is understandable by your users

```
<permission
    android:name="vnd.tlagency.sekrits.SEE_SEKRITS"
    android:label="@string/see_sekrits_label"
    android:description="@string/see_sekrits_description" />
```

This does not enforce the permission. Rather, it indicates that it is a possible permission; your application must still flag security violations as they occur.

Enforcing Permissions via the Manifest

There are two ways for your application to enforce permissions, dictating where and under what circumstances they are required. The easier one is to indicate in the manifest where permissions are required.

Activities, services, and intent receivers can all declare an attribute named android:permission, whose value is the name of the permission that is required to access those items:

```
<activity
    android:name=".SekritApp"
    android:label="Top Sekrit"
```

```
  android:permission="vnd.tlagency.sekrits.SEE_SEKRITS">
  <intent-filter>
    <action android:name="android.intent.action.MAIN" />
    <category
      android:name="android.intent.category.LAUNCHER" />
  </intent-filter>
</activity>
```

Only applications that have requested your indicated permission will be able to access the secured component. In this case, "access" means:

- Activities cannot be started without the permission

- Services cannot be started, stopped, or bound to an activity without the permission

- Intent receivers ignore messages sent via broadcastIntent() unless the sender has the permission

Content providers offer two distinct attributes: readPermission and writePermission:

```
<provider
  android:name=".SekritProvider"
  android:authorities="vnd.tla.sekrits.SekritProvider"
  android:readPermission="vnd.tla.sekrits.SEE_SEKRITS"
  android:writePermission="vnd.tla.sekrits.MOD_SEKRITS" />
```

In this case, readPermission controls access to querying the content provider, while writePermission controls access to insert, update, or delete data in the content provider.

Enforcing Permissions Elsewhere

In your code, you have two additional ways to enforce permissions.

Your services can check permissions on a per-call basis via checkCallingPermission(). This returns PERMISSION_GRANTED or PERMISSION_DENIED depending on whether the caller has the permission you specified. For example, if your service implements separate read and write methods, you could get the effect of readPermission and writePermission in code by checking those methods for the permissions you need from Java.

Also, you can include a permission when you call broadcastIntent(). This means that eligible receivers must hold that permission; those without the permission are ineligible to receive it. For example, the Android subsystem presumably includes the RECEIVE_SMS permission when it broadcasts that an SMS message has arrived – this will restrict the receivers of that intent to be only those authorized to receive SMS messages.

May I See Your Documents?

There is no automatic discovery of permissions at compile time; all permission failures occur at runtime. Hence, it is important that you document the permissions required for your public APIs, including content providers, services, and activities intended for launching from other activities. Otherwise, the programmers attempting to interface with your application will have to find out the permission rules by trial and error.

Furthermore, you should expect that users of your application will be prompted to confirm any permissions your application says it needs. Hence, you need to document for your users what they should expect, lest they get confused by the question posed by the phone and elect to not install or use your application.

CHAPTER 27

Creating a Service

As noted previously, Android services are for long-running processes that may need to keep running even when decoupled from any activity. Examples include playing music even if the "player" activity gets garbage-collected, polling the Internet for RSS/Atom feed updates, and maintaining an online chat connection even if the chat client loses focus due to an incoming phone call.

Services are created when manually started (via an API call) or when some activity tries connecting to the service via inter-process communication (IPC). Services will live until no longer needed and if RAM needs to be reclaimed. Running for a long time isn't without its costs, though, so services need to be careful not to use too much CPU or keep radios active too much of the time, lest the service cause the device's battery to get used up too quickly.

This chapter covers how you can create your own services; the next chapter covers how you can use such services from your activities or other contexts. Both chapters will analyze the MailBuzz sample application (MailBuzz), with this chapter focusing mostly on the MailBuzzService implementation. MailBuzzService polls a supplied email account, either on-demand or on a stated interval, to see if new messages have arrived, at which it will post a Notification (as described in the chapter on notifications).

Getting Buzzed

The MailBuzz application is an email monitoring application, combining an activity and a service. The activity allows you to specify an email account to monitor; the service does the actual monitoring. When new messages arrive, the service notifies the user.

Providing an application to actually read and write emails is left as an exercise for the reader.

Service with Class

Creating a service implementation shares many characteristics with building an activity. You inherit from an Android-supplied base class, override some lifecycle methods, and hook the service into the system via the manifest.

So, the first step in creating a service is to extend the Service class, in our case with our own MailBuzzService subclass.

Just as activities have onCreate(), onResume(), onPause() and kin, Service implementations can override three different lifecycle methods:

1. onCreate(), which, as with services, is called when the service process is created

2. onStart(), which is called when a service is manually started by some other process, versus being implicitly started as the result of an IPC request (discussed more in the next chapter)

3. onDestroy() which is called as the service is being shut down

Common startup and shutdown logic should go in onCreate() and onDestroy(); onStart() is mostly if your service needs data passed into it (via the supplied Bundle) from the starting process and you don't wish to use IPC.

For example, here is the onCreate() method for MailBuzzService:

```
@Override
public void onCreate() {
  super.onCreate();

  background=new Thread(new Runnable() {
    public void run() {
      try {
        String event=null;

        while (event!=SHUTDOWN) {
          event=queue.poll();

          if (event==POLL) {
            checkAccountImpl();
          }
          else if (event!=SHUTDOWN) {
            Thread.sleep(1000);
          }
        }
      }
      catch (Throwable t) {
        // just end the background thread
      }
    }
  });

  background.start();
  setupTimer();
}
```

First, we chain upward to the superclass, so Android can do any setup work it needs to have done. Next, we set up a background thread to monitor a ConcurrentLinkedQueue once every second, looking for new events. As we'll see, the queue allows us to do the actual polling for new messages in a separate thread than those used for either the periodic timer or the incoming IPC method calls from the MailBuzz activity.

The onCreate() method wraps up by calling a private setupTimer() method:

```
private void setupTimer() {
  if (getPollState()) {
    SharedPreferences settings=getPrefs();
    int pollPeriod=settings.getInt("pollPeriod", 5)*60000;

    task=new TimerTask() {
      public void run() {
        checkAccount();
      }
    };
```

```
    timer.scheduleAtFixedRate(task, pollPeriod, pollPeriod);
  }
  else if (task!=null) {
    task.cancel();
    task=null;
  }
}
```

This checks to see if we're supposed to be periodically checking for new messages or not. If we are, we set up a `TimerTask` to post a `POLL` message on our queue, and set up that task to be invoked based on an activity-supplied period, expressed in minutes. If we are not supposed to be periodically checking for message, we shut down the timer if it was already started. This may seem superfluous, but `setupTimer()` gets called not only from `onCreate()`, but when the periodic-check status changes.

The `onDestroy()` method is much simpler:

```
@Override
public void onDestroy() {
  super.onDestroy();

  timer.cancel();
  queue.add(SHUTDOWN);
}
```

Here, we just shut down the timer and background thread, in addition to chaining upward to the superclass for any Android internal bookkeeping that might be needed.

In addition to those lifecycle methods, though, your service also needs to implement `onBind()`. This method returns an `IBinder`, which is the linchpin behind the IPC mechanism. If you're creating a service class while reading this chapter, just have this method return null for now, and we'll fill in the full implementation in the next section.

When IPC Attacks!

Services will tend to offer inter-process communication (IPC) as a means of interacting with activities or other Android components. Each service declares what methods it is making available over IPC; those methods are then available for other components to call, with Android handling all the messy details involved with making method calls across component or process boundaries.

The guts of this, from the standpoint of the developer, is expressed in AIDL: the Android Interface Description Language. If you have used IPC mechanisms like COM, CORBA, or the like, you will recognize the notion of IDL. AIDL spells out the public IPC interface, and Android supplies tools to build the client and server side of that interface.

With that in mind, let's take a look at AIDL and IPC.

Write the AIDL

IDLs are frequently written in a "language-neutral" syntax. AIDL, on the other hand, looks a lot like a Java interface. For example, here is the AIDL for the MailBuzzService:

```
package com.commonsware.android.service;

// Declare the interface.
interface IBuzz {
  void checkNow();
  void enable(in boolean enabled);
  boolean isEnabled();
}
```

As with a Java interface, you declare a package at the top. As with a Java interface, the methods are wrapped in an interface declaration (interface IBuzz { ... }). And, as with a Java interface, you list the methods you are making available.

The differences, though, are critical.

First, not every Java type can be used as a parameter. Your choices are:

- Primitive values (int, float, double, boolean, etc.)

- String and CharSequence

- List and Map (from java.util)

- Any other AIDL-defined interfaces

- Any Java classes that implement the Parcelable interface, which is Android's flavor of serialization (see below)

In the case of the latter two categories, you need to include import statements referencing the names of the classes or interfaces that you are using (e.g., import com.commonsware.android.ISomething). This is true even if these classes are in your own package – you have to import them anyway.

Next, parameters can be classified as in, out, or inout. Values that are out or inout can be changed by the service and those changes will be propagated back to the client. Primitives (e.g., int) can only be in; we included in for the AIDL for enable() just for illustration purposes.

Also, you cannot throw any exceptions. You will need to catch all exceptions in your code, deal with them, and return failure indications some other way (e.g., error code return values).

Name your AIDL files with the .aidl extension and place them in the proper directory based on the package name.

When you build your project, either via an IDE or via Ant, the aidl utility from the Android SDK will translate your AIDL into a server stub and a client proxy.

Implement the Interface

Given the AIDL-created server stub, now you need to implement the service, either directly in the stub, or by routing the stub implementation to other methods you have already written.

The mechanics of this are fairly straightforward:

- Create a private instance of the AIDL-generated .Stub class (e.g., IBuzz.Stub)

- Implement methods matching up with each of the methods you placed in the AIDL

- Return this private instance from your onBind() method in the Service subclass

For example, here is the IBuzz.Stub instance:

```
private final IBuzz.Stub binder=new IBuzz.Stub() {
  public void checkNow() {
    checkAccount();
  }

  public void enable(boolean enabled) {
    enablePoll(enabled);
  }

  public boolean isEnabled() {
    return(getPollState());
  }
};
```

In this case, the stub calls corresponding methods on the service itself. Those methods are shown below:

```
private void checkAccount() {
  queue.add(POLL);
}

private void enablePoll(boolean enabled) {
  SharedPreferences settings=getPrefs();
  SharedPreferences.Editor editor=settings.edit();

  editor.putBoolean("enabled", enabled);
  editor.commit();
  setupTimer();
}

private boolean getPollState() {
  SharedPreferences settings=getPrefs();

  return(settings.getBoolean("enabled", false));
}
```

- checkAccount() pops a POLL message on our queue, so our background thread can poll the mail server

- enablePoll() updates our preferences so we know to start or stop polling when the service next runs, then calls setupTimer() to start or stop the polling

- getPollState() simply returns the preference updated by enablePoll()

Note that AIDL IPC calls are synchronous, and so the caller is blocked until the IPC method returns. Hence, your services need to be quick about their work. If checkAccount() were to directly check the mail server itself, instead of using the background queue, the activity calling checkAccount() would be frozen until the mail server responded. Since that takes a noticeable amount of time, putting the real checkAccount() work (checkAccountImpl()) in a queue-based background thread provides for a cleaner user experience.

Manifest Destiny

Finally, you need to add the service to your AndroidManifest.xml file, for it to be recognized as an available service for use. That is simply a matter of adding a service element as a child of the application element, providing android:name to reference your service class.

For example, here is the AndroidManifest.xml file for MailBuzz:

```
<manifest xmlns:android="http://schemas.android.com/apk/res/android"
  package="com.commonsware.android.service">
  <application>
    <activity android:name=".MailBuzz" android:label="MailBuzz">
      <intent-filter>
        <action android:name="android.intent.action.MAIN" />
        <category android:name="android.intent.category.LAUNCHER" />
      </intent-filter>
    </activity>
    <service android:name=".MailBuzzService" />
  </application>
</manifest>
```

Since the service class is in the same Java namespace as everything else in this application, we can use the shorthand dot-notation (".MailBuzzService") to reference our class.

If you wish to require some permission of those who wish to start or bind to the service, add an android:permission attribute naming the permission you are mandating – see the chapter on permissions for more details.

Where's the Remote?

In Android, services can either be local or remote. Local services run in the same process as the launching activity; remote services run in their own process. A detailed discussion of remote services will be added to a future edition of this book.

CHAPTER 28

Invoking a Service

Services can be used by any application component that "hangs around" for a reasonable period of time. This includes activities, content providers, and other services. Notably, it does not include pure intent receivers (i.e., intent receivers that are not part of an activity), since those will get garbage collected immediately after each instance processes one incoming Intent.

To use a service, you need to get an instance of the AIDL interface for the service, then call methods on that interface as if it were a local object. When done, you can release the interface, indicating you no longer need the service.

In this chapter, we will look at the client side of the MailBuzz sample application (MailBuzz). The MailBuzz activity provides fields for the account information (server type, server, etc.), a checkbox to toggle whether polling for new mail should go on, a button to push the account information to the service, and another button to check right now for new messages.

When run, the activity looks like this:

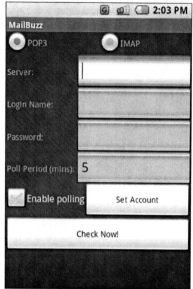

Figure 61. The MailBuzz service client

Bound for Success

To use a service, you first need to create an instance of your own ServiceConnection class. ServiceConnection, as the name suggests, represents your connection to the service for the purposes of making IPC calls. For example, here is the ServiceConnection from the MailBuzz class in the MailBuzz project:

```
private ServiceConnection svcConn=new ServiceConnection() {
  public void onServiceConnected(ComponentName className,
                IBinder binder) {
    service=IBuzz.Stub.asInterface(binder);
    checkNowButton.setEnabled(true);
    setAccountButton.setEnabled(true);
    setEnabled.setEnabled(true);

    try {
      setEnabled.setChecked(service.isEnabled());
    }
    catch (DeadObjectException e) {
      svcConn.onServiceDisconnected(null);
    }
  }
```

```
   public void onServiceDisconnected(ComponentName className) {
     service=null;
     checkNowButton.setEnabled(false);
     setAccountButton.setEnabled(false);
     setEnabled.setEnabled(false);
   }
 };
```

Your ServiceConnection subclass needs to implement two methods:

1. onServiceConnected(), which is called once your activity is bound to the service

2. onServiceDisconnected(), which is called if your connection ends normally, such as you unbinding your activity from the service

Each of those methods receives a ComponentName, which simply identifies the service you connected to. More importantly, onServiceConnected() receives an IBinder instance, which is your gateway to the IPC interface. You will want to convert the IBinder into an instance of your AIDL interface class, so you can use IPC as if you were calling regular methods on a regular Java class (IBuzz.Stub.asInterface(binder)).

To actually hook your activity to the service, call bindService() on the activity:

```
bindService(serviceIntent, svcConn, BIND_AUTO_CREATE);
```

The bindService() method takes three parameters:

1. An Intent representing the service you wish to invoke – for your own service, it's easiest to use an intent referencing the service class directly (new Intent(this, MailBuzzService.class))

2. Your ServiceConnection instance

3. A set of flags – most times, you will want to pass in BIND_AUTO_CREATE, which will start up the service if it is not already running

After your bindService() call, your onServiceConnected() callback in the ServiceConnection will eventually be invoked, at which time your connection is ready for use.

Request for Service

Once your service interface object is ready (`IBuzz.Stub.asInterface(binder)`), you can start calling methods on it as you need to. In fact, if you disabled some widgets awaiting the connection, now is a fine time to re-enable them (see the above `ServiceConnection` implementation).

For example, in `onServiceConnected()`, once we have the service interface object, we call `isEnabled()` to determine if the "Enable polling" checkbox should be checked or not (via `setChecked()`).

However, you will want to trap `DeadObjectException` – if this is raised, your service connection terminated unexpectedly. In this case, you should unwind your use of the service, perhaps by calling `onServiceDisconnected()` manually, as shown above.

Prometheus Unbound

When you are done with the IPC interface, call `unbindService()`, passing in the `ServiceConnection`. Eventually, your connection's `onServiceDisconnected()` callback will be invoked, at which point you should null out your interface object, disable relevant widgets, or otherwise flag yourself as no longer being able to use the service.

For example, in the MailBuzz implementation of `onServiceDisconnected()` shown above, we null out the `IBuzz` service object and disable the two buttons and checkbox.

You can always reconnect to the service, via `bindService()`, if you need to use it again.

Manual Transmission

In addition to binding to the service for the purposes of IPC, you can manually start and stop the service. This is particularly useful in cases where you want the service to keep running independently of your activities – otherwise, once you unbind the service, your service could well be closed down.

To start a service, simply call startService(), providing two parameters:

1. The Intent specifying the service to start (again, the easiest way is probably to specify the service class, if its your own service)

2. A Bundle providing configuration data, which eventually gets passed to the service's onStart() method

Conversely, to stop the service, call stopService() with the Intent you used in the corresponding startService() call.

For example, here is the MailBuzz code behind the "Enable polling" checkbox:

```
setEnabled=(CheckBox)findViewById(R.id.enabled);
setEnabled.setOnCheckedChangeListener(new
CompoundButton.OnCheckedChangeListener() {
  public void onCheckedChanged(CompoundButton buttonView, boolean isChecked) {
    try {
      if (isChecked) {
        startService(serviceIntent, new Bundle());
      }
      else {
        stopService(serviceIntent);
      }

      service.enable(isChecked);
    }
    catch (DeadObjectException e) {
      svcConn.onServiceDisconnected(null);
    }
  }
});
```

Not only do we call the service's enable() IPC method, but we also start and stop the service, based on the checkbox state. By starting the service, even if we later unbind from the service, the service will keep running and polling for new messages. Only when we both unbind from the service and stop the service will the service be fully shut down.

CHAPTER 29

Alerting Users Via Notifications

Pop-up messages. Tray icons and their associated "bubble" messages. Bouncing dock icons. You are no doubt used to programs trying to get your attention, sometimes for good reason.

Your phone also probably chirps at you for more than just incoming calls: low battery, alarm clocks, appointment notifications, incoming text message or email, etc.

Not surprisingly, Android has a whole framework for dealing with these sorts of things, collectively called "notifications".

Types of Pestering

A service, running in the background, needs a way to users know something of interest has occurred, such as when email has been received. Moreover, the service may need some way to steer the user to an activity where they can act upon the event – reading a received message, for example. For this, Android supplies status bar icons, flashing lights, and other indicators collectively known as "notifications".

Your current phone may well have such icons, to indicate battery life, signal strength, whether Bluetooth is enabled, and the like. With Android, applications can add their own status bar icons, with an eye towards having them appear only when needed (e.g., a message has arrived).

In Android, you can raise notifications via the NotificationManager. The NotificationManager is a system service. To use it, you need to get the service object via getSystemService(NOTIFICATION_SERVICE) from your activity.

The NotificationManager gives you two methods: one to pester (notify()) and one to stop pestering (cancel()).

The notify() method takes a Notification, which is a data structure that spells out what form your pestering should take. Here is what is at your disposal (bearing in mind that not all devices will necessarily support all of these):

Hardware Notifications

You can flash LEDs on the device by setting lights to true, also specifying the color (as an #ARGB value in ledARGB) and what pattern the light should blink in (by providing off/on durations in milliseconds for the light via ledOnMS and ledOffMS).

You can play a sound, using a Uri to a piece of content held, perhaps, by a ContentManager (sound). Think of this as a "ringtone" for your application.

You can vibrate the device, controlled via a long[] indicating the on/off patterns (in milliseconds) for the vibration (vibrate). You might do this by default, or you might make it an option the user can choose when circumstances require a more subtle notification than a ringtone.

You might also want to set insistent to true, indicating that the hardware notifications (e.g., vibration) should not be played just once, but rather should repeat until you cancel the notification.

Icons

While the flashing lights, sounds, and vibrations are aimed at getting somebody to look at the device, icons are designed to take them the next step and tell them what's so important.

To set up an icon for a Notification, you need to set statusBarIcon, where you provide the identifier of a Drawable resource representing the icon, and statusBarClickIntent, where you supply an Intent to be raised when the icon is clicked. You should be sure the Intent will be caught by something, perhaps your own application code, to take appropriate steps to let the user deal with the event triggering the notification.

You can also supply text blurbs to appear when the icon is put on the status bar (statusBarTickerText) and when the icon is selected but not yet clicked (statusBarBalloonText).

Letting Your Presence Be Felt

To raise a Notification, you can use the notify() method on the NotificationManager service object, where you specify the notification identifier and a Notification object. The identifier is simply a number, unique within your application, that identifies this specific notification (versus any others your application might be raising).

To cancel a notification, simply call cancel() on the NotificationManager service object, providing your identifier for the notification. You should do this when the notification icon is no longer needed (e.g., the user read the message and so there are no unread messages to alert the user about).

For example, the TourIt sample application uses notifications to alert riders that they are nearing waypoints on their chosen tour. How TourIt knows they are nearing waypoints is through the location services offered by Android, discussed later in this book. For the moment, assume that TourIt can find this out – here's how it notifies the users.

When a waypoint is near, TourIt invokes showNotification() on TourViewActivity:

```
private void showNotification() {
  NotificationManager nm = (NotificationManager)getSystemService(NOTIFICATION_SERVICE);
  Notification notif = new Notification(
      TourViewActivity.this,
      R.drawable.wheel_16,
      "Waypoint nearby!",
      System.currentTimeMillis(),
      null, null, null,
      R.drawable.wheel_16,
      "TourIt!",
      null);

  // after a 100ms delay, vibrate for 250ms, pause for 100 ms and
  // then vibrate for 500ms.

  if (alertVibrate) {
    notif.vibrate = new long[] { 100, 250, 100, 500};
  }

  if (alertSound) {
    notif.sound=Uri.parse("android.resource://com.commonsware.tourit/"+R.raw.alert);
  }

  notif.insistent=alertInsistent;

  nm.notify(R.string.go_button, notif);
}
```

This method:

- sets up the notification to show a wheel icon (16px high) and the message "Waypoint nearby!"

- sets up a vibration pattern, if the user chose (via the ConfigActivity) to be notified by vibration

- sets up the "waypoint-tone" to play, if the user chose to be notified by a sound

- configures the notification to be insistent, so the vibration or sound will keep playing

- displays the notification

Later on, when the waypoint is sufficiently distant, TourViewActivity cancels the notification:

```
private Handler handler=new Handler() {
  @Override
  public void handleMessage(Message msg) {
    long tmp=lastAlertSeen.get();

    if (tmp>-1L && System.currentTimeMillis()-tmp>2000) {
      NotificationManager nm=(NotificationManager)getSystemService(NOTIFICATION_SERVICE);

      nm.cancel(R.string.go_button);
      lastAlertSeen.set(-1L);
    }
  }
};
```

PART VI – Other Android Capabilities

CHAPTER 30

Accessing Location-Based Services

A popular feature on current-era mobile devices is GPS capability, so the device can tell you where you are at any point in time. While the most popular use of GPS service is mapping and directions, there are other things you can do if you know your location. For example, you might set up a dynamic chat application where the people you can chat with are based on physical location, so you're chatting with those you are nearest. Or, you could automatically "geotag" posts to Twitter or similar services.

GPS is not the only way a mobile device can identify your location. Alternatives include:

- The European equivalent to GPS, called Galileo, which is still under development at the time of this writing

- Cell tower triangulation, where your position is determined based on signal strength to nearby cell towers

- Proximity to public WiFi "hotspots" that have known geographic locations

Android devices may have one or more of these services available to them. You, as a developer, can ask the device for your location, plus details on what providers are available. There are even ways for you to simulate your location in the emulator, for use in testing your location-enabled applications.

Location Providers: They Know Where You're Hiding

Android devices can have access to several different means of determining your location. Some will have better accuracy than others. Some may be free, while others may have a cost associated with them. Some may be able to tell you more than just your current position, such as your elevation over sea level, or your current speed.

Android, therefore, has abstracted all this out into a set of LocationProvider objects. Your Android environment will have zero or more LocationProvider instances, one for each distinct locating service that is available on the device. Providers know not only your location, but their own characteristics, in terms of accuracy, cost, etc.

You, as a developer, will use a LocationManager, which holds the LocationProvider set, to figure out which LocationProvider is right for your particular circumstance. You will also need the ACCESS_POSITION permission in your application, or the various location APIs will fail due to a security violation. Depending on which location providers you wish to use, you may need other permissions as well, such as ACCESS_GPS, ACCESS_ASSISTED_GPS, or ACCESS_CELL_ID.

Finding Yourself

The obvious thing to do with a location service is to figure out where you are right now.

To do that, you need to get a LocationManager – call getSystemService(LOCATION_SERVICE) from your activity or service and cast it to be a LocationManager.

The next step to find out where you are is to get the name of the LocationProvider you want to use. Here, you have two main options:

1. Ask the user to pick a provider

2. Find the best-match provider based on a set of criteria

If you want the user to pick a provider, calling getProviders() on the
LocationManager will give you a List of providers, which you can then wrap in
an ArrayAdapter and use for the selection widget of your choice. The catch is
that LocationProvider does not have a useful toString() implementation, so
you need to do a little extra work, either overriding ArrayAdapter to populate
your views by hand, or wrapping each LocationProvider in your own object
that implements toString() by calling the provider's getName() method.
TourIt takes the latter approach in ConfigActivity:

```
@Override
public void onCreate(Bundle icicle) {
  super.onCreate(icicle);
  setContentView(R.layout.config);

  LocationManager mgr=(LocationManager)getSystemService(Context.LOCATION_SERVICE);

  for (LocationProvider p : mgr.getProviders()) {
    listWrappers.add(new ProviderWrapper(p));
  }

  ArrayAdapter<Waypoint> aa=new ArrayAdapter<Waypoint>(this,
                      R.layout.spinner,
                      (List)listWrappers);

  providers=(Spinner)findViewById(R.id.providers);
  aa.setDropDownViewResource(android.R.layout.simple_spinner_dropdown_item);
  providers.setAdapter(aa);
}
```

where ProviderWrapper is:

```
class ProviderWrapper {
  LocationProvider p;

  ProviderWrapper(LocationProvider p) {
    this.p=p;
  }

  public String toString() {
    return(p.getName());
  }
}
```

Or, you can create and populate a Criteria object, stating the particulars of
what you want out of a LocationProvider, such as:

- setAltitudeRequired() to indicate if you need the current altitude or not

- setAccuracy() to set a minimum level of accuracy, in meters, for the position

- setCostAllowed() to control if the provider must be free or if it can incur a cost on behalf of the device user

Given a filled-in Critieria object, call getBestProvider() on your LocationManager, and Android will sift through the criteria and give you the best answer. Note that not all of your criteria will be met – all but the monetary cost criterion might be relaxed if nothing matches.

Once you know the name of the LocationProvider, you can call getCurrentLocation() to turn on the location provider and get an up-to-date fix, or you can call getLastKnownPosition() to find out where you were recently. Note, however, that "recently" might be fairly out of date (e.g., phone was turned off). On the other hand, getLastKnownPosition() incurs no monetary or power cost, since the provider does not need to be activated to get the value.

These methods return a Location object, which can give you the latitude and longitude of the device in degrees as a Java double. If the particular location provider offers other data, you can get at that as well:

- For altitude, hasAltitude() will tell you if there is an altitude value, and getAltitude() will return the altitude in meters.

- For bearing (i.e., compass-style direction), hasBearing() will tell you if there is a bearing available, and getBearing() will return it as degrees east of true north.

- For speed, hasSpeed() will tell you if the speed is known and getSpeed() will return the speed in meters per second.

For example, TourEditActivity allows users to click a button to fill in the current location when editing waypoint – the theory being that the user is riding the tour and taking locations along the way to update the otherwise-complete tour definition. The user's preferred location provider is stored in a preference, filled in by the `ConfigActivity` and updated in `TourEditActivity`'s `onResume()`:

```java
@Override
public void onResume() {
  super.onResume();

  SharedPreferences prefs=getSharedPreferences(ConfigActivity.PREFS, 0);

  String providerName=prefs.getString(ConfigActivity.LOCATION_PROVIDER, null);

  if (providerName!=null) {
    for (LocationProvider p : myLocationManager.getProviders()) {
      if (p.getName().equals(providerName)) {
        provider=p;
        break;
      }
    }
  }

  if (provider==null) {
    Criteria crit=new Criteria();

    crit.setCostAllowed(true);
    crit.setSpeedRequired(false);
    crit.setBearingRequired(false);
    crit.setAltitudeRequired(false);

    provider=myLocationManager.getBestProvider(crit);
  }
}
```

Then, when the button is clicked, it gets a current fix and fills in the location in the appropriate fields:

```java
Button btn=(Button)findViewById(R.id.fillin);

btn.setOnClickListener(new View.OnClickListener() {
  public void onClick(View view) {
    if (provider!=null) {
      Location loc=myLocationManager.getCurrentLocation(provider.getName());

      pt_lat.setText(new Double(loc.getLatitude()).toString());
      pt_long.setText(new Double(loc.getLongitude()).toString());
      pt_ele.setText(new Double(loc.getAltitude()).toString());
    }
  }
});
```

On the Move

Now that you know where you are, you next might want to know where you're going.

LocationManager sports a pair of requestUpdates() methods, where you can register an Intent to be fired periodically, to keep you informed of your current position. Both flavors of requestUpdates() take a time (in milliseconds) and distance (in meters) – only if the requested time has elapsed *and* the position has changed by the requested distance will the Intent be dispatched. One flavor of requestUpdates() takes a LocationProvider, and you will only get updates based off of that provider; the other flavor takes a Criteria and will use the best-match provider.

It is up to you to arrange for an activity or intent receiver to respond to the Intent you register with requestUpdates(). Otherwise, the updates will never be acted upon.

When you no longer need the updates, call removeUpdates() with the Intent you registered.

Are We There Yet? Are We There Yet? Are We There Yet?

Sometimes, you want to know not where you are now, or even when you move, but when you get to where you're going. This could be an end destination, or it could be getting to the next step on a set of directions, so you can give the user the next turn. In TourIt, for example, it would be nice to know when a rider gets to a waypoint, so we can prompt them for the direction to go to get to the next waypoint on the tour.

To accomplish this, LocationManager offers addProximityAlert(). This registers an Intent, which will be fired off when the device gets within a certain distance of a certain location. The addProximityAlert() method takes, as parameters:

- The latitude and longitude of the position that you are interested in

- A radius, specifying how close you should be to that position for the Intent to be raised

- A duration for the registration, in milliseconds – after this period, the registration automatically lapses. A value of -1 means the registration lasts until you manually remove it via removeProximityAlert().

- The Intent to be raised when the device is within the "target zone" expressed by the position and radius

Note that it is not guaranteed that you will actually receive an Intent, if there is an interruption in location services, or if the device is not in the target zone during the period of time the proximity alert is active. For example, if the position is off by a bit, and the radius is a little too tight, the device might only skirt the edge of the target zone, or go by so quickly that the device's location isn't sampled while in the target zone.

It is up to you to arrange for an activity or intent receiver to respond to the Intent you register with the proximity alert. What you then do when the Intent arrives is up to you: set up a notification (e.g., vibrate the device), log the information to a content provider, post a message to a Web site, etc. Note that you will receive the Intent whenever the position is sampled and you are within the target zone – not just upon entering the zone. Hence, you will get the Intent several times, perhaps quite a few times depending on the size of the target zone and the speed of the device's movement.

In TourIt, when viewing the cue sheet for a tour (TourViewActivity), the user has a checkbox to enable alerts. When checked, TourViewActivity sets up proximity alerts for all of the waypoints in the tour, plus sets up the activity itself as being an intent receiver for the intent for these alerts:

```
private void enableAlerts() {
  if (provider!=null) {
    registerReceiver(receiver, proximitylocationIntentFilter);

    for (Waypoint pt : tour.getRoute()) {
      Intent i=new Intent(PROXIMITY_ALERT);
```

```
        myLocationManager.addProximityAlert(pt.getLatitude(),
                            pt.getLongitude(),
                            100.0f,
                            43200000,
                            i); // 12 hours max

        proximityIntents.add(i);
      }
    }
}
```

The official Android documentation says:

> The intent will have an extra added with key "entering" and a
> boolean value. If the value is true, the device is entering the
> proximity region; if false, it is exiting.

At the time of this writing, that does not seem to work properly. Hence, dealing with the incoming Intent stream is a bit tricky.

The way TourViewActivity (or, more accurately, its private ProximityIntentReceiver class) handles it is, when an alert Intent is first received, it sets up a notification to alert the user that she is nearing a waypoint:

```
private void showNotification() {
  NotificationManager nm = (NotificationManager)getSystemService(NOTIFICATION_SERVICE);
  Notification notif = new Notification(
        TourViewActivity.this,
        R.drawable.wheel_16,
        "Waypoint nearby!",
        System.currentTimeMillis(),
        null, null, null,
        R.drawable.wheel_16,
        "TourIt!",
        null);

  // after a 100ms delay, vibrate for 250ms, pause for 100 ms and
  // then vibrate for 500ms.

  if (alertVibrate) {
    notif.vibrate = new long[] { 100, 250, 100, 500};
  }

  if (alertSound) {
    notif.sound=Uri.parse("android.resource://com.commonsware.tourit/"+R.raw.alert);
  }
```

```
   notif.insistent=alertInsistent;

   nm.notify(R.string.go_button, notif);
}
```

For each `Intent` received, TourIt updates a timestamp of when the last Intent was received. It then uses a `Handler` to monitor for when the `Intent` stream stops – if it is stopped for two seconds or more, the notification is disabled and the mechanism is reset to await the next `Intent` stream:

```
private Handler handler=new Handler() {
  @Override
  public void handleMessage(Message msg) {
    long tmp=lastAlertSeen.get();

    if (tmp>-1L && System.currentTimeMillis()-tmp>2000) {
      NotificationManager nm=(NotificationManager)getSystemService(NOTIFICATION_SERVICE);

      nm.cancel(R.string.go_button);
      lastAlertSeen.set(-1L);
    }
  }
};
```

Finally, if the user un-checks the alert checkbox, or if the activity is positively closed, all of the proximity alerts are unregistered:

```
private void disableAlerts() {
  if (provider!=null && proximityIntents.size()>0) {
    unregisterReceiver(receiver);

    for (Intent i : proximityIntents) {
      myLocationManager.removeProximityAlert(i);
    }

    proximityIntents.clear();
  }
}
```

This is not a perfect system by any means. Ideally, the "entering" extra value would be set on the Intent, negating the need for the `Handler`. Better smarts are probably needed to handle other activity lifecycle events, as it is unclear what happens to registered proximity alerts if the activity that registered them is killed off.

Testing...Testing...

The Android emulator does not have the ability to get a fix from GPS, triangulate your position from cell towers, or identify your location by some nearby WiFi signal. Instead, it has abuilt-in fake GPS provider, set to simulate your movement around a loop of positions in the Silicon Valley area of California.

This, of course, is only nominally useful. Unless the other information you are tying location to happens to be in that area, you will need to simulate locations somewhere else.

The good news is that the fake GPS provider implemented by Android is actually part of a larger system for emulating location providers. You can either implement a full LocationProvider and tie it into the system, or you can create data files containing time offsets and positions, to simulate the movement of a device.

It is much simpler, though, to use TrackBuilder.

TrackBuilder is a sample application, posted to the anddev.org[29] site. It uses Android's own mapping logic to present you with a map, upon which you can click to note locations along a track of movement. TrackBuilder can then save the track, and you can move the data file into the proper spot for use with Android's fake-GPS provider. The track you recorded is then available for your testing use. Since the fake-GPS files require latitude and longitude positions to several significant digits, using TrackBuilder beats hand-writing those files in most situations.

Once you have the fake-GPS data file or custom LocationProvider in place, though, you need to have your application use that location source versus any other. This is made more complicated if you have several fake-GPS data files for different test scenarios. That is why it is probably a good idea to allow the user to configure the LocationProvider that your application uses, rather than merely relying upon Critieria-based selection – that way when

---

29 http://www.anddev.org/trackbuilder_for_mock_location_providers-t384.html

you are testing, you can choose the right provider to match the test you are running. It could be you only offer a manually-configured `LocationProvider` when your application is in some sort of test mode, if you do not want to expose that choice to actual users of your application.

CHAPTER 31

Mapping with MapView and MapActivity

One of Google's most popular services – after search, of course – is Google Maps, where you can find everything from the nearest pizza parlor to directions from New York City to San Francisco (only 2,905 miles!) to street views and satellite imagery.

Android, not surprisingly, integrates Google Maps. There is a mapping activity available to users straight off the main Android launcher. More relevant to you, as a developer, are MapView and MapActivity, which allow you to integrate maps into your own applications. Not only can you display maps, control the zoom level, and allow people to pan around, but you can tie in Android's location-based services to show where the device is and where it is going.

Fortunately, integrating basic mapping features into your Android project is fairly easy. However, there is a fair bit of power available to you, if you want to get fancy.

The Bare Bones

Far and away the simplest way to get a map into your application is to create your own subclass of MapActivity. Like ListActivity, which wraps up some of the smarts behind having an activity dominated by a ListView,

MapActivity handles some of the nuances of setting up an activity dominated by a MapView.

In your layout for the MapActivity subclass, you need to add an element named, at the time of this writing, com.google.android.maps.MapView. This is the "longhand" way to spell out the names of widget classes, by including the full package name along with the class name. This is necessary because MapView is not in the com.google.android.widget namespace. You can give the MapView widget whatever android:id attribute value you want, plus handle all the layout details to have it render properly alongside your other widgets.

For example, here is the layout for TourMapActivity, from the TourIt sample application:

```xml
<?xml version="1.0" encoding="utf-8"?>
<RelativeLayout xmlns:android="http://schemas.android.com/apk/res/android"
  android:layout_width="fill_parent"
  android:layout_height="fill_parent">
  <com.google.android.maps.MapView
    android:id="@+id/map"
    android:layout_width="fill_parent"
    android:layout_height="fill_parent"/>
  <LinearLayout
    android:orientation="horizontal"
    android:layout_width="fill_parent"
    android:layout_height="wrap_content"
    android:layout_alignParentBottom="true">
    <Spinner android:id="@+id/waypoints"
      android:layout_weight="1"
      android:layout_width="wrap_content"
      android:layout_height="wrap_content"
      android:drawSelectorOnTop="true"
      android:paddingTop="10dip"
      android:visibility="invisible"
      android:paddingBottom="10dip" />
    <ImageButton android:id="@+id/go"
      android:src="@drawable/go_to_point"
      android:layout_width="wrap_content"
      android:layout_height="wrap_content"
      android:gravity="center_vertical"
      android:layout_gravity="center_vertical"
      android:visibility="invisible"
      android:paddingTop="10dip"
      android:paddingBottom="10dip" />
  </LinearLayout>
</RelativeLayout>
```

That is pretty much all you need for starters, plus to subclass your activity from MapActivity. If you were to do nothing else, and built that project and tossed it in the emulator, you'd get a nice map of the world.

In theory, the user could pan around the map using the directional pad. However, that's not terribly useful when the user has the whole world in her hands.

Since a map of the world is not much good by itself, we need to add a few things...

Exercising Your Control

You can find your MapView widget by findViewById(), no different than any other widget. The widget itself then offers a getMapController() method. Between the MapView and MapController, you have a fair bit of capability to determine what the map shows and how it behaves. Here are some likely features you will want to use:

Zoom

The map of the world you start with is rather broad. Usually, people looking at a map on a phone will be expecting something a bit narrower in scope, such as a few city blocks.

You can control the zoom level directly via the zoomTo() method on the MapController. This takes an integer representing the level of zoom, where 1 is the world view and 21 is the tightest zoom you can get. Each level is a doubling of the effective resolution: 1 has the equator measuring 256 pixels wide, while 21 has the equator measuring 268,435,456 pixels wide. Since the phone's display probably doesn't have 268,435,456 pixels in either dimension, the user sees a small map focused on one tiny corner of the globe. A level of 16 will show you several city blocks in each dimension and is probably a reasonable starting point for you to experiment with.

MapView offers a `toggleEdgeZooming()` method, which takes a boolean parameter indicating if this feature should be on or off. If it is enabled, then the user can drag her finger down the right edge of the map to change the zoom level manually. In the emulator, use your mouse to simulate the dragging motion.

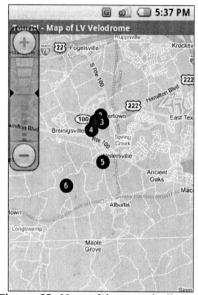

Figure 62. Map with zoom indicator

Center

Typically, you will need to control what the map is showing, beyond the zoom level, such as the user's current location, or a location saved with some data in your activity. To change the map's position, call `centerMapTo()` on the `MapController`.

This takes a `Point` as a parameter. A `Point` represents a location, via latitude and longitude. The catch is that the Point stores latitude and longitude as integers representing the actual latitude and longitude multiplied by `1E6`. This saves a bit of memory versus storing a `float` or `double`, and it probably speeds up some internal calculations Android needs to do to convert the

Point into a map position. However, it does mean you have to remember to multiple the "real world" latitude and longitude by 1E6.

Reticle

The "reticle" is the small circle showing the center of the map. Just as you can set the map center, you can retrieve it by calling getMapCenter() on the MapView. This will return a Point reflecting the position of the reticle. The user, in turn, can use the reticle to "point" at a specific spot, perhaps using the option menu to signal to your activity that it wants some information about that point.

Particularly if you will be implementing overlays (see below), you will probably want to add the following statement to your onCreate() method, where map is your MapView:

```
map.setReticleDrawMode(
    MapView.ReticleDrawMode.DRAW_RETICLE_UNDER
);
```

This will ensure anything you draw on the map will not be obscured by the reticle itself.

Traffic and Terrain

Just as the Google Maps you use on your full-size computer can display satellite imagery and, for some areas, traffic information, so too can Android maps.

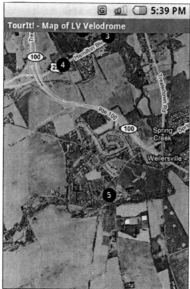

Figure 63. Map showing satellite view

MapView offers toggleSatellite() and toggleTraffic(), which, as the names suggest, toggle on and off these perspectives on the area being viewed. You can have the user trigger these via an options menu or, in the case of TourMapActivity, via keypresses:

```
@Override
public boolean onKeyDown(int keyCode, KeyEvent event) {
  if (keyCode == KeyEvent.KEYCODE_S) { // Switch on the satellite images
    map.toggleSatellite();
    return(true);
  }
  else if (keyCode == KeyEvent.KEYCODE_T) { // Switch on traffic overlays
    map.toggleTraffic();
    return(true);
  }

  return(super.onKeyDown(keyCode, event));
}
```

The third, default perspective is "street view", which can be turned on via toggleStreetView(). There is also isSatellite(), isTraffic(), and isStreetView() to test to see which of these perspectives is visible.

Follow You, Follow Me

When you use a GPS navigation system, the "normal mode" is for the map to follow your position. It's as if you are standing still and the world is moving underneath your wheels (or feet, or flippers, or...).

Android offers a similar feature via setFollowMyLocation(), available on MapController. With this, the map should re-center itself as you move.

At the time of this writing, though, there's one big problem with setFollowMyLocation() – it doesn't let you control which location provider to use. This is a serious limitation when working with the emulator, as you have no great means of controlling which location provider is used by the map, and so you might find yourself viewing the map of where the location provider thinks it is, rather than what you are trying to test.

The good news is that "rolling your own" follow-me logic is not that difficult.

The first step is figuring out which location provider you want to use, perhaps via an application preference. TourIt allows the user to choose a location provider via the ConfigActivity, as described in the previous chapter.

Next, you need to request updates from that location provider, via the requestUpdates() method on LocationManager. This method arranges for an Intent to be fired when the device moves a certain distance over a certain minimum period of time.

For example, here is onResume() from TourMapActivity:

```
@Override
public void onResume() {
  super.onResume();

  SharedPreferences prefs=getSharedPreferences(ConfigActivity.PREFS, 0);

  showMyLocation=prefs.getBoolean(ConfigActivity.SHOW_LOCATION, true);
```

```
followMe=prefs.getBoolean(ConfigActivity.FOLLOW_ME, true);

String providerName=prefs.getString(ConfigActivity.LOCATION_PROVIDER, null);

if (providerName!=null) {
  for (LocationProvider p : myLocationManager.getProviders()) {
    if (p.getName().equals(providerName)) {
      provider=p;
      break;
    }
  }
}

if (provider==null) {
  Criteria crit=new Criteria();

  crit.setCostAllowed(true);
  crit.setSpeedRequired(false);
  crit.setBearingRequired(false);
  crit.setAltitudeRequired(false);

  provider=myLocationManager.getBestProvider(crit);
}


if (provider!=null) {
  registerReceiver(intentReceiver, myIntentFilter);
  myLocationManager.requestUpdates(provider, MINIMUM_TIME_BETWEEN_UPDATE,
              MINIMUM_DISTANCECHANGE_FOR_UPDATE,
              myIntent);
}
}
```

We first find out what the chosen location provider is and whether or not
the follow-me feature should be enabled. If there is no specified location
provider, we use a Criteria to find one. Then, we register our intent receiver
(an instance of the private LocationIntentReceiver class) using our intent
filter:

```
new IntentFilter(LOCATION_CHANGED_ACTION);
```

Our LocationIntentReceiver class is trivial, simply telling the activity to
update its view:

```
class LocationIntentReceiver extends IntentReceiver {
  @Override
  public void onReceiveIntent(Context context, Intent intent) {
    TourMapActivity.this.updateView();
```

```
    }
}
```

The `updateView()` method on `TourMapActivity` checks to see if follow-me is enabled, and, if true, re-centers the map on the current position:

```
private void updateView() {
  if (provider!=null) {
    myLocation=myLocationManager.getCurrentLocation(provider.getName());

    if (followMe) {
      Double lat=TourMapActivity.this.myLocation.getLatitude() * 1E6;
      Double lng=TourMapActivity.this.myLocation.getLongitude() * 1E6;
      Point point=new Point(lat.intValue(), lng.intValue());

      mc.centerMapTo(point, false);
    }

    map.invalidate();
  }
}
```

By this mechanism, you can have your follow-me feature while offering more direct control over which location provider to use. It is eminently possible the Android API will be updated to "bake in" this type of capability, at which point the code shown here may become obsolete.

Layers Upon Layers

If you have ever used the full-size edition of Google Maps, you are probably used to seeing things overlaid atop the map itself, such as "push-pins" indicating businesses near the location being searched. In map parlance – and, for that matter, in many serious graphic editors – the push-pins are on a separate layer than the map itself, and what you are seeing is the composition of the push-pin layer atop the map layer.

Android's mapping allows you to create layers as well, so you can mark up the maps as you need to based on user input and your application's purpose. For example, TourIt uses a layer to show where all the waypoints of the tour are, in sequence, plus your current location relative to those waypoints.

Overlay Classes

Any overlay you want to add to your map needs to be implemented as a subclass of Overlay. This does not have to be a public class; TourMapActivity has a private inner class called RouteOverlay to show the waypoints and current device position.

To attach an overlay class to your map, you need to get your map's OverlayController and add the overlay to it:

```
map.createOverlayController().add(new RouteOverlay(this),
                                 true);
```

The first parameter is the Overlay instance, in this case a new RouteOverlay, attached to the activity. The second parameter is a boolean indicating if the overlay should be activated. You can define overlays and activate or deactivate them as needed, just as you toggle between regular and satellite views. In this case, since we want the overlay to be visible at all times, we use true to activate it immediately.

Drawing the Overlay

Overlay subclasses need to implement a draw() method to actually put their material onto their layer for superposition over the map surface. The draw() method takes three parameters:

1. A Canvas, used as the drawing surface

2. A PixelCalculator, to help you convert between pixels for your drawing and real-world dimensions on the map

3. A boolean indicating whether this is the "shadow" call or not

The draw() method is called twice in succession: once with shadow = true, indicating that if your layer has any sort of 3D effect (e.g., shadows cast by push-pins), you should draw those, and once with shadow = false for drawing the "regular" part of the layer. While you should chain upward to the superclass (via super.draw(canvas, calculator, shadow)), the default action for `draw()` is to do nothing. Hence, if you don't have a shadow, either ignore the parameter or only draw when `shadow = false`.

A `Canvas` offers a range of drawing methods, such as `drawCircle()`, `drawText()`, and so on. The catch is that the `Canvas` is expecting to be told where to draw in terms of pixels in canvas-space. You, on the other hand, have your data in terms of positions (latitude and longitude). And, of course, the user isn't viewing the whole world at once, so there's a question of which subset of things you want to draw actually appear on the `Canvas`.

Fortunately, Android encapsulates much of those problems inside the `PixelCalculator`. To draw things on the `Canvas`, you should:

1. Convert your latitude and longitude into a `Point`...as noted above, a `Point` uses a pair of integers for the latitude and longitude, scaled upwards by a factor of 1E6

2. Allocate an `int[2]` array to hold the pixel conversion of your `Point`

3. Call `getPointXY()` on the `PixelConverter`, supplying your `Point` and `int[2]` array

4. Use the `int[2]` array as x/y coordinates for your `draw...()` methods on the `Canvas`

For example, here is the implementation of `RouteOverlay`'s `draw()` method:

```
public void draw(Canvas canvas, PixelCalculator calculator,
        boolean shadow) {
  super.draw(canvas, calculator, shadow);

  if (showMyLocation() && TourMapActivity.this.myLocation!=null) {
    Double lat=TourMapActivity.this.myLocation.getLatitude() * 1E6;
    Double lng=TourMapActivity.this.myLocation.getLongitude() * 1E6;
    Point point=new Point(lat.intValue(), lng.intValue());

    int[] myScreenCoords = new int[2];
    calculator.getPointXY(point, myScreenCoords);

    canvas.drawCircle(myScreenCoords[0], myScreenCoords[1], 5, paint3);
  }

  int i=0;

  for (Waypoint pt : tour.getRoute()) {
```

```
   i++;

 Point position=pt.getPosition();

 if (position!=null) {
   int[] screenCoords=new int[2];

   calculator.getPointXY(position, screenCoords);
   canvas.drawCircle(screenCoords[0], screenCoords[1], 12, paint1);
   canvas.drawText(Integer.toString(i), screenCoords[0] - 4,
         screenCoords[1] + 4, paint2);
  }
 }
}
```

After chaining upward to the superclass, we first determine if we're supposed to be showing the device's position. If so, we build a Point, convert it to x/y coordinates, and draw a 5-pixel radius red circle at those coordinates (paint3 is defined up in onCreate() as being RGB red).

Then, for each waypoint in the tour, we do much the same thing: build a Point, convert it to x/y coordinates, draw a 12-pixel radius black circle, and write in the circle the waypoint number in white.

Handling Screen Taps

An Overlay subclass can also implement onTap(), to be notified when the user taps on the map, so the overlay can adjust what it draws. For example, in full-size Google Maps, clicking on a push-pin pops up a bubble with information about the business at that pin's location. With onTap(), you can do much the same in Android.

The onTap() method receives three parameters:

1. A "device type", indicating what generated the tap (touchscreen, trackball, etc.)

2. The Point representing the real-world location where the user tapped the map

3. A PixelCalculator to help you convert between Point and x/y coordinates, if needed

It is up to you to determine if the supplied `Point` represents something of interest and, if so, what to display.

In the case of `RouteOverlay`, `onTap()` looks like this:

```
@Override
public boolean onTap(com.google.android.maps.MapView.DeviceType deviceType,
            Point p, PixelCalculator calculator) {
  for (Waypoint pt : tour.getRoute()) {
    Point position=pt.getPosition();

    if (position!=null) {
      int[] screenCoords=new int[2];
      RectF rect=new RectF();

      calculator.getPointXY(position, screenCoords);
      rect.set(-12,-12,12,12);
      rect.offset(screenCoords[0], screenCoords[1]);
      calculator.getPointXY(p, screenCoords);

      if (rect.contains(screenCoords[0], screenCoords[1])) {
        Toast.makeText(parent, pt.getTitle(), 2000).show();
      }
    }
  }

  return(super.onTap(deviceType, p, calculator));
}
```

We iterate over the waypoints and use the `RectF` helper class to construct a 24x24 pixel square around each waypoint's on-screen representation. This square isn't drawn on screen; rather, it is used solely to determine if the tap (represented by the supplied `Point`) occurred within that square. If so, we consider the user to have tapped on that waypoint, and we show a `Toast` with the name of the waypoint (e.g., "Mosser St. @ Hamilton").

CHAPTER 32

Playing Media

Pretty much every phone claiming to be a "smartphone" has the ability to at least play back music, if not video. Even many more ordinary phones are full-fledged MP3 players, in addition to offering ringtones and whatnot.

Not surprisingly, Android aims to match the best of them.

Android has full capability to play back and record audio and video. This includes:

- Playback of audio, such as downloaded MP3 tracks
- Showing photos
- Playing back video clips
- Voice recording through the microphone
- Camera for still pictures or video clips

Exactly how robust these capabilities will be is heavily device-dependent. Mobile device cameras range from excellent to atrocious. Screen resolutions and sizes will vary, and video playback works better on better screens. Which codecs a device manufacturer will license (e.g., what types of video can it play?) and which Bluetooth profiles a device will support (e.g., A2DP for stereo?) will also have an impact on what results any given person will have with their phone.

You as a developer can integrate media playback and recording into your applications. Recording is outside the scope of this book, in large part because the current emulator has recording limitations at this time. And, viewing pictures is mostly a matter of putting an ImageView widget into an activity. This chapter, therefore, focuses on playback of audio and video.

As with many advanced Android features, expect changes in future releases of their toolkit. For example, at the time of this writing, there is no built-in audio or video playback activity. Hence, you cannot just craft an Intent to, say, an MP3 URL, and hand it off to Android with VIEW_ACTION to initiate playback. Right now, you need to handle the playback yourself. It is probably safe to assume, though, that standard activities for this will be forthcoming, allowing you to "take the easy way out" if you want to play back media but do not need to control that playback much yourself.

Get Your Media On

In Android, you have five different places you can pull media clips from – one of these will hopefully fit your needs:

1. You can package media clips as raw resources (res/raw in your project), so they are bundled with your application. The benefit is that you're guaranteed the clips will be there; the downside is that they cannot be replaced without upgrading the application.

2. You can package media clips as assets (assets/ in your project) and reference them via file:///android_asset/ URLs in a Uri. The benefit over raw resources is that this location works with APIs that expect Uri parameters instead of resource IDs. The downside – assets are only replaceable when the application is upgraded – remains.

3. You can store media in an application-local directory, such as content you download off the Internet. Your media may or may not be there, and your storage space isn't infinite, but you can replace the media as needed.

4. You can store media – or reference media that the user has stored herself – that is on an SD card. There is likely more storage space on

the card than there is on the device, and you can replace the media as needed, but other applications have access to the SD card as well.

5. You can, in some cases, stream media off the Internet, bypassing any local storage

Internet streaming seems to be somewhat problematic in this release of the Android SDK.

Making Noise

The crux of playing back audio comes in the form of the MediaPlayer class. With it, you can feed it an audio clip, start/stop/pause playback, and get notified on key events, such as when the clip is ready to be played or is done playing.

You have three ways to set up a MediaPlayer and tell it what audio clip to play:

1. If the clip is a raw resource, use MediaPlayer.create() and provide the resource ID of the clip

2. If you have a Uri to the clip, use the Uri-flavored version of MediaPlayer.create()

3. If you have a string path to the clip, just create a MediaPlayer using the default constructor, then call setDataSource() with the path to the clip

Next, you need to call prepare() or prepareAsync(). Both will set up the clip to be ready to play, such as fetching the first few seconds off the file or stream. The prepare() method is synchronous; as soon as it returns, the clip is ready to play. The prepareAsync() method is asynchronous – more on how to use this version later.

Once the clip is prepared, start() begins playback, pause() pauses playback (with start() picking up playback where pause() paused), and stop() ends playback. One caveat: you cannot simply call start() again on the MediaPlayer once you have called stop() – that may be a bug or may be the intended `MediaPlayer` behavior. We'll cover a workaround a bit later in this section.

To see this in action, take a look at the `AudioDemo` sample project. The layout is pretty trivial, with three buttons and labels for play, pause, and stop:

```xml
<?xml version="1.0" encoding="utf-8"?>
<LinearLayout xmlns:android="http://schemas.android.com/apk/res/android"
    android:orientation="vertical"
    android:layout_width="fill_parent"
    android:layout_height="fill_parent"
    >
  <LinearLayout
    android:orientation="horizontal"
    android:layout_width="fill_parent"
    android:layout_height="wrap_content"
    android:padding="4px"
  >
    <ImageButton android:id="@+id/play"
      android:src="@drawable/play"
      android:layout_height="wrap_content"
      android:layout_width="wrap_content"
      android:paddingRight="4px"
      android:enabled="false"
    />
    <TextView
      android:text="Play"
      android:layout_width="fill_parent"
      android:layout_height="fill_parent"
      android:gravity="center_vertical"
      android:layout_gravity="center_vertical"
      android:textAppearance="?android:attr/textAppearanceLarge"
    />
  </LinearLayout>
  <LinearLayout
    android:orientation="horizontal"
    android:layout_width="fill_parent"
    android:layout_height="wrap_content"
    android:padding="4px"
  >
    <ImageButton android:id="@+id/pause"
      android:src="@drawable/pause"
      android:layout_height="wrap_content"
      android:layout_width="wrap_content"
      android:paddingRight="4px"
    />
    <TextView
      android:text="Pause"
      android:layout_width="fill_parent"
      android:layout_height="fill_parent"
      android:gravity="center_vertical"
```

```
          android:layout_gravity="center_vertical"
          android:textAppearance="?android:attr/textAppearanceLarge"
      />
    </LinearLayout>
    <LinearLayout
      android:orientation="horizontal"
      android:layout_width="fill_parent"
      android:layout_height="wrap_content"
      android:padding="4px"
    >
      <ImageButton android:id="@+id/stop"
        android:src="@drawable/stop"
        android:layout_height="wrap_content"
        android:layout_width="wrap_content"
        android:paddingRight="4px"
      />
      <TextView
        android:text="Stop"
        android:layout_width="fill_parent"
        android:layout_height="fill_parent"
        android:gravity="center_vertical"
        android:layout_gravity="center_vertical"
        android:textAppearance="?android:attr/textAppearanceLarge"
      />
    </LinearLayout>
</LinearLayout>
```

The Java, of course, is where things get interesting:

```
package com.commonsware.android.audio;

import android.app.Activity;
import android.content.Context;
import android.content.SharedPreferences;
import android.media.MediaPlayer;
import android.os.Bundle;
import android.view.Menu;
import android.view.View;
import android.widget.ImageButton;
import android.widget.Toast;

public class AudioDemo extends Activity {
  private static final int CLOSE_ID = Menu.FIRST+2;

  private ImageButton play;
  private ImageButton pause;
  private ImageButton stop;
  private MediaPlayer mp;

  @Override
  public void onCreate(Bundle icicle) {
    super.onCreate(icicle);
    setContentView(R.layout.main);
```

```
play=(ImageButton)findViewById(R.id.play);
pause=(ImageButton)findViewById(R.id.pause);
stop=(ImageButton)findViewById(R.id.stop);

play.setOnClickListener(new View.OnClickListener() {
  public void onClick(View view) {
    mp.start();
    play.setEnabled(false);
    pause.setEnabled(true);
    stop.setEnabled(true);
  }
});
pause.setOnClickListener(new View.OnClickListener() {
  public void onClick(View view) {
    mp.pause();
    play.setEnabled(true);
    pause.setEnabled(false);
    stop.setEnabled(true);
  }
});

stop.setOnClickListener(new View.OnClickListener() {
  public void onClick(View view) {
    stop();
  }
});

try {
  mp=new MediaPlayer();
  mp.setOnPreparedListener(new MediaPlayer.OnPreparedListener() {
    public void onPrepared(MediaPlayer mp) {
      play.setEnabled(true);
    }
  });
  mp.setOnCompletionListener(new MediaPlayer.OnCompletionListener() {
    public void onCompletion(MediaPlayer mp) {
      stop();
    }
  });

  setup();
}
catch (Throwable t) {
  android.util.Log.e("AudioDemo", "Exception playing audio", t);
  Toast.makeText(this, "Ick!", 2000).show();
}
}

@Override
public boolean onCreateOptionsMenu(Menu menu) {
  menu.add(0, CLOSE_ID, "Close", R.drawable.eject)
      .setAlphabeticShortcut('c');
```

```
    return(super.onCreateOptionsMenu(menu));
}

@Override
public boolean onOptionsItemSelected(Menu.Item item) {
  switch (item.getId()) {
    case CLOSE_ID:
      finish();
      return(true);
  }

  return(super.onOptionsItemSelected(item));
}

private void stop() {
  mp.reset();
  setup();
}

private void setup() {
  play.setEnabled(false);
  pause.setEnabled(false);
  stop.setEnabled(false);

  try {
    mp.setDataSource("/system/media/audio/ringtones/ringer.mp3");
  }
  catch (Throwable t) {
    android.util.Log.e("AudioDemo", "Exception playing audio", t);
    Toast.makeText(this, "Ick!", 2000).show();
  }

  mp.prepareAsync();
}
}
```

During the preparation phase, we wire up the three buttons to shift us between the other states, plus prep the MediaPlayer (mp instance variable). Specifically:

- We use the empty constructor

- We hook it up to an OnPreparedListener via setOnPreparedListener() – this callback gets invoked when prepareAsync() is finished, and in our case it enables the play button

- We hook it up to an OnCompletionListener via setOnCompletionListener() – this callback gets invoked when the clip reaches the end, at which point we call stop(), just as if the user had clicked the Stop button

• We call a setup() method

Our stop() method simply resets the MediaPlayer and calls setup(). The setup() method – called during initial preparation and after the clip is stopped – disables the buttons, sets the clip to be a built-in ringtone MP3, and calls prepareAsync().

So, the flow is:

1. We prep the MediaPlayer with the clip

2. We enable the play button

3. The user clicks the play button and listens to the clip

4. The user possibly pauses playback, then clicks play again to resume

5. The user possibly stops playback, at which time the media player is completely reset to its post-prep state

6. The clip possibly ends on its own, at which time the media player is also reset

The whole reset-and-reconfigure process is how you can get a MediaPlayer back to being able to play again after you call stop().

The UI is nothing special, but we're more interested in the audio in this sample, anyway:

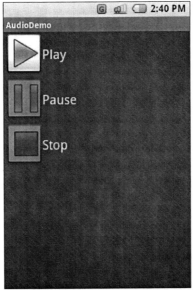

Figure 64. The AudioDemo sample application

Moving Pictures

Video clips get their own widget, the VideoView. Put it in a layout, feed it an MP4 video clip, and you get playback!

Right now, playback seems a bit rocky in the emulator, but that will likely clear itself up in future releases – VideoView was only made available in the SDK release prior to publication of this book.

Since VideoView is a widget, you can put it in a layout, such as this one from the VideoDemo sample project:

```xml
<?xml version="1.0" encoding="utf-8"?>
<LinearLayout xmlns:android="http://schemas.android.com/apk/res/android"
    android:orientation="vertical"
    android:layout_width="fill_parent"
    android:layout_height="fill_parent"
    >
  <VideoView
    android:id="@+id/video"
      android:layout_width="320px"
      android:layout_height="240px"
```

```
    />
  <Button android:id="@+id/show"
    android:text="Show Controller!"
    android:layout_height="fill_parent"
    android:layout_width="fill_parent"
    android:paddingRight="4px"
    android:enabled="false"
  />
</LinearLayout>
```

In addition to the VideoView, we also put in a Button that, when pushed, will pop up the VideoView control panel, known as the MediaController. This, by default, overlays the bottom portion of the VideoView and shows your current position in the video clip, plus offers pause, rewind, and fast-forward buttons:

```
package com.commonsware.android.video;

import android.app.Activity;
import android.graphics.PixelFormat;
import android.os.Bundle;
import android.view.View;
import android.widget.Button;
import android.widget.MediaController;
import android.widget.VideoView;

public class VideoDemo extends Activity {
  private VideoView video;
  private MediaController ctlr;

  @Override
  public void onCreate(Bundle icicle) {
    super.onCreate(icicle);
    getWindow().setFormat(PixelFormat.TRANSLUCENT);
    setContentView(R.layout.main);

    Button show=(Button)findViewById(R.id.show);

    show.setOnClickListener(new View.OnClickListener() {
      public void onClick(View view) {
        ctlr.show();
      }
    });

    video=(VideoView)findViewById(R.id.video);
    video.setVideoPath("/tmp/test.mp4");

    ctlr=new MediaController(this);
    ctlr.setMediaPlayer(video);
    video.setMediaController(ctlr);
    video.requestFocus();
```

```
        }
}
```

The biggest trick with VideoView is getting a video clip onto the device. While VideoView does support some streaming video, the requirements on the MP4 file are fairly stringent. If you want to be able to play a wider array of video clips, you need to have them on the device, either in the local filesystem or on an SD card.

The crude VideoDemo class assumes there is an MP4 file in /tmp/test.mp4 on your emulator. To make this a reality:

1. Find a clip, such as Aaron Rosenberg's *Documentaries and You* from Duke University's Center for the Study of the Public Domain's Moving Image Contest[30], which was used in the creation of this book

2. Use the adb push command (or the equivalent in your IDE) to copy the MP4 file into /tmp/test.mp4

Once there, the following Java code will give you a working video player:

---

30 http://www.law.duke.edu/cspd/contest/finalists/

Figure 65. The VideoDemo sample application, showing a Creative Commons-licensed video clip

NOTE: the /tmp directory is cleaned out periodically on the emulator, and so you may need to re-push the file if you intend to run this sample over an extended period of time.

The button is set up to call show() on the MediaController, which displays the control panel. The clip will automatically start playing back – you do not need to call play() on the VideoView, though that method is available (as is pause() and stopPlayback(), in case you need your own control over playback in addition to the MediaController's control panel).

CHAPTER 33

Handling Telephone Calls

Many, if not most, Android devices will be phones. As such, not only will users be expecting to place and receive calls using Android, but you will have the opportunity to help them place calls, if you wish.

Why might you want to?

- Maybe you are writing an Android interface to a sales management application (a la Salesforce.com) and you want to offer users the ability to call prospects with a single button click, and without them having to keep those contacts both in your application and in the phone's contacts application

- Maybe you are writing a social networking application, and the roster of phone numbers that you can access shifts constantly, so rather than try to "sync" the social network contacts with the phone's contact database, you let people place calls directly from your application

- Maybe you are creating an alternative interface to the existing contacts system, perhaps for users with reduced motor control (e.g., the elderly), sporting big buttons and the like to make it easier for them to place calls

Whatever the reason, Android has APIs to let you manipulate the phone just like any other piece of the Android system.

No, No, No – Not That IPhone...

To get at the phone API, you need to get an object implementing the IPhone interface from Android. Today, that works much like how you would access any other service's IPC interface, by calling IPhone.Stub.asInterface() with a suitable binder. The difference is in how you get that binder:

```
phone=IPhone.Stub.asInterface(svcMgr.getService("phone"));
```

What's Our Status?

Bear in mind that the phone capability might not always be on, even if Android is running. The phone might have the phone radio turned off in places where either it isn't allowed (airplanes, hospitals, etc.) or as a means of silencing the phone during meetings.

You can determine if the phone is ready for use by calling isRadioOn() on the IPhone interface. You can even call toggleRadioOnOff() to change the radio's status – though you really should make sure this is what the user wants, lest they accidentally toggle the phone on when they really shouldn't.

Of course, there's a more prosaic reason why you might not be able to use the phone – the user might already be on a call. The isOffhook() method – despite using the archaic "hook" terminology from a byegone era of phones – will tell if you if a call is in progress. Here, "off hook" means the phone is in use, so if isOffhook() returns true, you cannot place a call.

You Make the Call!

IPhone also offers three APIs related to call handling:

1. dial(), which takes a phone number and puts it on the Android Dialer screen, awaiting user confirmation to dial that number

2. call(), which immediately places a call, given a phone number

3. endCall(), which terminates the current call

Generally speaking, you probably should use dial() over call(), so the user gets confirmation that they're actually placing a call, in case they mis-clicked on something. Or, offer a configuration option, allowing users to choose whether you wind up using dial() or call(). If you feel you want to use call(), make sure the user has confirmed they truly want a call, or you may wind up with a bunch of unhappy users.

For example, let's look at the Dialer sample application. Here's the crude-but-effective layout:

```xml
<?xml version="1.0" encoding="utf-8"?>
<LinearLayout xmlns:android="http://schemas.android.com/apk/res/android"
    android:orientation="vertical"
    android:layout_width="fill_parent"
    android:layout_height="fill_parent"
    >
  <LinearLayout
    android:orientation="horizontal"
    android:layout_width="fill_parent"
    android:layout_height="wrap_content"
    >
    <TextView
      android:layout_width="wrap_content"
      android:layout_height="wrap_content"
      android:text="Number to dial:"
      />
    <EditText android:id="@+id/number"
      android:layout_width="fill_parent"
      android:layout_height="wrap_content"
      android:cursorVisible="true"
      android:editable="true"
      android:singleLine="true"
    />
  </LinearLayout>
  <LinearLayout
    android:orientation="horizontal"
    android:layout_width="fill_parent"
    android:layout_height="wrap_content"
    >
    <Button android:id="@+id/dial"
      android:layout_width="fill_parent"
      android:layout_height="fill_parent"
      android:layout_weight="1"
      android:text="Dial It!"
    />
    <Button android:id="@+id/call"
      android:layout_width="fill_parent"
      android:layout_height="fill_parent"
      android:layout_weight="1"
      android:text="Call It!"
```

```
    />
  </LinearLayout>
</LinearLayout>
```

We have a labeled field for typing in a phone number, plus buttons for dialing and calling said number.

The Java code wires up those buttons to dial() and call(), respectively, on the IPhone interface:

```java
package com.commonsware.android.dialer;

import android.app.Activity;
import android.os.Bundle;
import android.os.DeadObjectException;
import android.os.IServiceManager;
import android.os.ServiceManagerNative;
import android.telephony.IPhone;
import android.view.View;
import android.widget.Button;
import android.widget.EditText;
import android.widget.Toast;

public class DialerDemo extends Activity {
  IPhone phone=null;

  @Override
  public void onCreate(Bundle icicle) {
    super.onCreate(icicle);
    setContentView(R.layout.main);

    IServiceManager svcMgr=ServiceManagerNative.getDefault();

    try {
      phone=IPhone.Stub.asInterface(svcMgr.getService("phone"));
    }
    catch (DeadObjectException e) {
      android.util.Log.e("DialerDemo", "Error in dial()", e);
      Toast.makeText(DialerDemo.this, e.toString(), 2000).show();
      finish();
    }

    final EditText number=(EditText)findViewById(R.id.number);
    Button dial=(Button)findViewById(R.id.dial);

    dial.setOnClickListener(new Button.OnClickListener() {
      public void onClick(View v) {
        try {
          if (phone!=null) {
            phone.dial(number.getText().toString());
          }
```

```
      }
      catch (DeadObjectException e) {
        android.util.Log.e("DialerDemo", "Error in dial()", e);
        Toast.makeText(DialerDemo.this, e.toString(), 2000).show();
      }
    }
  });

  Button call=(Button)findViewById(R.id.call);

  call.setOnClickListener(new Button.OnClickListener() {
    public void onClick(View v) {
      try {
        if (phone!=null) {
          phone.call(number.getText().toString());
        }
      }
      catch (DeadObjectException e) {
        android.util.Log.e("DialerDemo", "Error in dial()", e);
        Toast.makeText(DialerDemo.this, e.toString(), 2000).show();
      }
    }
  });
  }
}
```

Some notes about the code:

- We keep the IPhone – created near the top of onCreate() – around in an instance variable in the activity, so we don't keep having to create new IPhone instances on every button push

- Since IPhone is, in effect, an interface to a service, we have to deal with the possible DeadObjectException if the service connection collapsed; here, we just log and display an error message

The activity's own UI is not that impressive:

Figure 66. The DialerDemo sample application, as initially launched

However, the dialer you get from clicking the dial button is better, showing you the number you are about to dial:

Figure 67. The Android Dialer activity, as launched from DialerDemo

Or, if you click the call button, you are taken straight to a call:

Figure 68. The Android call activity, as launched from DialerDemo

CHAPTER 34

Searching with SearchManager

One of the firms behind the Open Handset Alliance – Google – has a teeny weeny Web search service, one you might have heard of in passing. Given that, it's not surprising that Android has some amount of built-in search capabilities.

Specifically, Android has "baked in" the notion of searching not only on the device for data, but over the air to Internet sources of data.

Your applications can participate in the search process, by triggering searches or perhaps by allowing your application's data to be searched.

Note that this is fairly new to the Android platform, and so some shifting in the APIs is likely. Stay tuned for updates to this chapter.

Hunting Season

If your activity has an options menu, then you automatically "inherit" a hidden search menu choice. If the user clicks the menu button followed by the s key, it will display the search popup:

Figure 69. The Android search popup, showing a search for contacts

From here, you can toggle between applications by clicking the button on the left and enter in a search string. If the application you are searching supports a live filtered search, like the built-in Contacts activity, you can choose from an entry matching your search string as it appears below the search field:

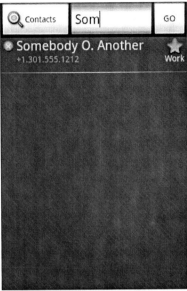

Figure 70. A filtered search for contacts

Or, you can click the Go button and be taken to an activity that will process your search and show the results.

If your activity does not have an options menu, you will need to trigger this manually by some other user interface element, such as a button. That is simply a matter of calling onSearchRequested() in your activity (e.g., from the button's callback method).

If your activity does not need keyboard entry, you can have keystrokes pull up the search popup by calling setDefaultKeyMode(SEARCH_DEFAULT_KEYS) in your activity (e.g., in onCreate()). Note that there are other options for setDefaultKeyMode(), such as DIALER_DEFAULT_KEYS, which routes number keypresses to a newly-launched Dialer activity.

Search Yourself

Over the long haul, there will be two flavors of search available via the Android search system:

1. Query-style search, where the user's search string is passed to an activity which is responsible for conducting the search and displaying the results

2. Filter-style search, where the user's search string is passed to an activity on every keypress, and the activity is responsible for updating a displayed list of matches

Since the latter approach is under heavy development right now by the Android team, let's focus on the first one.

Craft the Search Activity

The first thing you are going to want to do if you want to support query-style search in your application is to create a search activity. While it might be possible to have a single activity be both opened from the launcher and opened from a search, that might prove somewhat confusing to users. Certainly, for the purposes of learning the techniques, having a separate activity is cleaner.

The search activity can have any look you want. In fact, other than watching for queries, a search activity looks, walks, and talks like any other activity in your system.

All the search activity needs to do differently is check the intents supplied to onCreate() (via getIntent()) and onNewIntent() to see if one is a search, and, if so, to do the search and display the results.

For example, let's look at the Lorem sample application. This starts off as a clone of the list-of-lorem-ipsum-words application that we first built back when showing off the ListView container, then later with XML resources. Now, we update it to support searching the list of words for ones containing the search string.

The main activity and the search activity both share a common layout: a ListView plus a TextView showing the selected entry:

```
<?xml version="1.0" encoding="utf-8"?>
<LinearLayout xmlns:android="http://schemas.android.com/apk/res/android"
  android:orientation="vertical"
  android:layout_width="fill_parent"
  android:layout_height="fill_parent" >
  <TextView
    android:id="@+id/selection"
    android:layout_width="fill_parent"
    android:layout_height="wrap_content"
  />
  <ListView
    android:id="@android:id/list"
    android:layout_width="fill_parent"
    android:layout_height="fill_parent"
    android:drawSelectorOnTop="false"
  />
</LinearLayout>
```

In terms of Java code, most of the guts of the activities are poured into an abstract LoremBase class:

```
package com.commonsware.android.search;

import android.app.Activity;
import android.app.ListActivity;
import android.app.SearchManager;
import android.content.Intent;
import android.os.Bundle;
import android.view.Menu;
import android.view.View;
import android.widget.AdapterView;
import android.widget.ArrayAdapter;
import android.widget.ListAdapter;
import android.widget.ListView;
import android.widget.TextView;
import java.io.InputStream;
import java.util.ArrayList;
import java.util.List;
import org.xmlpull.v1.XmlPullParser;
import org.xmlpull.v1.XmlPullParserException;

abstract public class LoremBase extends ListActivity {
  abstract ListAdapter makeMeAnAdapter(Intent intent);

  private static final int CLOSE_ID = Menu.FIRST+1;
  TextView selection;
  ArrayList<String> items=new ArrayList<String>();

  @Override
  public void onCreate(Bundle icicle) {
    super.onCreate(icicle);
    setContentView(R.layout.main);
```

```
  selection=(TextView)findViewById(R.id.selection);

  try {
    XmlPullParser xpp=getResources().getXml(R.xml.words);

    while (xpp.getEventType()!=XmlPullParser.END_DOCUMENT) {
      if (xpp.getEventType()==XmlPullParser.START_TAG) {
        if (xpp.getName().equals("word")) {
          items.add(xpp.getAttributeValue(0));
        }
      }

      xpp.next();
    }
  }
  catch (Throwable t) {
    showAlert("Exception!", 0, t.toString(), "Cancel", true);
  }

  onNewIntent(getIntent());
}

@Override
public void onNewIntent(Intent intent) {
  ListAdapter adapter=makeMeAnAdapter(intent);

  if (adapter==null) {
    finish();
  }
  else {
    setListAdapter(adapter);
  }
}

public void onListItemClick(ListView parent, View v, int position,
              long id) {
  selection.setText(items.get(position).toString());
}

@Override
public boolean onCreateOptionsMenu(Menu menu) {
  menu.add(0, CLOSE_ID, "Close", R.drawable.eject)
         .setAlphabeticShortcut('c');

  return(super.onCreateOptionsMenu(menu));
}

@Override
public boolean onOptionsItemSelected(Menu.Item item) {
  switch (item.getId()) {
    case CLOSE_ID:
      finish();
      return(true);
  }
```

```
    return(super.onOptionsItemSelected(item));
  }
}
```

This activity takes care of everything related to showing a list of words, even loading the words out of the XML resource. What it does not do is come up with the `ListAdapter` to put into the `ListView` – that is delegated to the subclasses.

The main activity – `LoremDemo` – just uses a `ListAdapter` for the whole word list:

```
package com.commonsware.android.search;

import android.content.Intent;
import android.widget.ArrayAdapter;
import android.widget.ListAdapter;

public class LoremDemo extends LoremBase {
  @Override
  ListAdapter makeMeAnAdapter(Intent intent) {
    return(new ArrayAdapter<String>(this,
                    android.R.layout.simple_list_item_1,
                    items));
  }
}
```

The search activity, though, does things a bit differently.

First, it inspects the `Intent` supplied to the abstract `makeMeAnAdpater()` method. That `Intent` comes from either `onCreate()` or `onNewIntent()`. If the intent is a `SEARCH_ACTION`, then we know this is a search. We can get the search query and, in the case of this silly demo, spin through the loaded list of words and find only those containing the search string. That list then gets wrapped in a `ListAdapter` and returned for display:

```
package com.commonsware.android.search;

import android.app.SearchManager;
import android.content.Intent;
import android.widget.ArrayAdapter;
import android.widget.ListAdapter;
import java.util.ArrayList;
```

```
import java.util.List;

public class LoremSearch extends LoremBase {
  @Override
  ListAdapter makeMeAnAdapter(Intent intent) {
    ListAdapter adapter=null;

    if (intent.getAction().equals(Intent.SEARCH_ACTION)) {
      String query=intent.getStringExtra(SearchManager.QUERY);
      List<String> results=searchItems(query);

      adapter=new ArrayAdapter<String>(this,
                        android.R.layout.simple_list_item_1,
                        results);
      setTitle("LoremSearch for: "+query);
    }

    return(adapter);
  }

  private List<String> searchItems(String query) {
    List<String> results=new ArrayList<String>();

    for (String item : items) {
      if (item.indexOf(query)>-1) {
        results.add(item);
      }
    }

    return(results);
  }
}
```

Update the Manifest

While this implements search, it doesn't tie it into the Android search system. That requires a few changes to the auto-generated `AndroidManifest.xml` file:

```xml
<manifest xmlns:android="http://schemas.android.com/apk/res/android"
  package="com.commonsware.android.search">
  <application>
    <activity android:name=".LoremDemo" android:label="LoremDemo">
      <intent-filter>
        <action android:name="android.intent.action.MAIN" />
        <category android:name="android.intent.category.LAUNCHER" />
      </intent-filter>
      <meta-data android:name="android.app.default_searchable"
            android:value=".LoremSearch" />
    </activity>
```

```
<activity
    android:name=".LoremSearch"
    android:label="LoremSearch"
    android:launchMode="singleTop">
    <intent-filter>
        <action android:name="android.intent.action.SEARCH" />
        <category android:name="android.intent.category.DEFAULT" />
    </intent-filter>
    <meta-data android:name="android.app.searchable"
            android:resource="@xml/searchable" />
</activity>
</application>
</manifest>
```

The changes that are needed are:

1. The `LoremDemo` main activity gets a `meta-data` element, with an `android:name` of `android.app.default_searchable` and a `android:value` of the search implementation class (`.LoremSearch`)

2. The `LoremSearch` activity gets an intent filter for `android.intent.action.SEARCH`, so search intents will be picked up

3. The `LoremSearch` activity is set to have `android:launchMode` = `"singleTop"`, which means at most one instance of this activity will be open at any time, so we don't wind up with a whole bunch of little search activities cluttering up the activity stack

4. The `LoremSearch` activity gets a `meta-data` element, with an `android:name` of `android.app.searchable` and a `android:value` of an XML resource containing more information about the search facility offered by this activity (`@xml/searchable`)

That XML resource provides two bits of information today:

1. What name should appear in the search domain button to the left of the search field, identifying to the user where she is searching

2. What hint text should appear in the search field, to give the user a clue as to what they should be typing in

Try It Out

Given all that, search is now available – Android knows your application is searchable, what search domain to use when searching from the main activity, and the activity knows how to do the search.

If you pop up the search from the main activity (Menu+S), you will see the Lorem Ipsum search domain appear as your default area to search:

Figure 71. The Lorem sample application, showing the search popup

Typing in a letter or two, then clicking Go, will bring up the search activity and the subset of words containing what you typed, with your search query in the activity title bar:

Figure 72. The results of searching for 'co' in the Lorem search sample

PART VII – Appendices

APPENDIX A
The TourIt Sample Application

In several chapters of this book, we used TourIt as a source of sample code for features ranging from content providers to mapping and location services. This appendix discusses the application as a whole, so you can see all facets of it from front to back.

Installing TourIt

Installing the application itself is straightforward: with the emulator running, fire up `ant install` in the base of the TourIt project directory, and let Ant do the heavy lifting.

However, TourIt has two other requirements – a demo location provider and an SD card image – that are somewhat more complicated to install.

Demo Location Provider

As mentioned in the chapter on locations, Android has a built-in fake, or demo, location provider, that has the device moving through a loop around the Google campus in California. The author of this book does not live in Silicon Valley. As such, he had no good way of developing a bicycle tour matching that loop. It was more expedient to develop another demo location provider, this one handling a loop around the author's home base in eastern Pennsylvania, with the tour starting at the Lehigh Valley Velodrome.

This means, though, that you will probably want to install this demo location provider yourself, so the TourIt application's tour lines up with a location provider.

In the project's location/velo/ directory, you will find three files:

- location, which holds the most-recent position of the device along this track

- properties, which describes the characteristics of this location provider (e.g., doesn't support altitude, has a low power requirement)

- track, which is the actual roster of time offsets from the starting time and the position the device is in at that point, defined as latitude and longitude

To install this location provider in your emulator, do the following:

1. Use adb shell to create a velo/ directory under /data/misc/location/ (e.g., adb shell "mkdir /data/misc/location/velo")

2. Use adb push to push each of those three files into your newly created directory

3. Restart your emulator

At this point, for TourIt and any other location-aware application on your emulator, you will be able to use both the built-in fake GPS data and this new "velo" set of fake GPS data.

SD Card Image with Sample Tour

Future editions of TourIt will support multimedia clips, once some standard players start shipping with the Android SDK (versus the player components described in an earlier chapter). Hence, the long-term vision is for a tour and its associated media clips to reside on an SD card, either downloaded there off the Internet, or transferred there via USB cables, Bluetooth, or similar means.

For the purposes of this early incarnation of TourIt, you will need an SD card image you can use with the Android emulator and upload a tour there, before the TourIt application will be useful.

To create an SD card image, use the `mksdcard` tool supplied by the Android SDK. In this case, though, a small SD card image is supplied as `sdcard.img` in the TourIt project directory with the sample code for this book.

To use that card in the emulator, pass the `-sdcard` switch with a path to the image file:

```
emulator -sdcard path/to/sdcard.img
```

That will mount the card under `/sdcard/` in the emulator's filesystem.

Running TourIt

Like most Android applications, TourIt is available from the Android launcher:

Figure 73. The Android launcher, showing the TourIt main activity

Clicking on that icon brings up the main TourIt activity.

Main Activity

The main activity provides two distinct screens:

1. A "home page" showing version information and some navigation buttons

2. A list of available tours loaded into the application

Figure 74. The TourIt "home page"

The three navigation buttons shown on the home page are duplicated in the options menu, along with a Close menu choice to proactively exit the activity:

Figure 75. The TourIt "home page" with option menu

If you click on the show-tours button, you will see a list of available tours. If your SD card image is mounted properly, TourIt should automatically find the sample tour when it lazy-creates its database, so you should see:

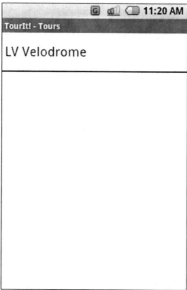

Figure 76. The TourIt list of tours

Configuration Activity

However, before looking at a tour, it is a good idea to visit the configuration activity, so we can use the right sample location provider when drawing the map. If you choose the "configure" button or option menu choice, you will bring up that configuration activity:

Figure 77. The TourIt configuration activity

As mentioned, the most important setting to change is the location provider, using the supplied spinner. If you uploaded the mock provider described earlier in this appendix, the "velo" location provider should be listed – choose it.

Beyond that, you can configure:

- Whether TourIt starts with the "home page" or the list of tours when you click the icon from the launcher

- Whether your current location should be shown on the map, and if the map should scroll to follow your location as you move

- What should happen when you near a waypoint on a tour you are taking – play a sound, vibrate, or both, and whether it should do that once or continuously while you are near the waypoint

Cue Sheet Activity

Of course, the interesting part of TourIt are the tours themselves. On the tours list, if you choose the "LV Velodrome" tour, it will bring up the cue sheet:

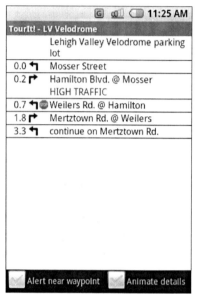

Figure 78. A tour's cue sheet in TourIt

The starting point is the first entry, called a "waypoint". Subsequent waypoints are given based on a direction from the preceding waypoint – for example, from Hamilton Blvd. at Mosser, you will travel 0.7 miles and make a left at the stop sign to turn onto Weilers Rd.

If you choose one of the waypoints in the list, a panel will appear towards the bottom showing more details about that waypoint:

Figure 79. The TourIt cue sheet with waypoint details

There are several bits of information that can appear in this panel. Use the left and right buttons on the D-pad to rotate between them, or check the "Animate details" checkbox at the bottom to have them scroll by automatically.

The other checkbox at the bottom, "Alert near waypoint", means you want the device to beep or buzz when you are near the waypoint. You would turn this on if you were actually taking the tour shown on this cue sheet, to help let you know you are nearing a place where you need to turn or stop.

Map Activity

The options menu from the cue sheet activity includes one to spawn a map showing your location and the location of the waypoints on the tour:

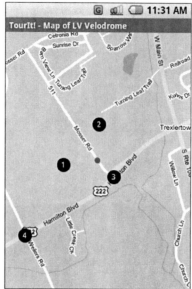

Figure 80. The TourIt map view

Your position is shown by the red dot (if you enabled that in the configuration). The waypoints are shown by numbered dots, starting with 1 for the first waypoint. If you turned on the follow-me feature in the configuration, the map will shift to show your position no matter where you go on the map.

The options menu for this activity has a few distinctive choices:

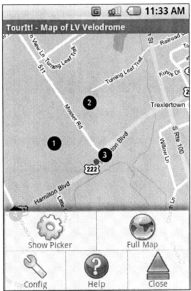

Figure 81. The TourIt map view, with options menu displayed

The "Show Picker" menu choice will bring up a spinner and button, allowing you to choose a waypoint and jump to that location. Note, however, if you are set with follow-me turned on, it will then pop the map back to your current location.

The "Full Map" menu choice will launch the built-in Android map activity on your current location, to access mapping features not available in TourIt's own simplified map view.

Tour Update Activity

TourIt does not allow you to define new tours from scratch inside the application, mostly because there would be a fair amount of typing involved, and that would be tedious on a phone. However, it does allow you to update the position information associated with waypoints. In theory, you would use some external program to define a tour, upload it to TourIt, then take the tour and update the waypoints as you go, then publish the resulting updated tour. There are a few pieces missing in this version of TourIt to make this a reality (e.g., easily adding and publishing tours), but the ability to update the location is provided. You can get to this via the Update menu choice from the cue sheet:

Figure 82. Updating a cue sheet within TourIt

Via the spinner, you can choose a waypoint. Then, you can update the distance travelled along the course from the preceding waypoint to here, and click "Fill In My Location!" to update the latitude, longitude, and (in theory) elevation of your position. When done, choose Save from the option menu to save your changes back out to the tour for later reuse.

Help Activity

TourIt also provides a very limited amount of online help, to explain how to use the application. Choosing the Help option menu choice from any activity takes you to online help for that activity:

Figure 83. A TourIt help page

TourIt's Manifest

TourIt has a somewhat more complicated AndroidManifest.xml file than the rest of the samples shown in this book:

```
<manifest xmlns:android="http://schemas.android.com/apk/res/android"
    package="com.commonsware.tourit">
  <uses-permission android:name="android.permission.ACCESS_LOCATION" />
  <uses-permission android:name="android.permission.ACCESS_GPS" />
  <uses-permission android:name="android.permission.ACCESS_ASSISTED_GPS" />
  <uses-permission android:name="android.permission.ACCESS_CELL_ID" />
    <application android:icon="@drawable/wheel">
      <provider android:name=".Provider"
            android:authorities="com.commonsware.android.tourit.Provider" />
      <activity android:name=".TourListActivity" android:label="TourIt!">
        <intent-filter>
          <action android:name="android.intent.action.MAIN" />
          <category android:name="android.intent.category.LAUNCHER" />
        </intent-filter>
      </activity>
      <activity android:name=".TourViewActivity">
        <intent-filter>
          <action android:name="android.intent.action.VIEW" />
          <category android:name="android.intent.category.DEFAULT" />
          <data android:mimeType="vnd.android.cursor.item/vnd.commonsware.tour" />
        </intent-filter>
      </activity>
      <activity android:name=".TourEditActivity">
        <intent-filter>
```

```
                <action android:name="android.intent.action.EDIT" />
                <category android:name="android.intent.category.DEFAULT" />
                <data android:mimeType="vnd.android.cursor.item/vnd.commonsware.tour" />
            </intent-filter>
        </activity>
        <activity android:name=".TourMapActivity">
        </activity>
        <activity android:name=".ConfigActivity" android:label="TourIt! - Configuration">
        </activity>
        <activity android:name=".HelpActivity" android:label="TourIt! - Help">
        </activity>
    </application>
</manifest>
```

Next, we wire in the content provider, supplying data about the available tours to our activities.

Finally, we describe all the available activities. One – TourListActivity – is set to appear in the application's launch menu. Two others – TourViewActivity and TourEditActivity – are available to be launched by intents looking to manipulate data supplied by our content provider. The rest are simply listed without an intent filter, so they can only be accessed via their class names.

TourIt's Content

TourIt's content is comprised of tours. Tours are made up of waypoints and directions between them. Waypoints and directions each have discrete bits of data, such as the coordinates of waypoint and the distance to travel for a direction. Later, tours and their waypoints will also have multimedia clips, either to show off features of a given location, or to help guide travelers through tricky directions.

Data Storage

Given that TourIt will eventually have multimedia clips, and given that Android's approach is to store such clips in the file system, and since clips could be big, TourIt assumes the existence of an SD card containing the tours. Right now, each tour gets its own directory on the card, containing a JSON data structure (tour.js) with the tour details (e.g., waypoints). Later, those directories will also hold the media clips associated with that tour.

There is also a SQLite database, with a tours table, to hold the master roster of available tours. This eliminates the need to scan the SD card just to populate the list of available tours. More importantly, it makes for a better sample application for this book.

Content Provider

The SQLite database is managed by an Android content provider, cunningly named Provider. Right now, it only deals with a single table – tours – which contains the roster of all available tours, loaded off the SD card. Eventually, the provider might be expanded to encompass other tables, should that prove necessary.

Model Classes

Android applications tend not to map all that cleanly to the model-view-controller (MVC) architecture popular in GUI development. An activity tends to blend both elements of the view (e.g., setting up and managing widgets) and controller (handling menu choices, button clicks, etc.). And some Android applications use the "dumb model" approach, putting business logic in the activity and using the content provider as just a data store.

TourIt's first step on the road to a cleaner MVC implementation are the model classes: Tour, Waypoint, and Direction. The Tour class knows how to read and write the JSON data structure and turn that into tour information, plus the Waypoints and Directions that make up the guts of the tour itself. Over time, more and more logic will move into the models, leaving the content provider still as a dumb store, but trying to make the activity more of a thin controller.

TourIt's Activities

TourIt breaks its user interface up into a series of activities, each covering a different facet of working with tours:

- TourListActivity is the home page plus the list of installed tours

- TourViewActivity shows the cue sheet for a selected tour

- TourMapActivity shows the waypoints for the tour, plus (optionally) your location

- TourEditActivity allows you to update location information for a tour, based on Android's reported location

- HelpActivity is the gateway to online help for using TourIt

- ConfigActivity allows you to set various options for customizing how TourIt works for you

This section isn't going to go through these activities line-by-line, but instead will highlight a few interesting bits that show off various Android features.

TourListActivity

TourListActivity handles both the home page and the list of installed tours. To do this, it uses ViewFlipper – think of it as the guts of a TabActivity, minus the tabs. Given a ViewFlipper and the appropriate means to get from view to view, this shows how you can build an arbitrarily complex activity instead of treating each individual activity as a separate construct.

In the layout (res/layout/main.xml), we declare a ViewFlipper. Each child element of the ViewFlipper represents a separate "page" to be flipped between. You flip between them via the child's 0-based index, as illustrated in showList(), which toggles the view to the list of available tours:

```
private void showList() {
  flipper.setDisplayedChild(0);
  setTitle("TourIt! - Tours");

  if (flipMenu!=null) {
    flipMenu.setTitle("Go Home");
    flipMenu.setIcon(R.drawable.home);
  }
}
```

The tour list itself is a simple ListView, backed by a SimpleCursorAdapter, in turn backed by the content provider. However, we do tailor the look of the individual list entries, by referencing our own layout (res/layout/tourlist_item.xml):

```
<?xml version="1.0" encoding="utf-8"?>
<TextView xmlns:android="http://schemas.android.com/apk/res/android"
    android:id="@android:id/text1"
    android:layout_width="fill_parent"
    android:layout_height="?android:attr/listPreferredItemHeight"
    android:textAppearance="?android:attr/textAppearanceLargeInverse"
    android:gravity="center_vertical"
    android:paddingLeft="5dip"
/>
```

TourViewActivity

At 500+ lines of code, TourViewActivity is far and away the most complicated class in all of TourIt. It handles displaying the cue sheet plus notifying users when they approach a waypoint. Here are a few of the interesting facets of this class, besides the location services documented in a previous chapter:

Custom List Contents

The individual items in the cue sheet – the waypoint title plus the direction of how to get there – is a trifle more complicated than the stock list formats supplied by Android. It's sufficiently complicated that even just providing a custom layout would not handle the need. So, TourViewActivity has a private class, RouteAdapter, that subclasses ArrayAdapter and builds the list item views as needed.

The problem is that there are several flavors of view that goes into the list:

- The typical direction plus waypoint title

- The first entry, which is just the starting waypoint with no direction

- Entries where the waypoint has a note (e.g., traffic alert) that calls for a two-line display

TourIt makes a simplifying assumption: the first waypoint has no note. Given that, we have the three scenarios listed above (versus having a fourth, where the first entry is a two-line variant).

`RouteAdapter#getFirstView()` handles the first entry, inflating a layout (`res/layout/tourview_std.xml`) and populating it:

```
private View getFirstView(View convertView) {
  ViewInflate inflater=context.getViewInflate();
  View view=inflater.inflate(R.layout.tourview_std, null, null);
  TextView label=(TextView)view.findViewById(R.id.waypoint);

  label.setText(tour.getRoute().get(0).getTitle());

  return(view);
}
```

`RouteAdapter#getStandardView()` handles the typical scenario, including converting codes in the tour's JSON into resources to display turn arrows, signs, etc.:

```
private View getStandardView(Waypoint pt, boolean stripe, View convertView) {
  ViewInflate inflater=context.getViewInflate();
  View view=inflater.inflate(R.layout.tourview_std, null, null);
  TextView distance=(TextView)view.findViewById(R.id.distance);
  ImageView turn=(ImageView)view.findViewById(R.id.turn);
  ImageView marker=(ImageView)view.findViewById(R.id.marker);
  TextView waypoint=(TextView)view.findViewById(R.id.waypoint);

  distance.setText(distanceFormat.format(pt.getCumulativeDistance()));
  turn.setImageResource(getResourceForTurn(pt.getFromDirection().getTurn()));

  if (pt.getFromDirection().getMarker()!=null) {
    marker.setImageResource(getResourceForMarker(pt
                                      .getFromDirection()
                                      .getMarker()));
  }

  waypoint.setText(pt.getTitle());

  return(view);
}
```

Finally, `RouteAdapter#getTwoLineView()` inflates a two-line layout and populates it as well:

```
private View getTwoLineView(Waypoint pt, boolean stripe, View convertView) {
  ViewInflate inflater=context.getViewInflate();
  View view=inflater.inflate(R.layout.tourview_2line, null, null);
  TextView distance=(TextView)view.findViewById(R.id.distance);
  ImageView turn=(ImageView)view.findViewById(R.id.turn);
  ImageView marker=(ImageView)view.findViewById(R.id.marker);
  TextView waypoint=(TextView)view.findViewById(R.id.waypoint);
  TextView hint=(TextView)view.findViewById(R.id.hint);

  distance.setText(distanceFormat.format(pt.getCumulativeDistance()));
  turn.setImageResource(getResourceForTurn(pt.getFromDirection().getTurn()));

  if (pt.getFromDirection().getMarker()!=null) {
    marker.setImageResource(getResourceForMarker(pt
                                      .getFromDirection()
                                      .getMarker()));
  }

  waypoint.setText(pt.getTitle());
  hint.setText(pt.getFromDirection().getHint());

  return(view);
}
```

Clearly, some refactoring is called for here to reduce code duplication. This is left as an exercise for the reader, or eventually for the author.

Details Panel

The details panel – the black panel that is displayed when you select an entry in the cue sheet – is a ViewFlipper. In the layout (res/layout/view.xml), it is set to be invisible (android:visibility = "invisible"), which is why it does not show up at first. Then, when you select an item, it is made visible again (detailsPanel.setVisibility(VISIBLE)) and is filled in with the details for that waypoint/direction pair, in the onItemSelected() method.

To support manually flipping the pages of the details panel, TourViewActivity implements onKeyUp():

```
public boolean onKeyUp(int keyCode, KeyEvent event) {
  if (keyCode==KeyEvent.KEYCODE_DPAD_LEFT ||
      keyCode==KeyEvent.KEYCODE_DPAD_RIGHT) {
    stopAnimation();

    if (keyCode==KeyEvent.KEYCODE_DPAD_LEFT) {
      detailsPanel.setInAnimation(AnimationUtils.loadAnimation(this,
```

```
                            R.anim.push_right_in));
        detailsPanel.setOutAnimation(AnimationUtils.loadAnimation(this,
                            R.anim.push_right_out));

        if (detailsPanel.getDisplayedChild()==0) {
          detailsPanel.setDisplayedChild(detailsPanel.getChildCount()-1);
        }
        else {
          detailsPanel.setDisplayedChild(detailsPanel.getDisplayedChild()-1);
        }
      }
      else {
        detailsPanel.setInAnimation(AnimationUtils.loadAnimation(this,
                        R.anim.push_left_in));
        detailsPanel.setOutAnimation(AnimationUtils.loadAnimation(this,
                        R.anim.push_left_out));
        detailsPanel.showNext();
      }
    }

    return(super.onKeyUp(keyCode, event));
}
```

Or, the checkbox can toggle automatic animation, courtesy of the flipping features built into ViewFlipper:

```
private void startAnimation() {
  detailsPanel.startFlipping();
  isFlipping=true;
}

private void stopAnimation() {
  detailsPanel.stopFlipping();
  isFlipping=false;
}
```

TourMapActivity

The guts of TourMapActivity are covered extensively in the chapter on mapping services and are not repeated here for brevity.

TourEditActivity

By and large, TourEditActivity is just a form for the user to fill in waypoint details. Two things are interesting here.

First, for the distance traveled field, we use a custom `FloatInputMethod` class, that constrains input to be positive or negative floating-point numbers:

```
class FloatInputMethod extends NumberInputMethod {
  private static final String CHARS="0123456789-.";

  protected char[] getAcceptedChars() {
    return(CHARS.toCharArray());
  }
}
```

Also, when the "Fill In My Location!" button is clicked, we do just that – find the current location and fill in the latitude, longitude, and elevation fields accordingly, as is described in the chapter on location services.

HelpActivity

The `HelpActivity` is a thin shell around the WebKit browser. It loads static HTML out of the project's `assets/` directory, which is referenced in code as `file:///android_assets`, as shown below:

```
@Override
public void onCreate(Bundle icicle) {
  super.onCreate(icicle);
  setContentView(R.layout.help);
  browser=(WebView)findViewById(R.id.browser);
  browser.setWebViewClient(new Callback());
  browser.getSettings().setDefaultFontSize(browser
                                    .getSettings()
                                    .getDefaultFontSize()+4);

  String page=getIntent().getStringExtra(PAGE);

  if (page==null) {
    browser.loadUrl("file:///android_asset/index.html");
  }
  else {
    browser.loadUrl("file:///android_asset/"+page+".html");
  }
}
```

By default, it will load the home page. If, however, the activity was started by another activity that passed in a specific page to view, it loads that page instead.

HelpActivity hooks into the WebKit browser to detect clicks on links. Since the only links in the help are to other help pages, it simply loads in the requested page:

```
private class Callback extends WebViewClient {
  public boolean shouldOverrideUrlLoading(WebView view, String url) {
    view.loadUrl(url);

    return(true);
  }
}
```

ConfigActivity

The ConfigActivity class mostly loads data out of preferences, updates the layout's widgets to match, then reverses the process when the activity is paused (e.g., when the user clicks Close from the options menu).

The most interesting thing here is the spinner of location providers – this is covered in detail in the chapter on location services.

Keyword Index

Command

Constant

Method

Property

Printed in the United States
125628LV00007B/35/P

9 780981 678009